Robt. B. Caverly

HEROISM
of
HANNAH DUSTON
Together with the Indian Wars of New England

Robert B. Caverly

HERITAGE BOOKS
2008

HERITAGE BOOKS
AN IMPRINT OF HERITAGE BOOKS, INC.

Books, CDs, and more—Worldwide

For our listing of thousands of titles see our website at
www.HeritageBooks.com

Published 2008 by
HERITAGE BOOKS, INC.
Publishing Division
100 Railroad Ave. #104
Westminster, Maryland 21157

Copyright © 1875 Robert B. Caverly

All rights reserved. No part of this book may be reproduced or transmitted in any form or by any means, electronic or mechanical, including photocopying, recording or by any information storage and retrieval system without written permission from the author, except for the inclusion of brief quotations in a review.

International Standard Book Numbers
Paperbound: 978-1-55613-301-5
Clothbound: 978-0-7884-7011-0

PREFACE.

NORTH BILLERICA, MASS., March 20, 1874.

MY DEAR SIR, — I am delighted to learn that you are engaged in the laudable work of raising a monument to the memory of the heroic Mrs. Hannah Duston. Among the heroines of New England's Indian history she stands forth pre-eminent; and her deeds are worthy to be enshrined by the hand of genius in the choicest prose and sweetest poetry.

I am glad that you are contemplating the perpetuation of her memory, also, in a book soon to be given to the public. Now, why not incorporate in this work a concise history of the early Indian wars of New England? Pardon me, my dear sir, for the suggestion; but it does appear to me that a brief *resumé* of the romantic enterprises, cruel sufferings, and bloody wars which characterized the colonization of this section of our land would greatly enhance the value of your work. Our young people know but little of the history of the early settlers; and this just for the want of a popular and able record of the brave and manly deeds of those old times of savage warfare.

PREFACE.

Please give us such a work, concise in diction, clear in arrangement, true in regard to fact, — such a work, indeed, as your practised pen can easily produce; and you will confer a very great service upon the present and every coming generation.

Set down, if you please, to my love of our New England history, the freedom I have used; and believe me ever your sincere and faithful friend,

ELIAS NASON.

ROBERT B. CAVERLY, Esq.

Replication and Dedication.

TO

MY LEARNED FRIEND,

ELIAS NASON,

HEROIC IN HISTORY;

AND TO ALL THE DONORS OF THE DUSTON MONUMENT,

GENEROUS IN THIS AND IN ALL,

This Volume,

TRUTHFUL IN ALL OF ITS TRAGICAL INTEREST,

Is Respectfully, Thankfully Inscribed.

ROBERT B. CAVERLY.

CONTOOCOOK ISLAND, June 17, 1874.

CONTENTS.

Arrowsick, Battle, &c., 306.
Appleton, Capt., 236.
Andover, 319.
Albany, 361.
Amoskeag Falls, 316.
Army raised, 236.
Adams, 364.
Athol, 365.
Albany, 371.
Address, historical, 389.

Bradley, Hannah, 40, 45, 54, 56, 57.
Bradley, Isaac, Story of, 47.
Battles, 153, 164, 210, 223, 227, 228, 238, 243, 272, 276, 312, 343, 349, 356, 360.
Beers, Capt., 224, 226.
Blind Will, 315.
Black Point, 316.
Billerica, 270, 319.
Block Island, 147.
Brookfield, 221, 222, 278, 369.
Bedford, N.H., 362.
Bradford, 244.
Bridgewater, 262, 263.
Bloody Brook.
Barnard, 367.
Burton, 370.
Bride of Burton (a poem), 372.

Court trials, 197.
Contoocook, 20, 217, 331.
Canonicus, 124, 125, 143, 144.
Clergy, 172, 206.
Church, Capt., 28, 215, 216, 284.
Cudworth, Capt., 216.
Colonies, 172, 187.

Concord, 271.
Concord, N.H., 221, 349, 352.
Casco, 40, 295, 302, 307, 309, 319.
Cocheco, 297, 317.
Connecticut, 129.
Chelmsford, 178, 271.
Canonchet, 256, 257.
Cutter, Capt., 272.
Charlestown, N.H., 367.
Chocorua, 370.

Duston Hannah, 14, 17, 380; her children, 21, 24.
Duston, Thomas, 32; his petition, 38.
Drake, Sir Francis, 63.
Deerfield, 225, 227.
Davenport, Capt., 236, 241.
Dedham, 236, 282.
Dover, N.H., 32, 195, 301, 314, 317.
Dorchester, 140.
Durham, N.H., 195.
Dunstable, 343, 349.
Donahew, 358, 359.
Dennison, Capt., 257, 261.
Dutch, Robert, 228.
Dutch Nation, 131, 138, 258.
Donors, names of, 382.

Eliot, 97, 175.
English, 139, 115, 163.
Endicot, Capt., 147, 148, 184.
Exeter, N.H., 297, 315.
East Stamford.
Expeditions, 261.
Epic Poem, 397.

CONTENTS.

Foreign Wars, 189.
Falmouth, 302.
Franklin, N.H., 57.
French Jesuits, 179, 354.
French and Indian War, 356.

Gauntlet, 18.
Gallop, John, 141, 236, 241.
Gardner, 148, 226, 236, 245.
Garrisons, 236.
Groton, 224, 264, 265.
Groton, Conn., 152.
Gookin, Capt., 176, 244, 264, 265.

History of Natives, 100.
Habits, 74, 76.
Hunt, Thomas, 101.
Henchman, Capt., 178, 210, 217, 218, 231, 277, 278.
Hutchins, Capt., 222.
Hatfield, 225, 226, 363, 364.
Hadley, 221, 225, 230, 274, 363.
Hassameneset, 231.
Haverhill, 15, 24, 32, 36, 40, 47, 54, 56.
Hamilton, 124.
Hartford, 131, 162, 170, 188, 229.
Hooksett, 362.
Hawks, Col., 364.
Hoosac Fort, 367.
Horton, Lieut., 367.
House, Capt., 368.

Incriptions, 387.
Indian Nations, 72, 73.
" Language, 94.
" Clothing, 78.
" Medical Practice, 93.
" Mode of Life, 81, 83.
" Painting, &c., 85.
" Depravity, 83.
" Mode of Attack, 97.
" First Insurrection, 105.
" Use of Fire-Arms, 134.
" Spies, 268.
" Ignorance, 77.
Isinglass River, 316.
Ipswich, 123, 124.
Kennebeck, 205, 303.
Kittery, 317.
Keene, N.H., 360.

Leonardson, Samuel, 23.
Lakes and rivers of N. E., 65, 71.
Lothrop, Capt., 224, 227, 228.
Long Beach, 316.
Lowell, 57.
Long Island, 133, 188.
Lancaster, 221, 246.
Lovewell, 343.
Lieut. Oaks, 211.

Mothers, valor of, 13.
Massasoit, sons of, 96, 173; his apparel, 115.
Mascanonomo, squaw of, 113.
Mohawks and Mass., 122.
Moseley Capt., 217, 236, 237, 235; at Concord, 221.
Miantonimo, 127, 150, 160, 167, 180, 207.
Mason, Capt., 151, 236.
Mystic, Battle at, 153.
Mohawks, 154, 172, 315, 349.
Massacre of Miantonimo, 169, 171.
Marshall, Capt., 236, 244, 339.
Madacawando, 304, 310.
Mugg, 307, 310.
Marlboro, 311, 319, 357.
Methuen, 55.
Mexam, 181.
Mather, Cotton, Rev., 183, 185, 206.
Mohegans, 185, 219, 258.
Manhattan, 191.
Mayano, 191.
Mt. Hope, 194, 211, 341.
Mendham, 217, 232.
Medfield, 253, 256.
Melvin, Capt., 367.
Monument, 381.

Neff, Mary, 22, 24, 55.
Norton, Capt., 133, 183..
New-England landscape, 65.
Names of tribes, 86, 88, 96.
Narragansetts, 140, 185, 235.
Nipmucks, 208, 219, 222, 245.
Northampton, 226, 231, 269.
Northfield, 226.
Ninegret, 180, 181, 132, 245, 257.
New Amsterdam, 191..
North Hill, 317.

CONTENTS. 9

New London, 129.
Norwich, 164.
New Haven, 188.
New Amsterdam, 190.
Names of Donors, 380.
Nianticks, 258.
Newbury, 260, 367.

Oldham, 140, 141, 145.
Oliver, Capt., 236.
One-Eyed John, 267.
Oyster River, 296.
Ossipee, 309.
Oweneco, 208.
Old and New Style, 357.
Orators, 416.

Poems, 24, 25, 32, 58, 397.
Pilgrims, 113.
Pequots, 129, 132, 138, 131, 185, 187, 207.
Philip, 193, 198, 206, 208, 209, 220, 301, 287, 202, slain, 286.
Prentice, Capt., 210, 217, 236.
Page, Capt., 217.
Parker, Capt., 224.
Passaconaway, 173, 175, 176.
Prayer, 292.
Plantations in the East, 293.
Piscataqua, 295.
Portsmouth, 316.
Plymouth, 131, 144, 188, 208, 216, 220.
Pembroke, N.H., 173, 174, 343, 347.
Pawtucket, 173, 341.
Passiqueno, 174.
Pawtucket Falls, 176.
Pessacus, 181, 366.
Pometacon, or Metacon, 193.
Podunks, 208.
Pocasset, 215, 216.
Paugus, 346.
Pennacooks, 351, 362.
Patuxet, 256.

Quabaug, 363.

Rolfe, Benj., slain, 25, 29, 30.
Rowlandson, Mary, 247, 251, 255, 259, 260, 346, 349.
Rowlandson, Joseph, Rev., 260.

Ramkamagus, 317.
Rhode Island, 129, 168, 182, 194.
Rattlesnake skin, 144.
Roxbury, 150.
Rehoboth, 216, 256.
Robbins, Ensign, 346.
Rewards, 357.
Royalton, 367.
Randolph, 368.

Scalping, 19.
Smith, John, 101.
Samoset, 107, 110.
Squanto, 113, 117.
Sachems, 120, 160.
Shawmut Sagamores, 120.
Sassacus, 131, 135, 154, 156, 158.
Stone, Capt., 132, 133, 136.
Swanzey, 201, 208, 209, 210.
Savage, Capt., 217, 256.
Sequessan, 162.
Sugar-Loaf Hill, 225.
Springfield, 224, 229, 232.
Stone-wall John, 237.
Siely, Capt., 236, 241, 245.
Sassamon, 196.
Sudbury, 258, 260, 270.
Sagamore John, 284.
Salmon Falls, 296, 315, 319.
Sturgeon Creek, 297.
Squando, 304, 314.
Simon, 316.
Shapleigh, 317.
Saybrook, 149, 150, 151.
Sagamore Sam, 179.
Saco, 206.
Scituate, 262, 363.
Swansey, 262.
Sill, 272, 363.
South Hampton, 365.
Stockbridge, 365.
Sharon, 368.
Subscription, 380.
Statute, Description of, 387.

Tarratines, 102, 103, 108.
Tisquantum, 103, 128.
Treaties, 112, 127, 130, 134, 211, 347, 361.
Tribes (hostile), 207, 281, 300, 354.

CONTENTS.

Taunton, 216, 262, 283.
Totonic Fort, 302.
Turner, Capt., 184.
Tyng, Capt., 346, 347, 348.
Tunbridge, 366.

Uncas, 159, 165, 207–8, 366.
Upham, 241.
Underhill, 184, 192.

Vandyck, 192.
Vernon, Vt., 366.

Whittaker, Joseph, Story of, 37, 47.
Women in war, 46.
War-whoop, 105.
Williams, Roger, 125, 126.
Wheeler, Capt., 222.

Bradford and Canonicus, 144.
Wethersfield, 139, 151, 185.
Willard, Major.
Watts, Capt., 224, 236, 245.
Winslow's force, 197, 236.
Wonalancet, 128, 179.
War on Long Island, 188.
Warwick Neck, 256, 280.
Wells, 40, 297, 316, 317, 319.
Waldron, 301, 304, 309, 311, 313, 315, 317, 318.
Wamsutta, 193, 272.
Wyman, Lieut., 345.
Weymouth, 256, 270.
Wadsworth, 259.
Wrentham, 364.
Williams, Col. 365.

Young Men of Essex, 227.

ILLUSTRATIONS.

1. PORTRAIT OF THE AUTHOR . . . . Title-Page.
2. DUSTON KILLING INDIANS 28
3. SIR FRANCIS DRAKE 62
4. MAN IN THE MOUNTAIN . . , . . . 66
5. THE PEMIGEWASSET 82
6. SAMOSET AND THE PILGRIMS 106
7. TREATY, MASSASOIT WITH CARVER . . . 114
8. TISQUANTUM IN THE CLOUD 128
9. INDIAN CONFLICT 150
10. DEATH OF KING PHILIP 200
11. THE OLD GARRISON-HOUSE 286
12. CHOCORUA AT THE GRAVE 374
13. CROSSING TO THE CONTOOCOOK 392
14. DUSTON STATUE, DIAGRAM 404

HEROISM OF HANNAH DUSTON.

CHAPTER I.

HER HISTORY.

Faith and Valor of the Mothers. — Hannah's Biography. — Her Children. — Their Names and Ages. — Her Captivity with Mary and Samuel. — Indians surround Haverhill. — Their Mode of Warfare. — What they then did. — What Thomas, her Husband, did. — His Biography. — His Heroism then poetized. — Names of the Twenty-seven slain by the Tribes. — Island Contoocook. — Its Location, and Distance from Haverhill. — What Hannah did there. — Names, &c., of her Thirteen Children. — Mrs. Neff's Biography. — Her Generous Deeds. — Samuel's Brief History. — The Gantlet. — Mode of Scalping. — Savages: Number slain. — Captives' Arrival Home. — Cotton Mather greets them in Boston. — General Court makes them Presents; Governor of Maryland also. — Recapitulation as an Epic.

HEROISM is a divine attribute. Patriotism approves and honors it. Humanity fervently and ambitiously inclines to cherish it.

To make a record of its achievements becomes the pleasure as well as the duty of a generous people, who are never unmindful of their heroes.

Hence the exploit of our heroine, with her assistants Neff and Leonardson (the boy), will ever be revered.

Forever will its history be remembered, transmitted, and cherished as a household treasure. Like an heir-loom, it imparts inspiration, — an inspiration which, diffusing itself, shall tend to elevate the heart-felt aspirations of the sons and daughters, descendants of the old New-England mothers throughout the uncounted ages yet to come, — *mothers* who lived in a day of trial, but whose truthfulness historic hath never been surpassed, and whose endurance, faithfulness, and valor, *tried* and made manifest in the midst of savages, are in this volume truthfully exemplified.

HER BIOGRAPHY.

Hannah Duston was born in Haverhill, Mass., Dec. 23, 1657; was the daughter of Michael and Hannah Webster Emerson; was married to Thomas Duston Dec. 3, 1677; and, up to the date of her captivity, had become the mother of a family of children, twelve at that date, thirteen in all.

THE INDIAN ONSET.

She was captured at Haverhill March 15, 1697; her infant then being only a week old.

Mary Neff, then a widow, a neighbor, and friend, was with her, and, for the time being, was having a care for the household.

The tribes throughout New England, as appears, had, for several years prior to this attack, beset the English settlements by trespassing upon their cornfields, killing their cattle, taking and carrying away captives, and daily and nightly murdering the inhabitants, burning down their barns, their lonely cots, and their infant villages.

Always, in their depredations upon the Pilgrim settlers, they had been cunning, ferocious, coy, and cruel. Previous to this Duston massacre, they had taken at Worcester, Mass., Samuel Leonardson, a youth of some fourteen summers, and had him along with them among their captives.

.At Haverhill, on that fifteenth day of March, 1697, according to the tactics of Indian warfare, they divided their tribes into small parties, and made the attack all around the town, everywhere very nearly at the same moment; so that on that day, in and about that little inland, rural village, they took and carried away thirteen captives, burned down nine dwelling-houses, and killed twenty-seven of its inhabitants, — men, women, and children.

THE SLAIN.

The individuals then and there killed were John Keezer, his father, and son George; John Kimball and his mother Hannah; Sarah Eastman; Thomas

Eaton; Thomas Emerson, his wife Elizabeth, and two children, — Timothy and Sarah; Daniel Bradley, his wife Hannah, and two children, — Mary and Hannah; Martha Dow, daughter of Stephen Dow; *Joseph, Martha,* and *Sarah Bradley,* children of Joseph Bradley; Thomas and Mehitable Kingsbury; Thomas Wood and his daughter Susannah; John Woodman and his daughter Susannah; Zechariah White; and Martha, the infant daughter of Mrs. Duston.

THE OLD COT.

Mrs. DUSTON's house stood not far from the left bank of the Merrimack River, on the north side of the road, about a mile and a half from that little hamlet, now the city of Haverhill, populous, opulent, and thriving.

FIRST SIGHT OF SAVAGES.

On that day, THOMAS DUSTON (the husband) was in some way startled in his field at the approach of savages. He seized his gun, mounted his horse, and driving his children before him, seven in number, — ages from two to seventeen years, — all escaped. It has been said that guns were fired at him, and that he returned the shots; but this statement is beclouded with at least some doubt. It is, however, said, and perhaps correctly, that the Indians did not pursue him far, for fear of the English; and that he with the children took shelter in an old house supposed to have been used occasionally as a garrison.

In the mean time the Indians at the homestead had seized Mrs. Duston, Mary, and the infant; forced the child from Mary's arms, and killed it against an apple-tree; and, pillaging and setting fire to the dwelling-house, drove their captives away into the wilderness, — a wilderness then dense, dark, pathless, and thorny; in the confusion, Mrs. Duston having but one shoe to her feet.

The cold snows of winter had not entirely disappeared. Yet were they compelled to advance, reclining at night upon the frosty earth to obtain rest and strength, and then up at break of day, continuing their ramblings northward, by and near to the Merrimack, through the wilderness; thus onward until they reached that Indian fort on the island between the waters of the Contoocook and Merrimack Rivers.

ISLAND CONTOOCOOK.

As appears, this island, containing about two acres, then (and now) covered with a dense forest, was the adopted home of one of the tribes; and, from its surroundings, it served to be a strong fortification against their common enemy, the English settlers.

For fifteen days they had continued their march through the forest, — a distance of seventy-five miles, according to our reckoning; but, according to the Indian computations of that time, two hundred and fifty miles.

But, before they reached the island, the tribe divided into two parts: the one with several captives (among whom was Hannah Bradley, whose brief biography will appear on a subsequent page) continued still farther onward to another place; while the other company, with Mrs. Duston, Neff, and Samuel, crossed over in their birch canoes, to dwell, at least for a night, on the island between the safe surroundings at the junction of these two beautiful rivers.

On their way the Indians had talked of another fort of theirs in Canada; and had intimated to the captives, that, upon their arrival there, they would be held to run the gantlet, according to the law and custom of the tribes.

GANTLET.

This was usually performed thus: The group was made up by "two files of Indians of both sexes, of all ages, containing all who could be mustered in the village; and the unhappy prisoners were obliged to run between them, when they were scoffed at and beaten by each one as they passed, and were made marks of, at which the younger Indians threw their hatchets."

As if to add to these worst of cruelties, the tribes often made sale of their captives to the FRENCH in Canada, — then hostile to the English settlers in New England, — to be held to service by them as slaves.

In sight of all the severities to which they had already been subjected, and in view of impending disgrace and danger, these *three* (Duston, Neff, and Samuel) secretly took counsel together, and resolved to liberate themselves.

HOW TO KILL AN INDIAN.

Thereupon the boy Samuel inquired of one of the tribe ("Bampico") as to where he would strike if he would kill a man instantly, and how he would take off the scalp.

The Indian, bringing his finger against his temple, made answer, "Strike him there!" and he then proceeded to tell him how to take off the scalp.

SCALPING.

This feat is performed by the savage as follows: Placing his foot upon the neck of his prostrate victim, he twists the fingers of his left hand into the scalp-lock; and then, cutting with a knife in his right hand a circular gash around the lock, he tears the scalp from the head, and fastens it to his girdle with a yell of triumph.

The scalps upon their belts on public occasions were worn to designate the warriors.

ON THE ISLAND.

There, on that night, March 30, 1697, the camp-fires in front of the wigwams blazed pleasantly; and the tribe in front of them, reclining, and burdened with the fatigue of a restless journey, of course slept soundly.

Having a heed to all this, the captives patiently awaited the midnight hour; and then, cautiously, noiselessly, obtaining the tomahawks, and moving with concert of action, they struck the deadly blow. None of the Indians escaped alive, save one old squaw covered with wounds, and an Indian boy, whom the captives did not incline to pursue.

NUMBER OF VICTIMS.

Ten of them were slain. The captives, in their haste, at first left the wigwams without full evidence of what had been done; yet soon returned, took off the ten scalps, taking also with them an Indian gun and tomahawk; and then, seeking to avoid pursuit, they scuttled the canoes, all but one; and in *that* they floated down the Merrimack as far as they could come for the falls, and thence along its left bank, as tradition has it, until they arrived home safely at Haverhill.

On the 21st of April in the same year (1697), they visited Boston; carrying with them, as evidence of their achievement, the scalps, the gun, and tomahawk; and, on the 8th of June thereafterwards, the General Court awarded to Mrs. Duston a gift of £25, and to Mary Neff and Samuel Leonardson £12 10s. each. Col. Nicholson, then governor of Maryland, upon hearing of the transaction, also transmitted complimentary presents to them. Many thanks, as well as material gifts, were extended to them by many others.

SONS AND DAUGHTERS.

The children of Thomas and Hannah Duston were, —

Hannah, born Aug. 22, 1678.
Elizabeth, born May 7, 1680.
Mary, born Nov. 4, 1681 (died Oct. 18, 1696).
Thomas, born Jan. 5, 1683.
Nath., born May 16, 1685.
John, born Feb. 2, 1686 (died Jan. 28, 1690).
Sarah, born July 4, 1688.
Abigail, born October, 1690.
Jona., born Jan. 15, 1691-92.
Timothy, born Sept. 14, 1694.
Mehitable, twin-sister to Timothy (died Dec. 16, 1694).
Martha, born March 9, 1696-97; slain by the Indians March 15, 1697.
And Lydia, born Oct. 4, 1698.

MARY NEFF.

Mary was a native of Haverhill, born Sept. 18, 1646; was the daughter of George and Joanna Corliss; and married William Neff June 23, 1665.

William died in February, 1681. Mary died Oct. 22, 1720, aged seventy-four years.

Mary, at her marriage, left the parental homestead; and, up to the time of her captivity, resided on the rise of ground on the left side of the road leading from the compact part of Haverhill to the old farm where little Martha Duston, the infant, was murdered against an apple-tree, and where the Duston dwelling-house, on that day, was burnt down by the Indians.

Mary's residence was at the same place, now or formerly owned by William Swasey. It was, in fact, a gift on her nuptial day from her father. It was situated about a mile north of the village of Haverhill.

Mary, as well as Mrs. Duston, was indeed a New-England mother. At her capture by the Indians she was a widow, and was Mrs. Duston's senior eleven years. Upon notice that her neighbor and friend Mrs. Duston was sick and in need of care, Mary was at her bedside.

From this and other evidence, we may well cherish

the belief, that the conduct of the household, the good health, and in fact the well-being, of that whole neighborhood, belonged mostly to Mary. They found in her, daily, not only a generous, genial disposition, but great strength of mind, and force of character, — a force in the sight of justice and duty too strong to be abashed or dismayed by the war-whoop cry, or to be disconcerted at sight of the tomahawk and scalping-knife. In fact, through all trial, Mary persistently adhered to the matron of her charge; hugged little Martha to her bosom until the child was torn from her embrace to be slain of the furious tribe ; and then, as ever, adhering to the care and encouragement of its sick, heart-stricken, bereaved mother.

SAMUEL LEONARDSON.

Of Samuel's parentage, of his birth, death, or burial, we have obtained no account. The three extraordinary incidents of Samuel's life — involved in his capture at Worcester by the Indians, his agency in the slaughter of savages in the Contoocook, and of his sedate, unostentatious presence in Boston April 21, 1697, and then again on the 8th of June the then next following, there to receive from "the Great and General Court" of Massachusetts a complimentary reward for the heroic manhood of his youth — are probably the first and last that earth will ever hear of that heroic, generous-hearted, gallant boy.

The account herein given of the war and blood at Haverhill, and of the slaughter of the tribe in the Contoocook, well known of tradition and general history, was carefully written down by that celebrated historian and divine, Cotton Mather, from the lips of Duston, Neff, and Leonardson, then in Boston, while they were receiving the plaudits of that afflicted generation of English settlers, and while they still held in their hands the sanguine trophies of their world-renowned victory.

Several years since, I published in my "Merrimack," page 36, in epic, descriptive form, a brief statement of that event at Haverhill and in the Contoocook, a part of which is here inserted as a

RECAPITULATION.

And this is war! and such in wrath makes haste
To lay the white man's cot and village waste;
That deals in daggers poisoned, coated o'er,
The fagot-torch, and gluts on human gore.
Against such crime the settlers strong unite:
In various ways they rally for the fight:
Some seek defence by force of gun and dogs;
Some take to garrisons strong built of logs;

And some in squads with weapons rude assail
The foe, and fierce pursue the hidden trail.

'Twas so at Newbury and at Bradford town,
Far further north, and seaward further down;
Along the vale, where'er the white man dwelt,
Still unprovoked the self-same scourge was felt.
And at old Haverhill, as Mather tells,
The flaring fagot burns where Duston dwells.
That faithful father, frenzied to dismay,
Hastens the flight of children far away:
But not the infant: that in wrath is slain.
Its mother, captured, trudges in the train
Of savages; while in the clouds are shown
The crackling ruins of an English home.

The tribes evade pursuit: they skirt the glen,
Fast hastening through the fields away; and then
Dense woods and sable night conceal the foe.
There, couched on broken boughs, in beds of snow,
Repose they seek. Still mindful of the past,
Her heart depressed, by sleep benumbed at last,
There dreams that mother, weary, sick, at rest,
Of happy home, of father, children blest;
Of life's sweet joys, profusely, kindly given;
Of angel-visits from the throne of heaven;

Of that true bliss religious life inspires,
That wafts the soul above earth's frail desires.
Thus moved congenial thought her dreamy mind
As moved that mighty forest in the wind;
Thus on, till twilight gray with breaking beam
Now turns the tenor of a fleeting dream;
When, half aroused, before her vision gaze,
Appear grim visages and fagot-blaze;
Tall spectres gaunt, whose garments drip with gore
From that infanticide the day before,
Wrought strange convulsions. Whence that fearful wail?
'Twas Hannah Duston, waking for the trail.

Her dark brown hair back on her shoulders spread;
The frosts of night still on her garments laid.
At sight of death, at sound of war-whoop cry,
Avenging justice flashes in her eye.
Still, far beyond the cloud-capt tree-tops shown,
There gleamed in prospect yet another home.
Light paints a tinge upon her pallid brow;
And up to God above she made a vow:
For on the trees are marks of kindred blood;
And vengeance just is whispered in the wood.
Firm as the granite hills that brave the storm
That mother's will is fixed, and waxes warm.

Yet, held to follow through the rugged way,
Kept equal step for many a weary day,
('Twas death to falter 'mid a savage throng,)
With Mary Neff and boy, all move along
Through winding paths and tangled wildwood fens,
Where prowled the wolf, and where the serpent dens:
Declivities they wind, and ford the brooks
That leap the mountain-pass from granite rocks;
Thence in dark thicket, then in sunlight gleam,
And then in boats of birch on spacious stream,
Up where old Contoocook unites in pride
With Merrimack, profound in rolling tide;
There, on an island wild, are captives shown
The wigwam rude, an Indian's favored home.
And there, on mats, around the camp-fire flame
Seated in group, they glut the slaughtered game
Which hunger sought; and Night, now gathering in,
Spreads her dark mantle o'er the woods within;
While from afar a gentle zephyr-breeze
Plays grateful music on the waving trees,
Inviting rest from the rambling drudge of day,
That lulls the spirit from the world away.
Still does that zephyr omens strange portend, —
A baleful bickering, some tragic end:
Yet ne'er more safe, ne'er less by danger pressed,
Than felt the drowsy foe reclined at rest;

And sleep sonorous, which fatigue inspires,
Drowns deep the tribe in front of midnight fires.
Then rose that mother, noiseless, moving near
To Neff; breathes mandates startling to her ear:
To Samuel, too, her vent of vengeance went
That fired his heart.   They move with joint intent,
And signal stealth.   Around the foe they felt,
And drew a tomahawk each from the belt
That touched his loins; and then erect they stand,
Lifting that bloody blade with heedful hand:
Down on his guilty head three times they strike;
And three times three death follows each alike.
No groan nor sigh is heard, nor sign of woe;
But stiff and cold there lies the bloody foe
'Neath clouds of night.   The wigwam embers fade;
And phantom shadows stalk along the glade
In depth of woods; the hills are hushed aloof;
No voice, save from the owl or hungry wolf
That clamors for his prey.   Yet as these three,
Once captive bound, now turn away thus free,
Bright, beaming stars through parted clouds be-
    tween,
True guides intent, from heaven's arch serene
Look down; while Truth, still valiant to prevail
O'er wrong, and Justice stern, with even scale,
Approve the deed: and from that crimson glade.
That dark, lone wigwam with unburied dead,

DUSTIN, NEFF, AND LEONARDSON.

Relieved, yet sad, they board a light canoe,
To dip the oar in hope of home; pursue
Adown bright Merrimack in generous tide,
That bears the craft on high through borders wide:
Thence paddling east, they gain a favored shore
Above the fall, where troubled waters roar
Below, — all safe at land. The day-star rose;
Nature anon awakes from night's repose;
Wild birds from far, thick gathered in the trees,
Warble sweet welcome on the morning breeze
To strange adventurers; while all that day,
Along the winding shore that leads the way
To Haverhill, they thoughtful trudge, and talk
What each had seen in life's bewildered walk, —
Of childhood years beguiled with favorite toys,
Of love, of home delights, of buried joys.

I will close the incidents of this chapter by inserting in this place a brief account of the murder, at Haverhill, of the

REV. BENJAMIN ROLFE.

On the 29th of August, 1708, at break of day, a force of two hundred and fifty French and Indians from Canada, after devastating other villages, came past the frontier garrisons undiscovered; and were first seen near the pound in Haverhill, marching two and two. John Keezer saw them first, near his house; and ran into the village, and alarmed the inhabitants by firing a gun near the meeting-house.

The enemy came on, making the air ring with terrific yells and " a sound like whistling." Scattering their forces, they commenced their bloody work. Mrs. Smith, the first person seen, as she took towards a garrison, they shot. The foremost party proceeded to the house of Rev. Mr. Rolfe; and, although guarded by three soldiers, his family were awakened by the war-whoop. Alas! it was but the death-knell of their own departure.

Mr. Rolfe leaped from his bed, placed himself against the door, which they were trying to force in, and called to his soldiers for assistance; but they fled like sheep. The tribe fired bullets through the door. Mr. Rolfe, wounded, fled from the back-door: the savages, following in pursuit, killed him with their tomahawks.

They soon found Mrs. Rolfe, killed her, and then murdered her infant against a stone at the door.

Hagar, a negro slave, ran away with two of the children, six and eight years of age; hid them under tubs in the cellar; and thus their lives were saved. Yet they murdered many. There were other invasions and other murders in Haverhill besides *these* and those which have been referred to on our fifteenth page.

CHAPTER II.

THOMAS DUSTON.

Thomas Duston's Bravery. — Saves his Children. — Poetry to his Praise by Mrs. Sarah J. Hale. — Order to Duston in his Garrison. — Story of Joseph Whittaker. — Petition of Thomas Duston. — Captivity of Hannah Bradley. — Her Return. — After Six Years, her Second Capture. — Her Long Sufferings. — Birth and Slaughter of her Infant. — Two Years a Slave to a Frenchman in Canada. — Her Husband finds and redeems her. — Their Return to Boston and to Haverhill. — How the Indian Battle-Axe fell Heavily upon the New-England Mothers. — A Word to the Praise of their Faith and Valor.

IT is an axiom commonly conceded, that great occasions — as when the lives of men or the well-being of a republic are endangered — operate to bring forth the brightest examples of truth, of self-sacrifice, and of valiant heroism.

Hence many modest, unpretending hearts, men and mothers, who else would have remained forever retired and unknown, sprang forth as against the invasions of barbarism in New England, and have left to us and to the world valuable enduring legacies.

Among these instances of bravery may be reckoned the gallant feat of Thomas Duston, husband of Hannah, in protecting the lives of his and her children at the massacre in Haverhill.

This hero, as is supposed, emigrated from a family at Dover, N.H., where it is said there were many of that name.

At Haverhill he seems to have been a man of considerable note and influence; was a constable, a maker of bricks, and also of almanacs on rainy days, as they say; and was the keeper of a garrison at his new brick house, his headquarters at the homestead having been consumed.

His sagacious effort in saving his seven children from the cruel grasp of savages on that terrible day when his little Martha was slain, his house burnt to ashes, and his wife carried away captive, was indeed praiseworthy. It has been poetized by Mrs. S. J. Hale. Her poetry runs thus:—

THE FATHER'S CHOICE.

Now fly as flies the rushing wind!
Urge, urge thy rushing steed!
The savage yell is fierce behind;
And life is on thy speed.

And from those dear ones make thy choice!
    The group he wildly eyed;
When " Father!" burst from every side,
    And " Child!" his heart replied.

There's one will prattle on his knee,
    Or slumber on his breast;
And one whose joys of infancy
    Are still by smiles expressed.

They feel no fear while he is near;
    He'll shield them from the foe:
But, oh! his ear must thrill to hear
    Their shriekings should he go.

In vain his quivering lips would speak;
    No words his thoughts allow:
There's a burning tear upon his cheek,
    Death's marble on his brow.

And twice he smote his clinchèd hands;
    Then bade his children fly,
And turned; and even that savage band
    Cowered at his wrathful eye.

Swift as the lightning winged with death
    Flashed forth the quivering flame:
Their finest warrior bows beneath
    The father's deadly aim.

Ambition goads the conquerer on ;
　　Hate points the murderer's brand :
But love and duty — these alone
　　Can nerve the good man's hand.

Not the wild cries that rend the skies
　　His heart of purpose move :
He saves his children, or he dies
　　The sacrifice of love.

The hero may resign the field,
　　The coward murderer flee :
He cannot fear, he will not yield,
　　That strikes, sweet Love ! for thee.

They come ! they come ! He heeds no cry
　　Save the soft child-like wail :
" O father, save ! " — " My children, fly ! " —
　　Were mingled on the gale.

And firmer still he drew his breath,
　　And sterner flashed his eye,
As fast he hurled the leaden death,
　　Still shouting, " Children, fly ! "

No shadow on his brow appeared,
　　Nor tremor shook his frame,
Save when at intervals he heard
　　Some trembler lisp his name.

THOMAS DUSTON.

In vain the foe — those fiends unchained —
Like famished tigers chafe:
The sheltered roof is neared, is gained;
All, all the dear ones safe!

This Indian massacre was a terrible blow to Haverhill. "Some of its most useful citizens and promising youth, as already appears, were among the slain; and, well knowing that they were daily and hourly liable to similar attacks, it needs no stretch of imagination to declare that fear seized the hearts of the inhabitants.

"The most vigorous measures were speedily taken to prevent, if possible, another similar bloody onset: guards were stationed in many of the houses; and the brick house of Thomas Duston, that had been partly finished the preceding year, not being occupied, was ordered to be garrisoned."

The following is a copy of the order to Thomas Duston when appointed to command it: —

ORDER.

"*To Thomas Duston, upon the Settlement of Garrisons.*

"APRIL 5, 1697. — You being appointed master of the garrison at your house, you are hereby in his Majesty's name required to see that a good watch is kept at your garrison, both by night and by day, by those persons hereafter named, who are to be under your command and inspection in building or repairing your garrison; and, if any person refuse or neglect their duty, you are accordingly required to make return of the same, under your hand, to the committee of militia in Haverhill. The persons appointed are as followeth: Josiah Heath, sen., Josiah Heath, jun., Joseph Bradley, John Heath, Joseph Kingsbury, and Thomas Kingsbury.

"By order of the committee of militia.

"SAMUEL AYER, *Captain.*"

Mr. DUSTON was a constable in Haverhill; and, for the times, was largely engaged in brick-making. The business, however, was attended with no little danger, on account of the Indians, who were almost continually lurking in the vicinity, watching an opportunity for a successful attack. The clay-pits were only a short distance from the garrison; but the enemy were so bold, that a file of soldiers constantly guarded those who brought the clay from the pits to the yard near the house, where it was made into bricks.

There is a story of Joseph Whittaker, one of this guard; and it may be well to tell it.

THE STORY.

JOSEPH was young. He had become deeply in love with one Mary Whittaker, who was then being protected within the garrison. Joseph had struggled long and manfully to escape the silken meshes, but in vain. At last, summoning all his courage, he improved a favorable opportunity to make a declaration of his passion and purpose. But ah! — most unfortunate Joseph! — Mary did not heed him. He pleaded, he entreated, he implored, but all to no purpose. Mary declared most emphatically that she would not have Joe Whittaker. Thereupon his blood was up. He told her, that, unless she accepted his offer, he would jump into the well. But Mary avowed that she wouldn't. Joe hastened from the garrison, seized a log that lay near by, and plunged it into the dark, deep waters. Mary heard the plunge, and her heart relented. Remembering her love, and with her hair streaming in the night-wind, she rushed to the well, crying in the agony of her heart, " O Joseph, *Joseph!* if you are in the land of the living, I *will* have you."

Joseph, immediately emerging from his hiding-place, fell into her arms, exclaiming, "*I will take you at your word!*"

The two Whittakers were soon afterwards made

one; and, from the records of Haverhill, it does not appear that the Whittakers were in any way diminished by that operation.

On the 21st of April, after a little rest from the fatigue of her wearisome captivity, Mrs. Duston with her husband and two captive companions were in Boston. Cotton Mather then and there wrote from their own account of it the entire outlines of this tragedy; while the ten scalps, the gun, and the tomahawk were still there as witnesses also to the truthfulness of the narrative. Duston at the same time presented to the General Assembly, then in session, a petition as follows: —

PETITION.

"*To the Right Honorable the Lieut.-Governor, and the Great and General Assembly of the Province of Massachusetts Bay, now convened in Boston.*

" The humble Petition of Thomas Duston of Haverhill sheweth: That the wife of ye petitioner (with one Mary Neff) hath, in her late captivity among the Barbarous Indians, been disposed & assisted by Heaven to do an extraordinary action, in the just slaughter of so many of the Barbarians, as would by the law of the Province which a few months ago would have entitled the actors unto considerable recompense from the Publick.

"That tho' the [want] of that good law [warrants] no claims to any such consideration from the Publick; yet your petitioner humbly —— that the merit of the action still remains the same; & it seems a matter of universall desire thro' the whole Province that it should not pass unrecompensed. And that your petitioner having lost his estate in that calamity wherein his wife was carried into her captivity, render him the fitter object for what consideration the Publick Bounty shall judge proper for hath been herein done; of some consequence not only unto the persons more immediately delivered, but also unto the generall interest.

"Wherefore, humbly requesting a favorable Regard on this occasion, your petitioner shall pray, &c.

"THOMUS DU(R)STUN."

On the 8th of June the House of Representatives "*voted* that the above-named Thomas Durstan, in behalf of his wife, shall be allowed and paid out of the publick Treasury Twenty-five pounds, and Mary Neff the sum of Twelve pounds Ten shillings, and the young man (named Samuel Lenerson) concerned in the same action the like sum of Twelve pounds Ten shillings."

HANNAH BRADLEY.

Contemporaneously with the capture of Hannah

Duston and Mary Neff, on the same 15th of March, 1697, Hannah Bradley was also taken and carried into captivity. She, as a captive, followed Mrs. Duston, and in the same trail constituted one of the number at the command of the same savages, until they arrived near and opposite to the Contoocook ; when she with one branch of the tribe took a different route, and camped at another Indian home not far away.

Hannah Bradley, however, afterwards escaped, and returned home to Haverhill, probably the same year.

In 1703, six years later, the same Mrs. Bradley was again captured by the savages, and at this time, as appears, remained nearly two years in captivity. In the mean time, she was sold by the Indians to the French in Canada, who were hostile to our English settlers.

Joseph Bradley the husband, at Haverhill, hearing of his wife in Canada, started off on that then long journey, and persevered until he found, purchased, obtained, and brought her back to Haverhill.

Of this Myrick says, " On that first general attack in that war of Queen Anne's time, Aug. 10, 1703, five hundred French and Indians ravaged the settlements from Casco to Wells, and killed and captured one hundred and thirty persons."

He says, " On the 8th of February then next following, a party of six Indians attacked the garrison of Joseph Bradley, which was unhappily in an unguarded state: even the sentinels had left their stations, and their gates open. As appears, Bradley lived on the parsonage road, near the northerly brook.

"The Indians approached cautiously, and were rushing into the open gates before they were discovered. Jonathan Johnson, a sentinel, who was standing in the house, shot at and wounded the foremost; and Mrs. Bradley, who had a kettle of boiling soap over the fire, seized her ladle, and, filling it with the steaming liquid, discharged it on his tawny pate, — a *soap*-orific that brought on a *sleep* from which he never awoke.

"The rest of the party immediately rushed forward, killed Johnson, and took captive the intrepid woman and some others.

"The Indians then, fearing lest they should soon be attacked by a stronger party, commenced a hasty retreat, aiming for Canada; which was then a place of resort often whenever they had been so successful as to take a number of prisoners. Mrs. Bradley was in delicate circumstances, and in slender health: still she received no kindness from her savage conquerers. No situation of woman would ever protect her from their demon-like cruelties.

"The weather was cold the wind blew keenly over

the hills, and the ground was covered with a deep snow; yet they obliged her to travel on foot, and to carry a heavy burden, — too large, even, for the strength of man.

"In this manner they proceeded through the wilderness; and Mrs. Bradley informed her family after she returned, that, for many days in succession, she subsisted on nothing but bits of skin, ground-nuts, the bark of trees, wild onions, and lily-roots. While in this situation, with none but savages for her assistants and protectors, and in the midst of a thick forest, she gave birth to a child. The Indians then, as if they were not satisfied with persecuting the mother, extended their cruelties to the innocent and almost friendless babe.

"For the want of proper attention, it was sickly, and probably troublesome; and, when it cried, these remorseless fiends showed their pity by throwing embers into its mouth.

"They told the mother, that, if she would permit them to baptize it in their manner, they would suffer it to live. Unwilling to deny their request, lest it should enrage their fierce and diabolical passions, and hoping that the little innocent would receive kindness at their hands, she complied with their request. They took it from her, and baptized it by gashing its forehead with their knives.

"The feelings of the mother, when the child was returned to her with its smooth and white forehead gashed with a knife, and its warm blood coursing down its cheeks, can be better imagined than described.

"Soon as Mrs. Bradley had regained sufficient strength to travel, the Indians again took up their march for Canada. But, before their arrival to their place of rendezvous, she had occasion to go a little distance from the party; and, when she returned, she beheld a sight shocking to a mother and to every feeling of humanity. Her child, which was born in sorrow and nursed in the lap of affliction, and on which she doted with maternal fondness, was piked upon a pole. Its excruciating agonies were over; it could no more feel the tortures of the merciless savages; and its mother could only weep over its memory."

HANNAH BRADLEY WITH THE FRENCH.

"Soon after, they proceeded to Canada, where Mrs. Bradley was sold to the French for eighty livres.

"She informed her friends after her return, that she was treated kindly by the family in which she lived. It was her custom morning and evening, when she milked her master's cow, to take with her a crust of bread, soak it with milk, and eat it: with this, and with the rations allowed her by her master, she eked out a tolerable existence.

"In March, 1705, her husband, hearing that she was in the possession of the French, started for Canada with the intention of redeeming her.

"He travelled on foot, accompanied only by a dog that drew a small sled, in which he carried a bag of snuff as a present from the governor of this province to the governor of Canada. When he arrived he immediately redeemed her, and set sail from Montreal for Boston, which they reached in safety, and from thence travelled to Haverhill."

THEY TRIED TO TAKE HER A THIRD TIME.

In 1706, "during the summer of that year," Myrick says, "a small party of Indians again visited the garrison of Joseph Bradley; and it is said that he, his wife and children, and a hired man, were the only persons in it at the time. It was in the night: the moon shone brightly; and they could be easily seen silently and cautiously approaching. Mr. Bradley armed himself, also his wife and man, each with a gun, and such of his children as could shoulder one.

"Mrs. Bradley, supposing that they had come purposely for *her*, told her husband that she would rather be killed than be again taken.

"The Indians rushed upon the garrison, and endeavored to beat down the door. They succeeded in pushing it partly open; and, when one of the Indians began to crowd himself through the opening, Mrs. Bradley, firing upon him, shot him dead.

"The rest of the party, seeing their companion fall, desisted from their purpose, and hastily retreated."

The story of Mrs. Bradley's captivity as a companion of Hannah Duston is here told briefly, perhaps imperfectly, — how she was taken a second time, carried to Canada, and sold as a slave; how during that time she had seen her own dear infant slain by the tribe; how amid Indian exultations she had seen it piked upon a pole; and how, after her deliverance from bondage, a third attack being made upon her husband's garrison, she arose in her heroism, shot the leader, and thereby put to flight the stealthy, cowardly invaders. The experiences of her gallant little son, who was indeed her senior in captivity, will appear in our next chapter.

From all this it must be seen how sadly in that day, and with what crushing weight, the Indian battle-axe at noonday and at midnight fell upon the women and children of New England.

A brief poem from my "Merrimack," page 35, given on the following page, may be of interest: —

WOMAN IN WAR.

From war-whoops wild, and earth in crimson glow,
A wail goes up, — a note of woman's woe.
Fierce vengeance tempts her singleness of heart,
Her heroism true, her guileless art,
Her purity, her own maternal care;
Her faith in God, that never knows despair;
Her love indeed, that triumphs most and best
In trial sad, when most by danger pressed;
Whose truth endures when fails our vital breath,
Inspires fond hope, and smooths the bed of death.
Such were the hearts, whose wails went up afar,
That brooked the fury of King William's war;
Whose just protection savages defied,
And dearest hopes of house and home denied.
Around her hearth from hidden ambush springs
The lurking foe, and death with horror brings.

CHAPTER III.

THE TWO BOYS.

Their Captivity. — Their Treatment by the Tribes. — They learn the Indian Language. — Their Schemes. — Their Escape at Midnight. — They hide in a Hollow Log. — The Tribes with Hounds pursue them. — The Boys appease the Dogs. — They remain undiscovered. — Advance mostly by Night. — They lose their Way. — Subsist on Roots. — Are Nine Days in the Forest homeward. — Their Arrival at Saco. — They fall Sick. — Isaac plods his Way Home. — Joseph's Father finds and takes him to Haverhill. — General Court grants Land to Isaac's Mother; also to Joseph Neff, Son of Mary. — Mrs. Bradley's Deposition. — Descendants from the Captives. — Their Talk from the Contoocook to Haverhill.

IN the fall of 1695, as history has it, a party of Indians appeared in the northerly part of Haverhill; where they surprised and made prisoners of Isaac, son of Hannah and Joseph Bradley, aged fifteen years, and Joseph Whittaker, aged eleven, who were at work in the open fields near Joseph Bradley's house. The Indians instantly retreated with their prisoners, without further violence; and pursued their journey through the forest until they arrived at their homes on the shores of the Winnipiseogee. Isaac, says tradition, was rather small in stature, but full of vigor, very active, and possessed more shrewdness than most boys of that age; but Joseph was larger and less active. Immediately after their arrival at the lake, the two boys were held in an Indian family consisting of the man, his squaw, and two or three children. While they were there they became acquainted with the Indian language; and learned from their conversations with other Indians that they intended to carry them to Canada the following spring. This discovery afflicted them. If such design were carried into execution, they knew there would be but little chance for their escape; and from that time the active mind of Isaac was continually planning a mode to effect it. A deep and unbroken wilderness, pathless mountains, and swollen and almost impassable rivers, lay between them and their homes; and the boys feared, if they were carried still farther northward, that they should never again hear the kind voice of a father, or feel the fervent kiss of their then afflicted mother, or the fond embrace of a sister. They knew, that should they die in a strange land, among savages, there would be no friend there to place the green turf upon their graves, and no fond one near to announce their fate or to treasure up their memories.

Such were the melancholy musings of the young boys; and they determined to escape before their master started them for Canada. The winter came with its storms of snow; the spring followed with its early buds, its flowers, and its pleasant south wind: still they were prisoners. Within that period Isaac was brought nigh to the grave: a burning fever came upon him, and for many days he languished; but by the care of a squaw, his mistress, usually kind, he recovered. And yet he felt a strong desire to escape, which increased; and in April he matured a plan for that purpose. He appointed a night in his own mind when to escape; and, on the day previously, he made known to his companion his intentions. Joseph expressed a desire also to escape: to this Isaac said, "I'm afraid you won't wake." Joseph promised that he would, and at night they laid down in their master's wigwam with the tribe. Joseph soon fell asleep, and began to snore lustily; but there was no sleep for Isaac: his strong desire to escape, the fear of a failure in the attempt, and of the punishment that would be inflicted if he did not succeed, and the danger, hunger, and fatigue that awaited him, all moved his imagination, and kept sleep far from his eyelids. His daring attempt was covered with danger, yet his resolution remained unshaken. At length the midnight hour came, and its holy stillness rested on the surrounding forest. At that moment he slowly and cautiously arose. All was silent there save the deep-drawn breath of the savage sleepers. The voice of the wind was scarcely audible on the hills; and the moon at times would shine brightly through the scattered clouds, and silver the broad lake, as though the robe of an angel had fallen on its sleeping waters. Isaac stepped softly and tremblingly over their tawny bodies, lest they should awake: he secured his master's fireworks, and a portion of his moose-meat and bread; these he carried to a little distance from the wigwam, and concealed them in a clump of bushes. He then returned, and bending over Joseph, who had all this time been snoring in his sleep, carefully shook him. Joseph, more asleep than awake, turned partly over and asked aloud, "*What do you want?*" This blunder alarmed Isaac; and he instantly laid down in his proper place, and again began to snore as loudly as any of them. Soon as his alarm had somewhat subsided, he again arose, and listened long for the heavy breath of the sleepers. Perceiving them all asleep, he resolved to escape without again attempting to awake Joseph, for fear of his indiscretion. He then arose, and, stepping softly out of the wigwam, walked slowly and cautiously from it until he had nearly reached the place where his provisions were concealed, when he heard footsteps approaching behind him. With a beating heart he looked backward, and saw Joseph, who had aroused, and, finding him absent, had followed him.

They then secured the fire-works and provisions, and, without chart or compass, struck into the woods in a southerly direction, aiming for the distant settlement of Haverhill. They ran at the top of their speed until daylight appeared, when they concealed themselves in a hollow log, deeming it too dangerous to continue their journey in the daytime. Their master and tribe, in the morning, finding their prisoners had escaped, aided by their dogs, pursued them in haste.

The dogs, taking their track, in a short time came up to the boys in the log, made a stand, and began to bark.

The boys trembled, fearing a re-capture, and death at the edge of the tomahawk. In this situation they knew not what to do, but spoke kindly to them. The dogs, knowing their voices, ceased barking, and wagged their tails with delight. They then gave them their moose-meat, which the dogs instantly seized and devoured. While they were thus concealed, trembling and meditating, the Indians made their appearance, and passed near to the log in which they were concealed; the dogs, being quiet, were unnoticed, and immediately followed on after the tribes. With breathless anxiety the boys followed them with their eyes as they advanced from their sight; and hope again revived within their bosoms. They lay in the log during the day, and at night pursued their journey, taking a different route from the one travelled by the Indians. Their bread was soon gone: after that, they subsisted on roots and buds. On the second day they again concealed themselves, but afterwards travelled night and day, without resting. On that day, towards night, they luckily killed a pigeon and a turtle, a part of which they ate raw, not daring to build a fire, lest they should be discovered. On their way they subsisted on fragments of these, and on such roots as they happened to find; continued their journey night and day as fast as their wearied legs would carry them. On the sixth day they struck an Indian path, and followed it till night, when they suddenly came within sight of an Indian encampment; saw their savage enemy seated around the fire, and distinctly heard their voices. This alarmed them exceedingly. They precipitately fled from it, fearing lest they should be discovered and pursued; then turning, all night long they retraced their steps. The morning came, and found them seated side by side on the bank of a small stream, their feet torn and covered with blood, and both sadly meditating upon their misfortunes. Thus far their hearts had been hopeful; but now their hopes had given way to despair. They thought of their homes, of the green trees under which they had played, of the hearth around which they had often gathered with brothers and sisters. They thought of these, and of more; still they were unwilling to yield. The philosophy of Isaac taught him that the stream must eventually lead to a large body of water: and, after refreshing themselves with a few roots, they again commenced their journey, and followed down the stream. Thus they continued onward. On the eighth morning Joseph found himself completely exhausted; his limbs were weak, and his mind was lost in despair. Isaac endeavored to encourage him to proceed; he dug roots for him, and brought water to quench his thirst, but all in vain. He laid himself down on the bank of the stream, in the shady deep forest, there to die unsought, unseen. Isaac left him to his fate; and, with a bleeding heart, slowly and wearily pursued his journey. He had travelled but a short distance when he came to a newly-raised building. Rejoiced at his good fortune, and believing that inhabitants were nigh, he immediately retraced his steps, and soon found Joseph in the same place, told him what he had seen, talked very encouragingly, and, after rubbing his limbs a while, induced him to stand on his feet. They then started together, Isaac now

5*

leading him by the hand, now carrying him on his back; and thus, with limbs tired with travelling, with bodies reduced to skeletons, they arrived at Saco Fort in the course of the next night.

Thus, on the ninth night — after travelling through an immense forest, subsisting on a little bread, on buds and berries, a raw turtle, and a pigeon, and without seeing a fire or the face of a friend — Isaac, soon as he regained his strength, started for Haverhill, and arrived safely at his father's dwelling-house, who had heard nothing from him since his capture, never expecting to see him again. But Joseph had more to suffer. As soon as he reached the fort his fever increased upon him; and there, for a long time, he remained confined to his bed. His father, obtaining intelligence by Isaac, went to Saco, and, as soon as circumstances would admit, conveyed his sick son safely to his home in Haverhill.

MRS. BRADLEY AGAIN.

Forty years farther along in our annals, to wit, in 1738, we again hear of the same *Hannah Bradley*, who on the same day with Hannah Duston, in 1697, had then for the first time been carried into captivity.

AT THE GENERAL COURT.

That year (1738) compensation was awarded her at that session, on the account of her suffering as a captive, *twice* taken, and pursued a *third* time.

It was the grant of two farms in Methuen, which were laid out to her by Richard Hazen, surveyor, May 29, 1739; the one containing one hundred and sixty acres, bordering on the westerly line of Haverhill, and the other ninety acres, which extended along the easterly line of Dracut.

MARY NEFF AGAIN.

In June, 1739, JOSEPH, a son of the same Mary, petitioned "the Great and General Court" for a grant of land in consideration of his mother's captivity, and of her services in assisting Hannah Duston "in killing divers Indians;" alleging that she was "*kept a prisoner for a considerable time*," and that "on their return home, they passed through the utmost hazard of their lives, and suffered distressing want, being almost starved before they could return to their dwellings."

On this petition Joseph was supported by the same Mrs. Bradley.

AN AFFIDAVIT.

"The deposition of the widow HANNAH BRADLEY of Haverhill, of full age, who testifieth and saith that about forty years past the said Hannah, with the widow Mary Neff, were taken prisoners by the Indians, and carried together into captivity; and above Pennacook the deponent was by the Indians forced to travel farther than the rest of the captives.

"And, *the next night but one*, there came to us one squaw, who said that Hannah Duston and the aforesaid MARY NEFF assisted in killing the Indians of her wigwam, except herself and a boy, herself escaping very narrowly, showing to myself and others *seven* wounds, as she said with a hatchet, on her head, which wounds were given her when the rest were killed."

"And further saith not."

"HANNAH X BRADLEY."
(her mark)

Signed and sworn to at Haverhill, "June 28, 1739."

"JOSHUA BAGLEY," *J. P.*

DESCENDANTS.

The descendants of these several captives whose brief biographies have been given, with the exception of Leonardson (if he had any) are quite numerous in New England.

HANNAH DUSTON has many, among whom are

Jonas B. Aikin, Walter Aikin, and *F. H. Aikin*, of Franklin, N.H., all men of wealth, noble and generous, and all of much use and profit in this generation.

MARY NEFF has also many descendants, among whom was the late Horatio G. F. Corliss, a distinguished lawyer of Lowell, Mass.; also Mr. John L. Corliss of the same city, who now resides on or near the spot upon which Passaconaway, when he had become old, in 1660, addressed the Pennacooks at Pawtucket Falls on the Merrimack. Another descendant of Mary is Charles Corliss, Esq., of Haverhill, who now holds the inheritance where Mary was born, and still lives in the same house; which, being fitted up, constitutes a kitchen to his modern mansion.

HANNAH BRADLEY'S descendants are to be found in New England almost everywhere. Prolific like Mrs. Duston, she left a numerous progeny; and from her the world has been blest with the best blood of a noble race, contributing much of life and stability to the various branches of New England enterprise. Among the many of them are Messrs. Ira Bradley and Son, formerly of Haverhill, now of Boston, far known to the book fraternity, and for these many years strong in wealth, truthful, faithful, and valiant.

It may here be observed that her son ISAAC, the

boy, was a comrade in captivity with Joseph Whittaker in 1695, as may be seen on page 47; the same Joseph who afterwards, in Duston's garrison at Haverhill, so adroitly obtained the hand of the heroic MARY WHITTAKER.

I close this chapter by inserting here from my "Merrimack," page 44, certain conversations supposed to have been had by the Contoocook captives, while on their way back to Haverhill, when and after the light of that tragic morning first discovered to little Samuel the stains of blood upon his garments.

THEY TRUDGE AND TALK.

Thus did the women mutual converse hold,
Till Samuĕl from mutest manner cold
Bespoke them thus: " What mean these signs of
    pain,
These crimson marks, that through my garments
    stain?
Did such from veins of Banpaco descend,
Who gave me bow and arrow as a friend?
Truth undisguised these morning beams disclose,
The sure avenger of his dying woes.
Unwelcome tints! they haunt my homeward way,
And at the threshold threaten to betray
Me there. Shall I, long lost, a mother's boy,
Return, and pangs impart instead of joy

To such a heart? No: leave me here unknown
To seek some hidden cave aloof from home;
Or send me captive bound, to dwell again
In tents, afar from her who mourns me slain,
Whence crime concealed shall never vent a stain,
Nor rumor sad to blot a cherished name,"—
He said, and there half halting stood,
Till Mary chides him thus in a different mood:—
"I pray thee, Samuel, list to me a while:
Misgivings sad attend but to beguile
Thy youth. But list! they move me to descry,
In wrong, if thou art guilty, so am I.
For at the war-whoop cry I could have fled,
And shunned captivity, its horrors dread;
Yet would not yield to fate that infant dear,
Nor fail my mistress kind, through selfish fear.
Alarmed, I seized it from the cradle there:
That life I begged a furied fiend to spare
At risk of self. Yet we no favor gain,—
Our plea, our prayers, most fervent, all in vain!
Impelled from horrors which this heart had stung,
To our liege mother and to thee I clung.
In bonds a comrade held, a volunteer
In all the dangers dread of such career,
I've more to fear than thou, who, found alone,
Wert forced at Worcester from parental home
By brutal foes. Grim cruelties they sought,
But on themselves relentless vengeance brought,

In which an agent I indeed was one
To bear a part in wrong, if wrong were done.
If, in the shed of blood, a crime it be
To break from hell-born bondage to be free,
Then is the fault in me much more than thee,
Who had no choice of lot nor chance to flee.
Yet have I faith, from inward teachings given,
Life's freedom gained is justified of Heaven;
Whose care paternal henceforth let us trust,
As did our fathers, faithful from the first."
Thus did they talk of self, of wrong and right,
Meandering along till late at night,
Through narrow pathways, hindered now and then
By tangled thicket dark, by brook and fen,
Then next by range of hills, where lies at length
A deep ravine, and there through lack of strength
They turn aside beneath a shelving rock,
O'ergrown of spreading pines, thither to stop,
Inclined to rest; but fain would wakeful keep
Yet, lost anon by force of needful sleep,
Remain still there till morn's refulgent ray,
Reflected on the wave of Nashua,
Cast varied shadows in the branchy wood
Around the group. There "Mother Duston" stood,
Invoking favors from the throne of God,
To be bestowed in coming time for good
For Mary Neff, for Samuel the same, —
Her pilgrim comrades, whence deliverance came;

And briefly now, as ended then her prayer,
Addressed them each in turn, still waiting there,
In kindness thus: "Mary, to thee I owe
Much more of debt than I can e'er bestow
Of earth's reward. Thy truthfulness of heart,
Thy generous constancy, thy guileless art,
In trial proved, this thankful soul reveres.
May blessings, Mary, crown thy future years!
My home is thine, if home I see again,
Devoutly favored thou shalt there remain.
And you, dear Samuel, valiant in the past,
Honest in purpose, faithful to the last,
No more should doubt. To savages belong
The retribution of relentless wrong,
And not to thee. Are not his dealings just
Who Israel led? Shall we our God distrust?
No. Brood no more of doubts, most noble boy!
Go, seek thy way to Worcester; bear true joy
To her who bore thee, and whose hallowed care
Shall haste thee onward to her presence there;
Still undisguised, in truth of God still led,
Wash not a stain from out thy garments red.
Thy deeds but known shall welcome truth impart:
They'll prove the valor of a valiant heart.
Take yonder skiff: 'twill be no trespass done:
For thee it drifted from a fate unknown.
For thee my voice in thanks shall hence ascend.
Away! and blessings on thy life attend."

Still loth to part, yet harboring doubts no more,
The lad, wide wafted on the westward shore,
His beckoning paddle raised: with aprons, too,
The women, answering, waved their last adieu.
Thence turning, tearful, meditating mild
On distant dear ones, wandered through the wild,
And Haverhill reached; to whom from governors even
Came generous gifts and thankful plaudits given.

And there they rest.   There upward points to-day
A monument of stone to Duston's clay.
Her noble deeds are held in high renown,
Sacred like heir-loom, in that ancient town;
And long as Merrimack's bright waters glide,
Shall stand that mother's fame still by its side.

SIR FRANCIS DRAKE.—FIRST WHITE MAN IN NEW ENGLAND.

CHAPTER IV.

INDIAN NATIONS: THEIR COUNTRY AND THEIR DESCENT.

Sir Francis Drake's Advent. — No Historic Record previously. — Outlines of the New-England Territory. — Beauties of its Landscape. — Poetical Description of its Creation, and of the Formation of its Rivers. — The Winnipiseogee, and other Lakes. — Rivers and Tributaries. — Origin of the Indian Nations of the New World. — Their Manners and Habits. — Their Numbers at the Coming of the Puritans. — Their Ignorance. — Their Government. — Their Fashions of Dress. — Kind at First. — Changing Gradually by the Machinations of the French, by Individual Indiscretion, and by their own unbridled Infirmities.

THE history of New England is brief and tragical. It dates back no farther than to Sir Francis Drake, that adventurous white man who in 1586 first touched upon its shores, named it, and then, leaving it, advanced onward upon his famous voyage around the world.

Up to that period, whatever had transpired in the affairs of this part of the New World is unknown. Oblivion covers it: nor is it within the power of mortal vision to trace or discover its outlines. Hence every thing historical in this region, anterior to the advent of Drake, becomes a matter of mere inference, or of curious speculation.

The countless years thus passed of man's career—
Fraught with achievements oft enacted here,
With works of skill, what human thought could do,
With grand exploits, or deeds of direful hue,
With kings and prophets, chief in note or worth,
Through generations vast transpired on earth—
Make but a blank in Time's historic lore,
Till voyagers from another world came o'er.

From my Merrimack, p. 22.

In Drake's time the length and breadth of territory then comprised within the outward lines of Maine, New Hampshire, Massachusetts, Rhode Island, and Connecticut, was a vast wilderness, crowned with its white mountains on the north-east, towering in the clouds, and sending forth ten thousand rills to the east, to the west, to the north, and to the south, from which the beautiful Merrimack, the Connecticut, and the Saco leaped forth as from the creation, and with silvery waters then flowing, rolling, meandering downward through the then vast wilderness,—

To form a sea, and on the world bestow
A vast highway, with tides to ebb and flow;

In light refulgent, in extent sublime,
To swarm with joyous life through endless time;
To float huge ships in commerce and in strife
Of unborn nations waking into life.

Through constant heat her atoms rise again,
Floating in transit backward whence they came,
Feeding the streams with purer founts anew,
Which, made eternal, onward still pursue.
Both flood and vapor in one circuit run,
Like planet in her orb about the sun,
Or like the life-blood coursing in the vein
By means of arteries, return again,
Sustaining man's frail body from his birth, —
So moving waters do the vital earth:
Pervading nature's germs and fibres free,
Upward in channels creep through herb and tree,
They deck the daisy in her checkered bloom,
And swell the rose to yield a sweet perfume,
Are felt in trunk, in branch, in bud, and leaves,
And thence escape in clouds borne on the breeze;
Emblem of the "Eternal" in their round,
E'er free to give, but ne'er exhausted found.

Standing on the lofty heights of New England, the historic spectator is entranced. He sees spread out before him, southward and eastward, in azure brilliancy, its vast expanse of field and forest, of mansion and village, interlaced with the meandering Saco and Connecticut; while rolling onward, as if to its eternal destiny, in the midst of this beautiful landscape is the

MERRIMACK.

Sweet river! thy true source which angels sung
At the creation when the world begun,
We seek; and how thy rills, of chaos born,
First leaped rejoicing in their native form;
When bleak New Albion's height began to rise,
And moon and stars, just formed, lit up the skies,
How the great God on high with outstretched hand
Divided waters from the massive land,
Scooped the vast concave of the ocean-bed,
And infant channels for the rivers made;
And how and when his wisdom next arranges
To move the stagnant floods by natural changes,
Compel the seas their rugged bounds forsake,
Becloud the hills, and shining rivers make;
To make thin vapors, heated to excess,
On ocean more, on *terra firma* less,
Out from the briny waves incessant rise
Above the hills, and back to other skies
Combine in clouds, and vast collections form,
Spreading the heavens with impending storm;

MAN IN THE MOUNTAIN.

Whence earth itself, full formed, begins to move
Through mighty conflicts by the hand of Jove,
Outward and onward from its native source,
Round with the whirling spheres to take its course.
Now then the forked light, ascending high,
Unveils the terrors of a troubled sky.
Tempestuous gales in darkness intervene,
Sweeping the world with howlings in extreme,
And thunderings loud: the clouds, let loose in drops,
Dash down their showers on the mountain-tops,
Then leap the streamlets from the mountain waste
As if by stern command requiring haste;
As if God's power, with screw and lever plied,
Squeezing the lofty hills to raise the tide,
Would drown the earth in awful floods sublime,
For local sin, or want of faith divine;
As since in wrath he did in Noah's time.
Thus at creation's dawn did Merrimack
Begin to flow. The storm subsides; and *light* —
Bright gleaming sunbeams — broke from sable night.
And now the sweeping wave, with banks o'erflown,
Brilliant and grand, 'mid azure splendor shown,
Rolls on: and — with accumulated force
Of mighty waters on their destined course
Through naked banks ne'er washed by waves be-
 fore;
Now curving o'er the cliff with dashing roar

Of cataract; now swelling far and wide
Down sloping vales in full majestic tide;
Then gliding smooth, as plain or meads ensue,
In tranquil pride resplendent bravely through —
Conveys her fountains to the untried shore,
Where wave or flood had never reached before.

From my Merrimack, p. 11.

Such have been the workings of these tragic waters from the creation. Such, indeed, was the landscape view of New England in 1586, when Drake discovered it; differing only in change of the revolving seasons, as when the bleak blast of stormy winter beat upon it, or when the zephyrs of sweet summer fanned the old forest to a tranquil repose.

Beautiful landscape! From its lofty mountain height, as if present, let us pause. The God of nature is here: we behold him in the air, in the river, in the cloud. Before us and around us is spread out that wild New-England wilderness, which in the advancing years is to become the great battle-field of the world, — a crimson field, where barbarism is to arise and manifest itself as never before, and where civilization, as opposed to it, at the hand of God and of the Pilgrim, is to live in its economy, and obtain a foothold.

Here, too, the great Winnepiseogee, shining forth

THE FINNY TRIBES.

as it did at creation's dawn, together with other innumerable beautiful lakes teeming with life, dotted the landscape. These, with the great rivers we have named, and their tributaries, had been made alive with sturgeon here, with salmon there, with shad, alewives, and the finny tribes generally in abundant varieties, of whose origin and advent we have speculated in "The Merrimack:"—

Next near the shore, now gliding, glittering, seen,
Minnows innumerous in the waters green;
Minute in size, some faster, fuller grown,
Each for an end, yet there unseen, unknown,
In caves now playful, cautious, prone to be;
Then out in depths of waters sporting free,
Each draws from heaven the fleeting breath of life,
Here to subsist through elemental strife,
Varied in species, color, and in form,
Some cold in temperament, others warm,
Each to its kind attached, prolific, free
To seek and share a common destiny.
In lapse of time from tiny minim grown,
The whale loomed up in vast proportion shown.
Now restless seeks more spacious depths to gain,
And finds a homestead in the briny main.
Huge sturgeons too, — all fish of larger growth
Swelled the deep current seaward splashing forth;

While smaller forms, as trout and pickerel,
Inhabit native streams, content to dwell
Fresh-water tenants, tranquil quite as yet
By foe unsought, unhurt by hook or net;
While others rove. The favorite salmon tries
The arctic seas in light of other skies;
Yet, when sweet spring betides the Merrimack,
His out-bound path he fondly follows back
With finny tribes. Then through the inlets trace
A countless progeny, an infant race
From hidden spawns, to swarm the harmless shore;
Then gambol outward, onward as before,
Quiet, yet quick in transit to and fro,
E'er keen to see what makes for weal or woe,
They drink sweet joys in light of nature given,
And fill a purpose grand, ordained of Heaven.

Thus, then, did the bright waters of New England teem with inhabitants, lined and surrounded as they were by that lofty old forest that had stood the tempestuous blast of the eternal ages, and never as yet had seen the woodman's axe. Majestic, lofty as ever it then stood, casting its shadows at the foot of the mountains, on the margin of the lakes and rivers of New England, and along the shores of the sea, as it loomed up in the sublimity of its beauty. Ancient, venerable old forest! Where, oh where are the tribes that knew thee of yore? Within and beneath the shadows of thy waving boughs various fruits of the earth had sprung forth; and the wild deer, the moose, the roebuck, the stag, the bear, the beaver, and other wild animals, have come forth and gambolled, each race in its turn passing away, unknown of the white man, from the beginning of the world.

Here also did the beautiful bird delight to dwell, in nearly all its varieties, from the noble, historic eagle to the sedate and lonely little sparrow.

Of the origin or advent of all these have we speculated in "The Merrimack:" —

Meanwhile, the tree, for fruit and forest sprung
From latent life beneath the soil, begun
To spread in varied shadows Mother Earth
Verdant and fruitful; in productive birth
Alike of insects strange, of beast or bird,
In pairs connubial, fit for flock or herd.
As thus 'mid thicket dense, or bower green,
In earth or air, at first half-hidden seen
The merest mites, thence, formed and fluttering, move
Unfeathered owls, the raven, hawk, and dove;
Whence flaunts the eagle due in course of time,
And songsters warbling wing for every clime;
Whence all the nervy tenants of the air,
From proudest swan to flitting insect rare,

Whence clods of earth, and drops of water pure,
First fraught with life, with life can but endure.
Of tardy growth, sleek whelps in tiny form,
From latent caverns in the hill-side warm,
Of panther race, and beasts of other kind,
At length emerge, and habits varied find.

But the most interesting production found on these shores by the first adventurers was the red man. How long he had lived and wandered in this wilderness with his tribes, subsisting from day to day almost entirely upon the productions of a New-England forest, and of its lakes and rivers, was and still remains a mystery.

HIS ORIGIN.

The origin of the natives of this new world is like a sealed book. All speculations in reference to it are attended with extreme doubt and uncertainty. No theory is satisfactory. These benighted sons, of themselves knew nothing, and had no definite idea of the paternity of their race; and in *this*, perhaps, we are no wiser than they. Many have believed them to be of Asiatic origin, and that they had crossed over here upon the ice that covers the northern coast of America.

Yet, opposed to such a theory, is the fact that there

is a vast dissimilarity now existing between the Asiatics, and the North-American Esquimaux and other Indians. Reason would seem to warrant the belief, that, in the absence of proof to the contrary, the same race of men that our forefathers first found had always been here.

That the " New World " had existed for thousands of years without having a race of men upon it, would seem but little short of a rash presumption.

That it had been left to accident; that it had been left to be peopled by the passing of a tribe from Asia over an unknown arctic region, too cold for human existence to get to it, — would seem to be a presumption quite as rash.

On the whole, we can but perceive that the wild forests of America, when discovered by the white race, were as well suited to the Indian as the Indian was to the forest. And that the Indian here was no more a matter of accident than was the forest itself; and that both were but parts of *one* and the same great design, — would seem to be the most reasonable theory.

In alluding to his origin, as may be seen in my " Merrimack " of years ago, we made suggestions as follows : —

HIS CREATION.

Then next from curious germ beneath the sod,
Now blest of needful care of nature's God,
Whose eye, all-seeing, here began to scan
The strange invention of mysterious man,
By vigorous thrift, as fell the beaming rays
Of Phœbus, fitly felt on vernal days,
Came forth an Indian's form divine,
First spawn of manhood on the stream of time,
Basking in valleys wild, earth-formed, earth-fed,
For ripened age by native reason led;
And chief o'er beast and bird in power became, —
A fitful terror to the timid game.

And so it was: the manners and habits of the native Indians, for aught we know, had always been the same as now. Tradition affords us nothing otherwise. They are known only as they were first found by the adventurer from the Old World.

Their history, circumscribed as it is within the limits of their short existence with the white man, comprises the record of their race for all time. Probably for thousands of years they had been nothing but *wild hunters*, with manners and habits the same, unimproved, unchanged, as is described in "The Merrimack:" —

And thus, o'er land and stream, for ages long,
A race of red men, vagrant, plod along
With language taught from rustic nature's throne,
And habits each peculiarly their own;
On growth spontaneous fed, content with prey,
What serves the purpose of a single day.
Their God is seen afar at rise of sun;
Their life in heaven is hunting, here begun.
By laws unwritten, sachems rule the tribes,
And lead the host wherever ill betides
To fatal war. By force of arrows hurled,
They reigned sole monarchs in this western world.

It is asserted, that, when the Pilgrims landed, there were then about twenty nations, or tribes, of Indians in New England. These nations were distinct from each other, but united sometimes for mutual protection, and for the purposes of war. In every tribe there was a chief, or sagamore, to whom all the others paid deference. But, as has already been stated, the Indian wars, and the plague of 1617–18, had greatly reduced their numbers.

In the same work I once briefly discoursed of

HIS HABITS.

Increased at length by nature's self-same laws
To numerous tribes, prolific men and squaws,

From artful wigwams new spread o'er the land,
First skill evinced in architecture grand,—
He wanders wild, belted with arrows keen,
And blest with knowledge right and wrong between,
A stately priest at peace. Provoked to strife,
He wields a hatchet and a scalping-knife
With dire revenge. E'er true to self and squaw,
He knows no faith, no code, but nature's law;
His footsteps fondly dwell where now we trace
Primeval heirlooms of the human race,—
The chisel smooth, and tomahawk, first made
Of stone, ere art had formed the iron blade;
Where, from a narrow dock, with native crew,
He launched in naval pride the first canoe,
And ploughed the Merrimack. His dripping oar
Ripples the waters, never pressed before;
Bestirs the scaly tribes to nervous fear
For rights most sacred thus invaded here,
As if by instinct they the chieftain knew
To be a tyrant and a glutton too,
Intent on native beast or bird or fish,
By slaughter dire to fill a dainty dish;
Whose webs are nets from bark of trees alone,
And mills that grind are mortars made of stone;
Who clothed his tribes, if clad they e'er appear,
In raiment plundered from the bounding deer;
Who maketh treacherous hooks from guiltless bones,
And drags a deadly net o'er sacred homes.

HIS IGNORANCE.

He was no artisan. His wigwam and birch canoe evinced the best skill in architecture which he ever had. His paintings were extravagant and gaudy, his colors brilliant. The flesh side of skins taken by the Indian hunter was generally taken on which to paint. These he spotted in curious, fantastic hues, and often with fantastic colorings such as none but a wild man could make, contrive, or invent. He knew but little, and sought for improvement in nothing.

HIS GOVERNMENT.

In other parts of the earth all societies or cohabitants are controlled by governments, and an absolute compelling power is lodged somewhere, and in some manner, in each and all of them; but not so with the North-American Indians. They had, substantially, no compelling power the one over another.

When a tribe or neighborhood sent delegates to treat with other tribes, or with bodies of white men, the conclusions were always carried home *memoriter;* and the young men, who were always to be depended on in war, must be persuaded to accede to all of their general articles of agreement for peace or for war. And, in the tide of events, if, from war and blood, they at any time were forced into a defeat or into an humble treaty of peace, the blame, as of course, would always fall upon their young men.

THEIR CLOTHING.

The Northern Indians wore skins of seals, cut in different ways, according to their curious, fantastic fashions, and sewed together with thongs. They had no threads of flax or hemp. In other parts of the country they wore skins from the various beasts of the forest.

After the first English settlements in New England, they wore duffels and blanketings of about two yards square, which the Romans would have denominated "togas." Their sagamores, or sachems, wore blankets with borders of different colors.

When the explorers of New England first made their appearance here, the Indians generally entertained them with a generous feeling, seldom if ever doubting their sincerity and truth. But after a series of years had elapsed, — partly by reason of the wild, cruel, and uncultivated nature of the Indian himself, and of his unstable, treacherous disposition; and partly by reason of the want of kindness, discretion, honesty, and fairness, of individual white men, who from time to time violated law and justice; and partly from the secret machinations of French Jesuits and their hirelings, who took an interest in advising and instigating the Northern and Eastern tribes to make war upon the English, — the native Indian, who had theretofore been master of the soil, began to consider himself in the place of a degraded servant. Hence he manifested himself true to his nature; and at every provocation, real or surmised, he sprang forth from his secret hiding-places, an implacable enemy to the white man, quick at resentment, and reckless in revenge. Notwithstanding the agency which some of the French in Canada had in starting and perpetuating at least a part of the Indian wars in New England, yet they were led to see the Indian's true nature and character: they named him (as some think) accurately, "*Les homines des bois,*" men-brutes of the forest.

MANNERS IN THE WIGWAM.

"The business of the women is to take exact notice of what passes, imprint it in their memories (for they have no writing), and communicate it to their children. They are the records of the council; and they preserve tradition of the stipulations in treaties a hundred years back, which, when we compare with our writings, we always find exact. He that would speak rises. The rest observe a profound silence.

When he has finished, and sits down, they leave him five or six minutes to recollect, that if he has omitted any thing he intended to say, or has any thing to add, he may rise again, and deliver it. To interrupt another, even in common conversation, is reckoned highly indecent. How different this is from the mode of conversation in many polite companies of Europe, where, if you do not deliver your sentence with great rapidity, you are cut off in the middle of it by the impatient loquacity of those you converse with, and never suffered to finish it!"

Instead of being better since the days of Franklin, we apprehend it has grown worse. The modest and unassuming often find it exceedingly difficult to gain a hearing at all. Ladies, and many who consider themselves examples of good manners, transgress to an insufferable degree, in breaking in upon the conversations of others. Some of these, like a ship driven by a north-wester, bearing down the small craft in her course, come upon us by surprise; and, if we attempt to proceed by raising our voices a little, we are sure to be drowned by a much greater elevation on their part. It is a want of good-breeding, which, it is hoped, every young person whose eye this may meet will not be guilty of through life. There is great opportunity for many even of mature years to profit by it. — *S. G. Drake.*

CHAPTER V.

INDIAN NATIONS, THEIR TRIBES AND HABITS.

Always at Leisure. — His Habits, and Mode of Living. — Fish as found in the New-England Rivers. — Indian Deceit, Revenge, and Barbarity. — Have but little Honesty. — No Faith. — Their Paintings. — Reckonings of Time, Distances, &c. — Names of some of the Tribes. — The Winnepiseogees. — Definitions of Indian Words. — The Abenaqui Indians. — Number of Several of the Tribes. — Their Locations. — Tribes Anciently. — Their own Hostilities favored the English in New England. — Never lay up Any Thing in Store. — Their Medical Practice. — Language and Reckonings. — Hieroglyphics. — Their Fashion of changing their Names. — Names of Massasoit's Two Sons changed. — Eliot prints a Bible in Indian Language. — Naticks. — Indian Mode of Attack.

AN Indian was always at leisure. He knew no overtasking of the brain, had no troublesome extensive trade, no taxes to pay, no rents, no national debts. All his surroundings were free to him. Each had a share in the cool and shady hunting-grounds, in the skies above them, and in the best fishing-places.

His corn-fields were where he sowed his seed. His tobacco was a constant luxury to him; and his fishing and hunting was a favorite pastime.

His wants, being few, were easily supplied. The

bow-arrow and the fishing-rod afforded him a competence in food and raiment: these were substantially the implements of his toil and of his care.

With his squaw, who often wandered from the wigwam in company with his tribe, he was usually contented and happy. His home was made glad with the song and the dance, and in the smoking or " drinking the pipe," as they usually termed it.

The large lakes and rivers always afforded him excellent fishing-places. The *rivers* were a constant income, as vast highways, which brought to him, at every returning spring, a full supply of salmon, alewives, and shad.

At that day, no dams or bars being in the way to impede the advent or progress of the finny tribes, they came in vast numbers, and ever proved a source of wealth to the Indian. At the forks of the Merrimack the salmon, which always seek the coldest climes, generally took the cold water, and went up the Pemigewasset; while the others took to the warm water, and followed the Winnepeseogee to the lake, or into the smaller streams.

From these rivers and their tributaries, the thirty thousand Indians that used to trail along these valleys obtained the principal share of their support. For thousands of years the waters of our rivers had

PEMIGEWASSET.

afforded the red man an abundant supply. Salmon weighing twenty or thirty pounds were not uncommon. There were then no gates to close up Nature's highway, no dashing wheels to frighten back the fish; nor was there then any need of artificial steps or fishways to lead the bewildered tribes (as are now invented, but as yet in vain) over high dams into the ponds above.

Kind Nature had given to the native Indian the waters of these rivers to run freely down, as from the creation they *had* run; and had given to the fish common highways to advance upward in them. Yet by what is now termed the progress of civilization, the tribes of fish, as well as the tribes of red men, have become almost extinct in and about the rivers of New England.

Sturgeons used to be caught in the Merrimack. As these large fish passed up the river, two Indians, the one to scull the boat, and the other to throw the weapon, would spear them. Many a noble sturgeon, from year to year, was thus slain, and tugged ashore from his native waters.

HIS DEPRAVITY AND REVENGE.

Douglas, who wrote a hundred and twenty-five years ago, says, "Indians are not so polite as the wandering Tartars. Like the wild Irish, they dread labor more than poverty. Like dogs, they are always either eating or sleeping, except in travelling, hunting, and their dances: their sloth and indolence incline them to sottishness. Before Christians arrived amongst them, they had no knowledge of strong drink: this Christian vice not only destroys their bodily health and that of their progeny, but creates feuds, outrages, and horrid murders. They are much given to deceit and lying, so as scarce to be believed when they speak the truth. Their temper is the reverse of *East Indians*, whereof some castes or sects will not kill any animal: the *West Indians*, or Americans, are barbarous, and upon small provocations kill their own species. Some of them exceed in barbarity, and in revenge and fury eat the flesh of their enemies, not from hunger or delicacy. Such were the *Florida Indians:* they said that the flesh of the *English* ate mellow and tender, that of the Spaniard, hard and tough, the *Bermudian,* fishy.

"The *Aboriginal Americans* have no honesty, no honor: that is, they are of no faith, but mere brutes in that respect. They generally have great fortitude of mind: without any appearance of fear or concern, they suffer any torture and death. In revenge they are barbarous and implacable: they never forget nor forgive injuries. If one man kills another, the nearest in kindred to the murdered watches an opportunity to kill the murderer; and the death of one man may occasion the deaths of many; therefore, when a man is guilty of murder, he generally leaves the tribe, and goes into a kind of voluntary banishment. They are a sullen, close people. The Indian wars ought to be called *massacres*, or inhuman barbarous *outrages*, rather than necessary acts of hostility."

PAINTING AND TIME-KEEPING.

"Indians in general," says Douglas, "paint their bodies, especially their faces (they affect red colors), as the Picts and Britons of Great Britain formerly were accustomed.

"In the higher latitudes the Indians reckon their time by winters (years), by moons (months), and by sleeps (nights).

"Between the tropics they reckon by rains (the seasons of rains: the end of summer and beginning of autumn are *periodical*, as are our winters), moons, and sleeps.

IN COMPUTING DISTANCES.

"They reckon by sleeps, or days' travel (as the Dutch do by hours), viz., so many sleeps or days' travel from one place to another."

THEIR NAVIGATION.

This was by the "crossing of rivers upon *bark-logs*, travelling along on the rivers or rivulets, and on the sides of the lakes, in canoes or 'schuyties,' portable by two men in their carrying-places from one river or pond to another: they are of birch-bark, upon ribs of ash, sewed together by some tough wooden fibres, and *paid* (as sailors express it), with rosin from the pine-tree. They use no sails or oars, only paddles and setting-poles. The boat is capable of carrying a man, his wife, children, and baggage.

"Narrow rivers are better travelling than ponds and lakes, because upon the lakes, if stormy or much wind, they cannot proceed, but must put to the shore."

THE TRIBES.

The names of the tribes led for the most part by the Pennacooks were, — the *Agawams* of Essex County, the Massachusetts, *Wamesits*, Nashuas, Souhegans, *Namoskeags*, and *Winnipesaukees*. Aside from these, there were other tribes, foreign to the Merrimack, yet acknowledging fealty to the great Pennacook in his confederacy, to wit, the Wachusetts, Coosucks, Pequakuakes, Ossipees, Squamscotts, Winnecowetts, Piscataquaukes, Newichewannocks, Sacos, and Amariscoggins.

NAMES AND DERIVATIONS.

"The Winnipesaukees for the most part occupied the lands and islands in and about their favorite lake of that name. Its outlet, the Weirs, had been for hundreds and perhaps thousands of years their rallying-point, to which they had been in the habit of returning from their wanderings. *Winnipesaukee* is derived from winne (beautiful), nipe (water), kees (high), and auke (a place), literally meaning the beautiful water of the high place. *Wachusetts* comes from wadcher (a mountain) and auke (a place): these centred near Wachusetts Mountain in Massachusetts. The *Coosucks:* this cognomen is derived from cooash (pines); and they mostly dwelt on and boated in and about the Connecticut River. The *Pequaquaukes* — from Pequaquis (crooked) and auke (a place) — lived, hunted, and fished up and down their favorite Saco, in Maine and New Hampshire. The *Ossipees*, from cooash (pines) and nipe (river), wandered in and about Ossipee Lake and its river, in the county of Carroll, N.H., and in York County, Me. The *Swamscotts* — from winne (beautiful), asquam (water), and auke (a place) — hunted upon Exeter River in Exeter, and Stratham in Rockingham County, N.H. The *Winnecowetts*,— from winne (beautiful), cooash (pines), and auke (a place) — lurked about in the same county. The *Piscataquaukes* — from pos (great), attuck (a deer), and auke (a place) — fished and hunted on the banks of the Piscataqua, between the southeastern part of New Hampshire and Maine. The *Newichewarnocks*, from me (my), week (a contraction of week-wam, a house), and ouannocks (come): they inhabited the upper branches of the same river, known as the Salmon Falls and the Cocheco. The name *Sacos* was taken from sawa (burnt), coo (pine), and auke (a place): they dwelt mostly upon Saco River, in the county of York, Me. And the *Amariscoggins* — derived from mamaos (fish), kees (high), and auke (a place) — had their dwelling-places and hunting-grounds upon the Amariscoggin River, which took its rise in the New-Hampshire hills, and empties its waters into the Kennebec."

All the tribes of the interior, as contradistinguished from those near to the shores of the sea, were known and designated in Indian parlance as *Nipmucks*, or fresh-water Indians. "*Nipmuck* is derived from nipe (still water), and auke (a place), with the letter 'm' thrown in for the sake of the euphony."

Northerly, and yet on the south side of the St. Lawrence River, there were tribes in the early days of New England who were denominated *Abenaqui Indians*, to wit, — *Delorette*, a very small tribe a little below Quebec; *Wanonoaks*, on the River Besancourt, or Puante, over against Les Trois Rivières, not exceeding forty fighting men; about ten leagues higher was the tribe *Areusiguntecook*, on the River St. François, about a hundred and sixty fighting men; on the east side of Lake Champlain was the tribe of *Mesiassuck*, sixty fighting men; a little above Montreal were the *Kabnuagas*, about eighty men, being a parcel of idle " *ave Maria* " praying Indians, runaways from the New-York *Mohawks* and River Indians. " They swallowed their flesh and fish raw, and went naked, or covered with seal and other skins. They were in small clans, very idle, much dispersed, and of no great benefit to trade or to the world."

Douglas says the northern tribes were small and distinct. A large parcel of land lying waste, in winter countries, for many months in the year, not fertile and not cleared of wood, cannot subsist many people; but these small tribes, though much dispersed, were allied by contiguity, language, and intermarriages. " Thus it is with our neighboring *Abnaquies*, who border upon New England; the *Iroquois*, or *Mohawks*, who border upon New York, Pennsylvania, and Virginia; and the *Chirakees*, who border upon Carolina. These may be called three distinct nations."*

Other distinct tribes were also to be found then or later. In Connecticut were what were called the *Pequots*, the *Quinnipiacs*, the *Tunxis*, and the *Hammonassets*. In Maine the *Etechemins* dwelt farthest towards the East: and the *Abenaquis*, of whom the *Terratines* were a part, hunted on both sides of the Penobscot; and at one time their boundaries extended from the English settlements on the Atlantic shore to the Bay of Fundy, Lake Champlain, and to the Rivers Hudson and St. Lawrence. The Indian population in New England at the beginning of its settlement by the English has been estimated at about fifty thousand, at which time the District of Maine contained about one-fourth part, and Connecticut and Rhode Island about one-half.

The *Pakanokets*, or *Wampanaogs*, hunted in Southeastern Massachusetts, near Buzzard's and Narraganset Bays; the *Narragansets*, in Massachusetts, Rhode Island, and some of them along the banks of the Thames; and the *Mohegans* at or near the shores of the Connecticut River. The *Wamesets* had a village dwelling-place in Wamesit, at the junction of the Concord and Merrimack Rivers, now Lowell, Massachusetts, where *Eliot* often preached to the tribes of Wonalancet.

* Douglas wrote in 1749.

TRIBES ORIGINALLY.

In Bible history, it appears, all mankind anciently lived in small tribes. Abraham and his allies could muster only three hundred and eighteen men: with these he defeated four great kings who had conquered several kings.

"Where lands lie *not* cultivated, the Tribes must necessarily be small."

"From a country thus reduced to a small stock we may investigate the various degrees of civil government. At first they were only distinct Families left isolated, and their government was patriarchal; that is, by heads of families. These heads of families soon became acquainted and neighborly, and for mutual protection and good neighborhood entered into associations by us called Tribes, Cantons, or Clans; and several of these Tribes, upon suspicion of some ambitious design of some neighboring powerful Tribes, for their better defence were obliged to enter into a federal Union, and at length were incorporated into one general direction called a Nation or Empire. Perhaps we may suppose that such were the empires of Mexico and Peru."

FEW AND FEEBLE.

Douglas also says that the Europeans, on account of their disparity of numbers, never could have succeeded in their settlement here, if the tribes (many of them) had not joined them by reason of hostilities among themselves. Thus Cortez in Mexico was assisted by several of the disaffected tribes; and on the other hand, after the landing of the Pilgrims, Massasoit was made formidable as against the Narragansets by the use of fire-arms obtained from the English.

A Spanish bishop of the West Indies, a man of observation, many years ago wrote as follows: " The Indians are of a tender constitution. No part of Europe was more populous than Mexico upon the Spaniards' first arrival there. The Spaniards in the first forty years destroyed about twenty millions of them. They left but a few Indians in Hispaniola, none upon Cuba, Jamaica, Bahama Islands, Porto Rico, and Caribee Islands, excepting upon Dominica and St. Vincent, where they remain to this day."

THEIR FOOD, AND MODE OF LIVING.

" Our Indians do not imitate the Bees, Ants, &c., in laying up Stores, but, like rapacious animals, live from Hand to Mouth: after long Fasting they are voracious, and upon a Glutonous Repast can fast many Days by bracing in or reefing their Girdles or Belts.

" The far North *Indians* of *West Greenland, Terra de Labarador,* &c., live upon the Blubber of Whales,

INDIAN MODE OF SUBSISTENCE.

Seals, and other Fish; and their most generous Beverage is Fish-Oil: scarce any Quadrupids or Fowls, not only from the Severity and long Continuance of their cold Weather, Frost and Snow, but also because their Meadows and other Lands instead of Grass and other Herbage bear only Moss.

"The *Indians* in the more moderate Climates live by Hunting, Fowling, and Fish. They do not clear and cultivate the Forest by planting and grazing: lately some of their Squaas or Women improve in planting of *Mays and Indian Beans*. Their Bread Kind are *Mays or Indian Corn, Phaseolus Kidney or Indian Beans*, several Sorts of tuberous Roots called Ground Nuts, several Sorts of Berries, particularly several Sorts of *Vitis Idea* in *New England* called Huckle-Berries. Upon a continued March, where Hunting and Fowling is inconsiderable, they carry with them for subsistence parched Indian Corn, called No-cake.

"The *Abnaquies*, or New England Northern and Eastern *Indians*, because of the Hunting and Fowling failing, during the Winter are obliged to remove to the Sea-side, and live upon Clams, Bass, Sturgeons, &c.

"*Their medical Practice* resembles that of officious old Women in some remote Country Villages of Europe, — meer Empiricism, or, rather, a traditionary blind Practice: they regard only the Symptoms that strike the gross Senses most, without Respect to any less obvious principal Symptom which may be called the Disease, or to Constitution, Sex, and Age.

INDIAN LANGUAGE.

"Their Manner of Expression is vehement and emphatick: their Ideas being few, their Language is not copious: it consists only of a few Words, and many of these ill contrived: by a rumbling Noise or Sound of many syllables they express an Idea or Thing which in the European Language is done by a Syllable or two.

"As their Ideas increase, they are obliged to adopt the *European* Words of adjoining Colonies.

"In numbering they use the same natural Way of reckoning by Tens, as in Europe, Ten being the Number of humane Fingers.

"No Cronocles, scarce any traditionary accounts of Things extending back further than two or three Generations: scarce any Indians can tell their own Age.

"They had no Characters, that is, *Hieroglyphics* or Letters: they had a few symbols or signatures, as if in a Heraldry Way to distinguish Tribes: the principal were the Tortois, the Bear, the Wolf.

"There was not the least Vestage of Letters in

America. Some years since a certain credulous Person and voluminous Author imposed upon himself and others: he observed in a tiding River a Rock, which, as it was not of uniform Substance, the ebbing and the flowing of the Tide made a Sort of *vermulure*, Honey-combing or etching on its Face: here he immagined that he had discovered the *America Indian* Characters, and, overjoyed, remits some lines of his imaginary Characters to the *Royal Society in London. See Philosophical Transactions, No.* 339.

" ' At *Taunton* by the Side of a tiding River, Part in, Part out, of the River, there is a large Rock, on the perpendicular Side of which, next to the Stream, are 7 or 8 Lines about 7 or 8 feet long, and about a Foot wide each of them, engraven with unaccountable Characters not like any known Character.'

" This may be supposed to have been written Anno 1714. At present (Anno 1747) by the continued ebbing and flowing, the Honey-combing is so altered as not in the least to resemble his Draught of the Characters.

" As the *Indians* were so rude as to have no letters or other Characters, there is no certain Way of writing their Names of Things: all we can do is to express their Sounds or Pronunciations as near as may be in our own letters.

" Father *Ralle* of *Norridgwog*, and some other scolastick *French* Missionaries, have imagined that the *Greek* Alphabet suits their Pronunciation best.

"The *Indians* have a figurative Way of expressing themselves, as if in Hieroglyphics: thus, renewing of Alliances they call brightening of the Chain.

"There is no general fixed Way of Writing *Indian Words;* therefore we shall not mind any particular Orthography in that Respect; only we shall endeavour to be understood. For Instance: the *Indian* Tribe upon *Quenebeck* River in *New England*, we write and pronounce it *Naridgwoag:* the *French* Missionaries write it *Narautsoack*.

"The Tribe of the Iroquois, or five New York allied *Indian* Nations, which we call *Sennekas*, the *French* call them *Sonontouans*.

"There is not the same Reason for preserving the *Indian* Names of their Countries, Nations, Tribes, Mountains, and Rivers, as there is for preserving the *Greek*, *Roman*, and other more modern Names of such Things in *Europe*. The Indians have no civil or classical History to require it.

The Indians change their own personal Names, and the Names of other Things upon trifling occasions.

"Our *Indians* affect to have *English* Names: thus *Massasoit's* two Sons desired of the Court at *Plymouth* to give them *English* Names: they were accordingly named *Alexander* and *Philip*.

"This *Philip*, formerly *Metacomet*, was Chief in a subsequent *Indian* War called King *Philip's* War.

"Capt. *Smith* the Traveller resided 19 years in Virginia and New England, and wrote a History of those Parts, Anno 1624: he enumerates the Names of many Tribes, Rivers, and other Things, which are now irrecoverably lost.

"As the *Indian's* Dealings and mutual Correspondence are much confined, their several Languages ' are of small extent.'."

Mr. Douglas, who was alive in 1747, adds to the foregoing the following:—

"Mr. Eliot, formerly Minister of Roxbury, adjoining Boston, with immense Labor translated and printed our Bible into Indian: it was done with a good pious Design, but must be reckoned among the " *Otiosorum hominum negotia;*" it was done in the *Natick* Language. Of the Naticks at present there are not twenty Families subsisting, and scarce any of these can read: *Cui Bono?*"

THEIR MODE OF ATTACK.

When the Indians go to battle they seldom make an attack in large bodies. After a general *rendezvous*, they divide into small skulking parties (their common unvarying art of war was in the hidden efficiency of small parties); and like carnivorous beasts of the forest they advanced to the onset, laying waste dwelling-houses, and committing cruel murders without regard to justice, honor, age, or sex.

As formerly among the Israelites, so it was in the early days of the New England settlements: a sagamore was considered as a mighty prince who could lead one hundred or two hundred fighting men. He prided himself in the loss of ten or twelve men as the sure and unmistakable evidence of a bloody battle.

In the first instances their weapons of war were arrows and darts; but latterly they had obtained and used the deadly musket, fusils, the hatchet, and long, sharp-pointed knives.

CHAPTER VI.

INDIAN WARS.

No Record here Anterior to the Advent of Drake. — No Serious Trouble for Twenty-eight Years. — In 1614 Hunt kidnaps and sells Twenty Indians. — It troubles the Adventurers. — The War and the Plague of 1616 and 1617. — Bones on the Battle-Grounds. — Tisquantum (Squanto). — Pilgrims land. — First Indian Insurrection. — The War-Whoop. — Their Wood-Cry. — Samoset greets the Pilgrims. — His Personal Appearance and Discourse. — Tarried at Night, and left them in the Morning. — Pilgrims feed the Indians. — Indians sang and danced. — Painted Faces. — First Treaty. — Massasoit with Sixty Warriors meets Gov. Carver and his Suite.

HAVING already glanced at the landscape of New England as it appeared prior to its becoming a general battle-field; and having made allusion to the nature and habits of the native Indian, and of his tribes, their various locations, hunting-grounds, and fishing-places, — I come next to notice the barbarous conflicts which from time to time happened among themselves.

This branch of our New-England annals must necessarily be brief, — brief from the fact that the natives were entirely unlettered, with a language somewhat vague, yet curious and comprehensive, and up to that day almost undefined, and entirely unwritten. They could have no record, historic or otherwise ; and none existed.

Hence, as we have hinted, the bloody conflicts that would have stained these pages, of the years and the ages that had transpired anterior to the advent of Sir Francis Drake, had entirely vanished from earthly vision ; so that in history *these*, as well as the events of peace, of love, or of joy among the tribes, as from time immemorial they had alternated, are all *covered* of oblivion, and can have no place in these our epics. In all that history, if we and the world had it, how much there would be to be learned from it! How much to amuse, how much to improve us, how much of love, and how much of anger or of wrath at which earth might be made sad, is now and forever to remain a mystery !

Since *that* day (1586) the red man in New England has had a history. A history varied, as the impulses of the human temper is various, where, in the end, the wrath of man has been suffered to achieve a mastery over his better nature ; and where, from the want of caution and culture, the inheritance of an entire nationality has been lost, almost entirely through its common frailties, and through its mad, ill-advised, unbridled ambition.

Prior to 1615 the history of Indian conflicts among

BATTLES AMONG THEMSELVES. 101

themselves remains, as forever it must, almost entirely unrecorded. Up to that period very little, if any thing, had occurred to create any conflict between the exploring, occasional adventurer and the native Indian or his tribe, as each party at that time was mutually interested in the novelty of the occasion, as well as in the traffic which from time to time tended in its promises to afford aid and sustenance to both nationalities. The first trouble between the tribes and the adventurers arose in manner as follows : —

Twenty-eight years after the advent of Sir Francis Drake, to wit, in 1614, Captain John Smith sailed along the New-England shore, surveying its coast from the Penobscot to Cape Cod. At this time he discovered the river Piscataqua. One of his ships he left behind him in the care of one THOMAS HUNT, who, forgetting his manhood, if he ever had any, decoyed on board it about twenty of the native Indians, kidnapped and carried them to Malaga, and sold them into slavery *to* the Spaniards.

This infamous outrage of course excited dread animosity in the tribes, and greatly enraged them against Hunt, engendering in their minds hatred and distrust towards succeeding adventurers. Some of those captives, however, through the friendly interposition of one Capt. John Mason and others, found their way back to the tribes; and peace again was restored. This was the act of ONE *white* English *man*, wherein and whereby the peace and well-being of many honest, generous explorers and settlers suffered, and in many instances lives were lost. Yet such perfidious acts by the first explorers here must have been few; for this is the only outrage of the kind which is noted in the history of that time; and thereafterwards peace, being declared, prevailed for many years between the red man and his more discreet and peaceable neighbors. But in about two years (1616) the first and most terrible war among and between the tribes themselves, of which we have any account, broke out. As it appears, the Northern and Eastern Tarratines came down upon the Patuxets, the Narragansets, and other neighboring tribes, and the battle was terrible; also the plague of 1617, raging at the same time, made sad havoc upon the red men: so that of all the sons and daughters of the Patuxets, not one of them remained alive save their chief, Squanto, Tisquantum. The bones of the slain at that time almost everywhere were seen by the Pilgrims, — around the sickly wigwam, in and about the numerous Indian battle-grounds of New England, on the hills, in the valleys, on the margin of the lakes, by the side of the beautiful river, and along the shores of the sea.

This was the first and last of all the bloody battles in New England of importance, of which we have any account, from the beginning of the New World up to the advent of the Pilgrims.

Tisquantum, above named, as appears, was one of the same twenty Indians who had been kidnapped by Hunt, and sold into slavery to the Spaniards. It further appears that he soon in some way escaped from Spain, and afterwards for a considerable time sojourned in London with a man by the name of *Slaine*, learned something of our language there; but at length, through the aid of the master of a ship, by the name of *Dermer*, he found his way back to New England; and upon his arrival became a great chief among the Patuxets. But alas! when the Pilgrims arrived, his tribe, as we have said, were dead; and Tisquantum (Squanto) was alone.

From my " Merrimack," page 23, I here insert a brief recapitulation, in which allusion is made to the arrival of the Pilgrims, and their intimate friendliness with

TISQUANTUM.

Columbus first of all; then many more
Within a hundred years then next before
The Pilgrims land, — adventurers indeed,
From Adam sprung, juniors in race and breed,
But versed in letters, statute, law, and art,
Seniors in science, just in head and heart.

They meet old Squanto wandering here alone,
Who, sore depressed, bereaved of friends and home,
Recounts events which true tradition brought
Of Indian life, what sad experience taught, —
How far and near the dead unburied lay,
His own Patuxet tribe all swept away;
Yet nations seaward, deep in woods afar,
Spared from the scourge of pestilence and war,
Still thrive. There Massasoit, whose power maintains
The peace of tribes, in full dominion reigns.

Tisquantum, while in Spain and in London, had excited the curiosity of foreigners, who never before had seen a red man, and who inclined to gaze at him as a choice production of the New World.

The Pilgrims, at their landing Dec. 11 (O. S.), 1620, forty-one in all, very soon fell in with this extraordinary personage, who, through his familiarity in conversations with Englishmen in London while there, had obtained some knowledge of our language. They of course soon sought him out, and made him their interpreter.

On the fifteenth of the same month, four days after their arrival here, they discovered five or six Indians approaching their encampments; but upon seeing the Pilgrims they appeared frightened at their friendly attempt to approach them, and fled.

FIRST INDIAN INSURRECTION.

On the 15th of November, 1620, as a Pilgrim of the forest relates it, " We went ranging up and down till the sun began to draw low; and then we hasted out of the woods, that we might come to our shallop.

" By that time we had done, and our shallop came to us, it was within night, and we betook us to our rest after we had set our watch.

" About midnight we heard a great and hideous cry, and our sentinel called ' ARM! ARM! '

" So we bestirred ourselves, and shot off a couple of muskets."

" About five o'clock in the morning, Dec. 8, we heard a great and strange cry, which we knew to be the same voice, though they varied their notes."

" One of our men, being abroad, came running in, and cried, ' They are men! Indians! Indians! ' And their arrows came flying amongst us."

THE WAR-WHOOP.

It was here at Namskekat that the Pilgrims first heard the terrible war-whoop cry of the savage, which from time immemorial to the present day in its startling vociferations has remained invariably the same. They do not move at the sound of the drum or trumpet. They rally at the cry, —

WOACH! WOACH! HA — HA — HA — HACK — WOACH! And their *wood-cry* is FO — HAU!

The Pilgrims represented the CRY as terrible: the Indian arrows came flying in among them, of which they afterwards picked up eighteen, which they sent to their friends in England, on the return of "The Mayflower." One savage fought from behind a tree; and an old Pilgrim had three shots at him with a musket: at the last the scamp gave an extraordinary yell, and away they all went in a hurry.

Some of those arrows were curiously headed with hart's horn, others with eagle's claws.

Whether any of the savages were slain or seriously injured in this first brief conflict does not appear. This was by the Nauset Indians, of whom *Aspinet* was chief.

Since their arrival on the 11th of November, they, as appears, had for the most part made the ship their abode up to the 11th of December, when they landed.

It was on this occasion that the famous chief *Samoset*, then and there, upon the shore of Cape Cod, came forth from the wilderness, and extended to them the friendly cry, " *Welcome, Inglishmen!* " In my "Merrimack," page 24, mention is made as follows of this

SAMOSET.

SAGAMORE.

From thence SAMOSET comes with heart and hand
To welcome Englishmen, and grant them land;
His visage dark, with long and raven hair,
No treacherous marks his beardless features bear,
His frame erect, and strangely painted o'er,
Belted around his loins; a sagamore,
Whose bony arm a bow and arrow held,
A heart unsoiled his tawny bosom swelled
To generous deeds. He broken English spake,
And talked anon of men, of Francis Drake,
That gallant white man, years before who came,
And gave New Albion her historic name;
Of Captain Smith, who since surveyed the coast,
And other voyagers, now a scattered host;
Of former days some history tried to give,
And "lay of land" where rambling red men live.
Truthful Samoset proves, and seeks to bring
The Pilgrim saints in audience with his king.

This interview of Samoset with the Pilgrims was on the 16th of March, 1621; and Mourt says he very boldly came all alone, and along the houses straight to the *rendezvous*, where he intercepted him, not suffering him to go in, as undoubtedly he *would*, out of his boldness. He was naked: " only a leather about his waist, with a fringe about a span long."

It was cold weather; and the PILGRIMS "*cast a horseman's coat about him.*" In his kindness *Samoset* gave them, as well as he could, much valuable information. He, as they said, had learned some broken English of adventurers who had come to fish at Wouhiggan, and knew by name most of the captains, masters, or commanders who had visited here. He was free in speech so far as he was able to talk our language. The Pilgrims "questioned him of many things;" and they say "*he was the first savage we could meet withal.*"

He told them " he was not of those parts, but of *Moratiggon*, and one of the sagamores or lords thereof; had been eight months in these parts; it lying hence to the eastward a day's sail with a great wind, and five days by land." " He discoursed of the whole country and of every province, and of their sagamores, their number of men, and strength;" had a bow and two arrows, one headed, and the other not. " He was tall and straight; hair black, long behind, short before, none at all on his face." " He asked for some beer; but we (as they say) gave him *strong water* and biscuit and cheese and pudding, and a piece of a mallard, all which he liked well."

He told us " the place where he now lives is called Patuxet; and that about four years ago all the inhabitants died of an extraordinary plague, and there is neither man, woman, nor child remaining, as indeed, we have found none; so there is none to hinder our possession, or lay claim unto it."

"All the afternoon we spent in communication with him: we would have gladly been rid of him at night, but he was not willing to go *this* night.

"Then we thought to carry him on shipboard, wherewith he was well content, and went into the shallop; but the wind was high and the water scant, that it could not return back.

"We lodged (with him) at *Stephen Hopkins'* house, and watched him."

It may seem strange that the Pilgrims should have been here so long without a friendly interview with the tribes previously to *this* with Samoset. But it will be remembered that the war of which we have spoken, and the plague of which Samoset here speaks, had destroyed almost all; and that these remnants of tribes most likely had been *made coy* from the fact, that, at their onset upon the Pilgrims, on the night of the 7th of December then last, they, perhaps for the first time in their lives, had been made to " smell gunpowder."

"Samoset left Plimouth the next morning to return to *Massasoit*, who, he said, was a sachem having under him sixty men."

"The English, having left some tools exposed in the woods, on finding that they were missing, rightly judged the Indians had taken them."

"They complained of this to Samoset in rather a threatening air. We willed him (they say) that they should be brought again, otherwise we would right ourselves."

When he left them "he promised within a night or two to come again," and bring some of Massasoit's men to trade with them in beaver-skins.

MODE OF DRESS.

As good as his word, Samoset came the next Sunday, " and brought with him five other tall, proper men. They had every man a deer's skin on him; and the principal of them had a wildcat's skin, or such like, on one arm. They had most of them long hosen up to their groins, close-made; and about their groins, to their waist, another leather; they were altogether like the Irish trousers. They are of complexion like our English gypsies; no hair, or very little, on their faces; on their heads long hair to their shoulders, only cut before; some trussed up before with a feather, broadwise like a fan; another a fox-tail hanging out."

The English had charged Samoset not to let any who came with him bring their arms; these, therefore, left " their bows and arrows a quarter of a mile from our town."

" We gave them entertainment as we thought was fitting them. They did eat liberally of our English victuals," and appeared very friendly; "sang and danced after their manner, like anticks." Some of them had their faces painted black from the forehead to the chin, four or five fingers broad: others after other fashions, as they liked. They brought three or four skins; but we would not truck with them all that day, but wished them to bring more, and we would truck for all, which they promised within a night or two, and would leave these behind them, though we were not willing they should; and they brought all our tools again, which were taken in the woods in our absence.

"So, because of the day (Sunday), we dismissed them so soon as we could. But Samoset, our first acquaintance, either was sick or feigned himself so, and would not go with them, and staid with us till Wednesday morning.

"Then we sent him to them, to know the reason they came not according to their words; and we gave him a hat, a pair of stockings and shoes, a shirt, and a piece of cloth to tie about his waist."

SAMOSET returned again the next day, bringing with him Squanto, mentioned in the last chapter. He was "the only native [says Mourt's Relation] of Patuxet, where we now inhabit, who was one of the twenty (or twenty-four) captives that by Hunt were carried away, and had been in England, and dwelt in Cornhill with Master John Slaine, a merchant, and could speak a little English with three others."

They brought a few articles for trade; but the most important news, " that their great sagamore, *Massasoit*, was hard by," whose introduction to them accordingly followed.

In June, 1621, a boy, *John Billington*, having been lost in the woods, several English, with Squanto and Tokamahamon, undertook a voyage to Nauset in search of him. Squanto was their interpreter.

FIRST TREATY.

On March 22, 1621, Samoset and Squanto brought to Plymouth the welcome news that Massasoit of Pokanoket, their chief, was near at hand; and " they brought with them [say the Pilgrims] some few skins to truck, and some red herrings newly taken and dried, but not salted, and signified unto us that their great sagamore, *Massasoit*, was hard by with Quadiquina his brother.

" They could not well say what they would; but after an hour the king came to the top of an hill [supposed to be what is now Watson's Hill on the south side of Town Brook] over against us, and had in his train sixty men, that we could well behold them, and they us."

CHAPTER VII.

FIRST TREATY.

The Tribes greet the Pilgrims. — Governor returns Presents to Them. — Address to the Natives. — The Repast. — The King's Dress. — His Ornaments. — Hostages. — Savages seated on the Floor. — Terms of their Treaty. — Squanto and Samoset are their Interpreters. — Death of Squanto. — His Will. — His Departure Poetized. — March of Civilization. — Peace Fifty Years. — Eruption between the Tribes. — Sachems and Sagamores, Names of, in New England. — An Expedition to attack the Mohawks. — Josias leads. — Mascanonomo degraded. — Battle with the Mohawks. — Tarratines attack his House. — They capture his Squaw. — He relents, and greets the English. — They make him Presents. — A Land Grant to his Widow. — Canonicus. — His Exemplary, Liberal Life. — His Peaceful Death.

"WE were not willing," the Pilgrims say, "to send our governor to Massasoit and his tribe; and they were unwilling to come to us: so SQUANTO went again unto him, who brought word that we should send one to parley with him; and we sent Edward Winslow, to know his intent, and to signify the mind and will of our governor, which was that we might have trading and peace with them.

"We sent to the king a pair of knives, and a copper chain with a jewel in it. To *Quadequina* we sent likewise a knife, and a jewel to hang in his ear, and withal *a pot of strong water*, a good quantity of biscuit, and some butter, which were all willingly accepted.

"The Englishman then made a speech to him about his king's love and goodness to him and his people, and that he accept of him as his friend and ally.

"He liked well of the speech (say the English), and heard it attentively, though the interpreters did not well express it.

"After he had eaten and drunk himself, and given the rest to his company, he looked upon our messenger's sword and armor, which he had on, with intimation of his desire to buy it; but, on the other side, our messenger showed his unwillingness to part with it.

"In the end he left him in the custody of *Quadequina* his brother, and came over the brook, and some twenty men following him. We kept six or seven as hostages for our messenger." As Massasoit proceeded to meet the English, they met him with six soldiers, who saluted each other. Several of his men were with him; but all left their bows and arrows behind. They were conducted to a new house which was partly finished; and a green rug was spread upon the floor, and several cushions, for Massasoit and his chiefs to sit down upon.

THE FIRST TREATY.

FIRST TREATY.

Then came the English governor, followed by a drummer and trumpeter and a few soldiers; and, after kissing one another, all sat down.

Some *strong water* being brought, the governor drank to Massasoit, who in his turn " drank a great draught, that made him sweat all the while after."

They now proceeded to make a treaty, which stipulated, that neither Massasoit nor any of his people should do hurt to the English; and that, if they did, they should be given up to be punished by them; and that, if the English did any harm to him or any of his people, they (the English) would do the like to them; that, if they did unjustly war against him, the English were to aid him; and he was to do the same in his turn; and by so doing King James would esteem him his friend and ally.

"All which [they say] the king seemed to like well; and it was applauded of his followers."

THE KING'S APPAREL.

Then Massasoit the king, and chiefs, appear;
As well the " governor and suit" draw near,
By music led, and soldiers at command,
Clad in the homespun of a foreign land,
And greet the king. The king no armor bears,
Save on his breast a knife-like weapon wears,

White beads about his neck, a gaudy ring,
And quaint tobacco-bag suspended by a string,
Comprise the insignia of his regal power,
Known and observed of nations as of yore.
Both king and chiefs, with painted features, wear
Feathers disjoined from birds of plumage rare,
But little else. Kindly in turn they greet
The Pilgrim band, and down in group now seat
Themselves, holding discourse of allied strength
In treaty; and, when all agreed at length,
They pass the pipe around: each drink* in turn:
A sacred compact thus they all confirm, —
A treaty wise, that full contentment gives
For fifty years while Massasoit lives.

From my Merrimack, p. 25.

Meanwhile it appears Squanto and Samoset remained with the English, instructing them, and acting as their interpreters. "Squanto went to fish, a day or two after Massasoit left, for eels. At night he came home with as many as he could lift in one hand, which our people were glad of. They were fat and sweet. He trod them out with his feet, and then caught them with his hands."

As we have said, this Indian was of great use to the English, with whom he was at all times kind

---

* If you smoke, the Indian calls it "*drinking.*"

and friendly in volunteering as an interpreter, and in giving aid and information during the two first years of the Pilgrim settlements. He believed in their religion, joined their church, lived two years in their society, and died in December, 1622.

The Pilgrim account of this event is *this:* " Here at *Manamoyk* [since Chatham], though they had determined to make essay to pass within the shoals of Cape Cod, yet God had otherwise disposed, who struck *Tisquantum* with sickness, insomuch that he there died. His disorder was bleeding much at the nose, which the Indians reckon a dangerous symptom."

" He desired the governor would pray for him, that he might go to the Englishmen's God, bequeathing his things to sundry of his English friends as remembrances of his love ; of whom (as they say) ' we have a great loss.' "

The reader will bear in mind, this was the same Squanto who in 1614 had been kidnapped by Hunt, sold into slavery in Spain, and had fled from there into London. In my " Merrimack," page 26, I wrote a word to his praise, as follows : —

TISQUANTUM.

Squanto, meanwhile, — who'd served a peaceful end,
And in the Pilgrims' God had found a friend,

Bereaved and worn by care of by-gone years
In mazy pathways through a vale of tears, —
Falls sick; and as by fever low depressed,
And life in doubt, to Pilgrims thus addressed
His sovereign *Will:* " This hunting-ground is mine,
The lakes, the vales, those mountain-heights sublime,
The green-grown banks where Merrimack bright glows,
And all the hills far as Patuxet goes:
These spacious wilds, my kindred (now no more)
In full dominion held and hunted o'er;
Then dying, all their titles thence descend
To me, Tisquantum, now so near this end
Of life. To thee, my Pilgrim friends, I give
This broad domain, — here may the white man live, —
My bow and arrow too: I give thee all;
Hence let me go, obedient to the call
Of Angel Death. Adieu!"

       Thus gracious dies
The last red man beneath Patuxet skies;
And thus the English sole possession share
By will from Squanto all this region fair,
Forever thence to lay the forest low,
To fence fair fields, and drive the crooked plow,
To waste the wigwams which for ages spread
The wild; and build broad mansions in their stead,
School-houses, temples to the God of grace,
And cities proud, peculiar to the race

Of Adam. Diligent through honest toil,
They reap rich harvest from the virgin soil.
From culture urged with bold aggressive sway,
Wild beasts, becoming frantic, flee away.
As ravenous bears and moose and wolves recede,
Neat-cattle and the noble horse succeed
In aid of husbandry. Full flocks abound;
The herds increase, as roll the seasons round;
The desert even, through culture's grateful care,
Soon set with fruit, begins to bloom and bear;
Fair nature smiles responsive to the plan
Of faith in God and industry of man.

It will be remembered that from this first treaty among the tribes in 1621, by Gov. Carver and Massasoit their king, an amicable peace of fifty years ensued.

This peace accordingly prevailed as between them. But in 1636 a war broke out between the Pequot tribes and Massasoit's tribes and the English.

SEVERAL WARS.

And then followed many eruptions, skirmishes, murders, and wars; including the Pokanekets and their allied nations under Philip, against the English; the French and Indian wars in King William's time; Queen Anne's War in Europe, and consequently, as a result of it, outrages, invasions, eruptions, murders, and devastations in and throughout the settlements of New England; and then, again, the eruptions and bloody conflicts that followed between 1722 and 1725; and another conflict transpired among the early settlers, growing out of a war originating or meditated by the French and Spaniards in Europe; and the war of 1747, — all tending to involve New England in conflagration, devastation, and death.

But, before advancing to a more specific account of the more prominent conflicts, we will here give the names of some of the sachems, chiefs, and sagamores who first and last were, to a greater or less degree, land-holders, and leaders of the multifarious tribes of New England.

SACHEMS AND SAGAMORES.

Samoset,	*Massasoit,*		*Tisquantum.*
Passaconaway,	*Pennacooks.*	Messambomet,	*Androscoggin.*
Wonalancet of **Wamesit,**	"	Wexar,	"
Hodgkins,	"	Egeremit,	*Tarratines.*
Kamkamagus,	"	Watambatet,	"
Adiwando,	"	Wassambomet,	"
Wehanonowit,	"	Washemet,	"
Hegans,	"	Wattanmeman,	"
Nahoba of **Wamesit,**	"	Tassuke,	"
Watchenoet,	"	Mugg,	"
Pangus,	*Pequawhets.*	Wattammon,	"
Wattanumon,	"	Wenemovet,	"
Moxus,	*Norrigewocks.*	Kennebis,	*Kennebecks.*
Hopegood,	"	Capt. Samuel.	"
Squando,	*Saco.*	Bomazine,	"
Manatagua,	"	Robinhood,	"

SACHEMS AND SAGAMORES.

Warnadugunbuent,	Penobscots.	Uncas,	Mohegans
Sussup,	"	Sunseto,	"
Apamaquid,	"	Oweneco,	"
Madacawando,	"	One-eyed John,	Nipmucks
Warrangunt,	"	Namapassamet,	"
Robin Doney,	Piscataquas.	Webcowit (squaw),	"
Miantonimo,	Narragansetts.	Aprimps,	"
Canonicus,	"	Wattapacoson,	"
Ponham,	"	Sagamore Sam,	"
Sassamon,	"	Sassacus,	Pequots.
Tupayaaman,	"	Tunxis,	"
Hobomoh,	"	Hammonasset,	"
Mossup,	"	Robert,	"
Quinnapin,	"	Sokoso,	"
Wauwamino,	"	Warandance,	Mohandsicks.
Tashtassuck,	"	Ascossasotick (Long Island),	"
Tassaquanawith,	"	Aspinet, } sachems of Nausett,	"
Kutshamaken, an interpreter,	"	Iyanough, }	
Mascus,	"	Kutchamaquin, { Sachems of Dorchester, &c., near Squantum.	
Wenew,	"		
Tawagason,	"	Ono Pequin,	Sachem of Quabaog.
Ninegret (Niantick),		John Tahattawan,	Chief of Praying Indians.
Walluspequin,	"	Wampatuck,	Massachusetts.
Philip (Metacom),	Wampanoags.	Chickataubut,	"
Alexander (Wamsutta),	"	Tampatuck,	"
Quaquath,	"	Cluchatabutt *alias* Jonas,	"
Peksuot,	"	Tahattawan, at Concord (Mustaquid),"	
Tokamahamon,	"	Masconomo, at Ipswich (Agawam),	"
Wecopaulum,	"	Montowampate, at Marblehead,	"
Wectamos (a princess),	"	Sam Hide, at Dedham (aged 105),	"
Watuspaquin,	"	Stonewall John,	"
Connecticote,	Mohegans.	Cononchet (Ch. Sachem of Philip),	

SHAMUT SACHEMS.

(Otherwise, those who signed the treaty of amity at Plymouth, Sept. 13, 1621.)

Ohquamehud,	Cawnacome,	Obbatinnua.
Natawahunt,	Caunbatant,	Chuckatabak.
Quadaquina,	Huthmoiden,	Apanno.

THESE SAGAMORES.

"*Some had expired in fight, the brands
Still rusted in their bony hands;
In plague and famine some.*" — CAMPBELL.

MASSACHUSETTS AGAINST THE MOHAWKS.

In the year 1669 the Massachusetts tribe, uniting with Englishmen, numbering in all about seven hundred strong, took a march into what was called the Maquas Country. They were mostly young men, and advanced, without direction or advice of the authorities at Boston, with revenge intent upon the Mohawks.

ELIOT, the New-England apostle, advised against it; and yet five of his Indian disciples, volunteering, went in for the fight. *Josias*, an ambitious, stout, middle-aged Indian, led off as if in command.

They thus advanced two hundred miles through the forest, and there falling in upon a Mohawk fort, and besieging it, several of their men were killed: others fell sick; and, after some hesitation and delay, they gave up the siege. On their retreat, the Mohawks, following in pursuit, obtained a position in the swamps or other ambushes in front of them; and there in battle, the great chieftain Chikatabutt, in the midst of his prodigies of valor, was killed; and nearly fifty of his warriors also fell in this conflict, on their way from the land of the Mohawks.

MASCANONOMO.

In the English court, June 28, 1631, as against this "sagamore of Agawam" (who had executed deeds of "all his lands in Ipswich," to one John Winthrop, jun.), a decree was recorded "*that the sagamore of Agawam be banished from coming into any Englishman's house for a year, under penalty of ten bear-skins.*"

This, as it seems, grew out of a difficulty which he had made in killing Indians, and making strife between the Tarratines and the English.

Soon the Tarratines came out in force against the tribe of Mascanonomo, with a hundred men; and on the 8th of August of that year they made an attack in the night-time upon his wigwams, wounded him, killed seven of his men, and mangled others, who afterwards died of their wounds. His squaw was carried away captive.

This chief, notwithstanding these admonitions, long afterwards, in 1644 (March 8), being friendly to the English, made them a call with some of his friends, assented to their articles of faith, were "*solemnly received;*" and then they were presented to the court.

They made him presents of twenty-six fathom of wampum; and the court gave him two yards of cloth, dinners to him and his men, and "a cup of sac" to each at their departure. He dies.

A GRANT TO HIS SQUAW.

And now on the old Town-Book of Ipswich, under date of June 18, 1658, a generous act of that municipality is to be found, wherein a grant is made to Mascononomo's squaw of

"*That parcel of land which her husband had fenced in,*" so long as she should remain a widow.

"Her husband was the last of the *sachems* of *Agawam;* and with him," says Mr. Felt, "descended his feeble and broken sceptre to the grave." He died March 6, 1658; and they buried him there, with his *gun,* his *tomahawk,* and *other implements* of the chase by his side, on "*Sagamore Hill,*" within the lines of Hamilton: *there* both squaw and sagamore *are at rest forever.*

Many of the chiefs whom we have named as well as we might in this chapter were men of note in their times, standing distinguished among the native nations, and at times were respected and favored of the colonies.

CANONICUS.

Among these also was this sachem, from whose good example and liberal kindnesses Connecticut was obtained and civilized by the white man. During the Pequot War great pains were taken to secure to the colonies the favor of *Canonicus,* then a sachem near to it in Connecticut. Hence Roger Williams wrote to Gov. Winthrop as follows: —

"*Sir, if any thing be sent to the princes, I find Canonicus would gladly accept of a box of eight or ten pounds of sugar; and, indeed, he told me he would thank Mr. Governor for a box-full.*"

Then again he sent another letter, saying, —

"*I am bold to request a word of advice concerning a proposition made by* CANONICUS *and* MIANTUNIMO *to me some half-year since. Canonicus gave an island in this bay to Mr. Oldham, by name Chibachuwese, upon condition, as it should seem, that he would dwell there near unto them,*" and desired to know if this proposition would be agreeable to Massachusetts. But the Pequot War soon intervened; and here, as we believe, this matter came to an end.

CANONICUS was much noted. He was poetized by some Boston writer in 1803, from which we quote, wherein, at the age of eighty-four years, he is made to announce his own departure from the stormy trials of earth: —

HIS LAST WORD.

"I die, my friends. You have no cause to grieve:
To abler hands my regal power I leave;
Our God commands: to fertile realms I haste,
Compared with which your gardens are a waste.

There in full bloom eternal *spring* abides,
And swarming fishes glide through azure tides;
Continued sunshine gilds the cloudless skies,
No mists conceal *Keesuckquand* from our eyes."

Roger Williams, in the year 1654, in alluding to the old Narragansetts says, —

"Their late famous long-lived Canonicus so lived and died; and in the same most honorable manner and solemnity (in their way) as you laid to sleep your prudent peacemaker Mr. Winthrop, did they honor this their prudent and peaceable prince; yea, through all their towns and countries, how frequently do many, and ofttimes our Englishmen, travel alone with safety and loving-kindness!"

In a deposition which he gave of this chief, June 18, 1682, Mr. Williams says in substance that Miantonimo was the marshal of Canonicus, was his youngest brother's son, and did nothing without the consent of Canonicus; and then he adds, "*I declare to posterity, that, were it not for the favor that God gave me with* CANONICUS, *none of these parts, no, not Rhode Island, had been purchased or obtained; for I never got any thing of* CANONICUS *but by gift.*"

CHAPTER VIII.

TREATY; PEQUOTS WITH THE ENGLISH.

The Advance of Civilization.—Pequot Hostilities and Depredations.— Their Numbers. — Location of their Tribes. — Sassacus their Sachem.— English Treaty with them.— Land conveyed by the Tribes to the Dutch.— Consideration.— In War they had conquered the Dutch Settlers.— Plymouth People seek Territory there.— Extent of the Dominions of Sassacus.— Stone and his Men; how slain. — Vessel Explosion, and Several killed. — Narragansetts and English unite against the Pequots.— SASSACUS seeks Reconciliation. — A Talk in Boston. — *Position*, as urged by the Pequots.— A Treaty is signed.— Boston in an Uproar. — Armed Men sent to Neponset to appease the Narragansetts.— Colonies try to pacify the Nations.— Englishmen seek Pequot Lands under Treaty.— Neither Party fulfils it.— English took Deeds.— Consideration of One of them.— Oldham is slain. — Gallop finds his Body, and pursues the Pequots.

IN the preceding chapters we have seen in brief how the Pilgrims started on these shores; the first insurrection of the natives against them; how after the lapse of about three months the friendly *Samoset* came to meet and greet them; how he brought in from afar the wise, the peaceful, the discreet and generous-hearted MASSASOIT; how they made their treaty, and formed a friendly alliance which, as between the Plymouth Colony and these tribes, endured for nearly fifty years; and how old Squanto (Tisquantum), after he had been taken by the heartless Hunt, carried into Spain, and sold as a slave, escaped; and after all his experience in London, and after his sad reverses in the loss of his own entire Patuxet tribe and kindred (all swept away by a war and by the pestilence), how he still lived, and loved the English; how he joined the Church; how then, within two brief years, giving up every thing, he took his final leave of a wilderness world, with an abiding, triumphant faith in the Pilgrims' God.

Since then (December, 1622), the onward march of civilization in New England has worked its wonders.

FROM THE CLOUD.

Come back, *Tisquantum,* if above ye dwell:
Behold thy Merrimack, once loved so well.
Thy race had traced it from creation's start:
The white man turns it to the works of art.
Survey its progress these three hundred years,
Since up and down ye wandered here in tears
Alone, bereaved. Call once again to view
Thy thick-set forest wild, thy birch canoe,
Where now thy kindred sleep as from the first;
Where Pilgrim saints since mingled in the dust;
Where now the ploughman trudges in his toil,
Thoughtless of what still lies beneath the soil;

TISQUANTUM IN A CLOUD.

Oh! let us know from what thy name inspires,
What is man's destiny, what Heaven requires,
More fully still. From realms eternal, fair,
Tell us of hunting-grounds, of glory there,
Where blissful prospect Heaven shall fulfil
To generations onward, upward still;
While purest fountains flowing, failing never,
Shall swell the tide of Merrimack forever, —
Sure sign here given of God's enduring care,
For what we see in heaven, in earth, or air.

From my Merrimack, p. 74.

THE PEQUOT WAR.

The Pequot tribes of 1635–6 and 7 were said to be at that period " the most numerous, the most warlike, the fiercest and bravest, of all the aboriginal clans of Connecticut. From the Niantic River on the west, their forts and wigwams extended along the rude and stony hills of New-London County to Wecapoag, ten miles east of Paucatuc River, which divides Connecticut from Rhode Island." Their dominions extended back a considerable distance from the sea, their northernmost tribes being mostly Mohegans, who usually hunted along the banks of the Thames. Sassacus was their grand sachem, having under him twenty-six sagamores; and he could muster from five hundred to seven hundred warriors.

The Narragansetts, their most formidable foes,

dwelt at the eastward, in Rhode Island and vicinity, and along the shores of the sea in Massachusetts where the Indian population was dense.

These Narragansetts at the time are said to have been very numerous, according to some accounts numbering more than twenty thousand, and that at one time they could have furnished five thousand fighting men.

It appears that on the 18th of June, 1633, there was a treaty of sale and purchase between the Dutch settlers in Connecticut and the Pequots. These Indians conveyed to those Dutchmen "a tract of land one Dutch mile in length along the river, extending one-third of a mile into the country." For this land "*Wopigwooit* received twenty-seven ells of a kind of coarse cloth called duffels, six axes, six kettles, eighteen knives, one sword-blade, one pair of shears, and some toys."

THE HOUSE OF GOOD HOPE.

The territory thus purchased for the purposes of trade was to be free to all nations of Indians, and "was to be a territory of peace. The hatchet was to be buried there. No warrior was to molest his enemy while within its bounds."

Yet *Van Curler*, " one of the Dutch," erected on it a small trading-fort, armed it with two pieces of cannon, and named it "*The House of Good Hope.*"

Thereupon "the Pequots soon broke through the conditions of the treaty aforesaid, by killing *Indians*, their enemies, who came there to trade. Upon that, the Dutch contrived to kill Wopigwooit their chief, and several of his men."

SASSACUS his son, a renowned warrior, succeeded Wopigwooit as chief; but alas! he proved in the end to be the last sachem of that tribe.

The war thus between the Dutch and the tribes commenced. It lasted nearly two years; bringing to the settlers all the horrors of a bloody conflict, interrupting trade, and producing unabated consternation throughout New England.

The Pequots for the time being prevailed over the Dutch. In October, 1633, while the war with the Dutch progressed, the Plymouth people resolved to make a settlement in the Pequot country, and sent one William Holmes up there with a vessel, a number of men, and the frame of a house. "He sailed up the river, passed the Dutch fort at Hartford, and, in spite of remonstrances and threats of the garrison, erected his trading-house in a place now called Windsor." Holmes, they say, carried back in his vessel the original sachems who had been driven away by the Pequots, probably thereby giving further offence.

The Pequots had then already conquered this part

of the Connecticut Valley; and their supremacy had been substantially acknowledged by the Dutch.

It may be observed that the English inclined to question the Dutch titles as well as those of the Pequots. But no open hostility commenced at this time between the English and the Pequot race; and yet the germ of hostility was beginning to move.

In the summer of 1633 *Capt. Stone* came here from Virginia in a small vessel to obtain trade on the coast of New England. He traded a short time at Massachusetts Bay, and then sailed with a Capt. Norton and seven others for the Connecticut River. Soon after his departure news came to Boston that Stone, Norton, and his whole company, were killed, his vessel burned, and all his articles of cargo taken and divided among the Pequots and Nehantics. It appears further that at or near this time others, to the number of thirty, had been slain somewhat in a similar manner.

ORIGIN OF THESE TRIBES.

This nation of Pequots, as we have seen, according to Hubbard, cruel and war-like as they were, had in former times " come down from the inland parts of the continent, and by force had seized upon one of the goodliest places near the sea, and had become a terror to all their neighbors." He says their domain extended over a part of Long Island, over the *Mohegans*, over the sagamores of *Quinnepeake* (now New Haven), yea, over all the people that dwelt upon Connecticut River, and over some of the most southerly inhabitants of the Nipmuck Country about Quinabaag. The principal seat from which these sagamores rallied was near the mouth of the Thames, now New London. They had here originally three kings, to wit, *Connecticote*, *Quinnipiog*, and *Sassacus*. CONNECTICOTE, as from a long line of descents, was chief of chiefs. They up to this time had conquered the Dutch settlers, having murdered many of them in a quarrel, arising mostly from the fact that the Dutch had traded with some of their enemies; and, now that they had begun to murder the English who came there to trade, we soon will begin to behold

"HOW GREAT A MATTER A LITTLE FIRE KINDLETH."

So it was that one Capt. Stone from Virginia, in 1634, while on a trading expedition, as he had at first touched at Massachusetts Bay, with his seven men on board of his vessel was brutally murdered.

STONE AND NORTON.

It happened thus: On reaching the mouth of the Connecticut, Stone opened a trade with the natives, and sent three of his men ashore to hunt for wild-fowl. The Indians appeared friendly, and were suffered to come on board the vessel at pleasure. Stone, being tired for want of rest, fell asleep in his cabin in presence of the sachem; and the rest of the crew unsuspiciously and without any precautions were in the galley.

Meantime the three men on shore had been attacked and slain by a party of the Indians, but so far off, it was not known of the ship's crew. Then the chief knocked out the brains of the unconscious captain; and instantly his followers seized the fire-arms of the vessel, and presented them against the startled English.

NATIVES AFRAID OF FIRE-ARMS.

One of the English, seizing a musket, aimed it in his own defence. Upon seeing such a weapon in the hands of a white man, they all fled, leaping overboard.

But, in the rush and confusion, the powder in the vessel ignited, blew up, damaging the vessel, and killing nearly the whole of the little crew then remaining.

Next then, the Indians clambered on board again, and, killing such as yet remained alive, plundered and sequestered the cargo. These murderers were Pequots, aided, perhaps, by some of the western

Nehantics. It was in this way the battles went on; for the Narragansetts, the Massachusetts, and tributaries had not forgotten, *as they never would forget*, their alliance as pledged to the English on their great first treaty in the peaceful days of Massasoit; and they now resolved to move together against the Pequots.

The Pequot nation had been besought to give up their murderers by the English through their governor at Boston, and, as of course, *in vain.* Yet their war with the Dutch settlers was still troubling them; and, in sight of the storm which they could but see gathering to becloud them, they in the following year, through Sassacus, undertook to conciliate the English, hoping thereby to escape danger, and to restore to his people a return of trade.

HE SENDS AN AMBASSADOR.

In October, 1634, a Pequot messenger arrived at "the bay," bearing, according to Indian fashions as an ambassador, a present for Deputy-Gov. Ludlow from his sachem.

He laid down before the governor "two bundles of sticks, indicative of the number of *beaver* and other skins which the Pequots would give the English, and promised also a large amount of wampum, and therefore requested a league between his people and the pale-faces."

Ludlow accepted the presents thus made to himself, and gave him in return a moose coat of equal value for the Pequot chieftain; but the governor kindly told the messenger, when he took leave of him, that *Sassacus* must show his respect for the English by sending deputies of greater quality than he was, and *enough* of them, before a treaty could be made with the colonies.

A fortnight afterwards, two Pequot *sagamores* arrived, bringing to Ludlow other presents.

The deputy-governor, *Dudley* being absent, received them with civility, conducted them to Boston, and their negotiations opened.

But the Pequots were told that there could be no consent to a treaty until the *murderers of Stone* and others were surrendered, nor until restitution was made for the plunder and destruction of his vessel.

PEQUOTS DEFEND THEIR ACTION.

These sagamores "did not deny that their nation was responsible for the murder, but asserted that *Stone had provoked his fate.*"

They said that "on entering the *Connecticut*, he forcibly seized two Indians of that region, and kept them on board his vessel to make them pilot it up the river; that after a while, he and two of his men landed, taking with them the two captives, *with their hands still closely bound behind them;*

"That nine Indians watched the party; and at night, when the English had gone to sleep on the shore, *they killed them*, and liberated their countrymen;" that the vessel, with the remainder of their crew, was afterwards blown up; but of this they knew nothing, neither the manner nor cause.

They further stated that the *sachem* whom they had when Stone was put to death *had been killed* by the Dutch, and that all the Indians concerned in the murder *had died* of the small-pox, except two.

These, they cautiously added, *Sassacus* would probably be willing to deliver to the English, provided the guilt could be proved upon them.

This story of the Pequot ambassadors, the English were inclined to believe, having no direct evidence to the contrary; and a treaty was then and there agreed upon, and was signed by the parties.

SECOND TREATY IN N. E. HISTORY.

By *this*, the English were to have as much land in the country of the Connecticut as they needed, provided they would make a settlement; and the Pequots were to give them all possible assistance in effecting their settlement.

The Pequots were to surrender the two murderers whenever they were demanded, and were to pay the

English forty beaver-skins, thirty otter-skins, and four hundred fathoms of wampum.

They were likewise to give all their custom to the English, who, on the other hand, were to send them a vessel immediately, not to defend them, but to trade with them.

Such was the treaty between the Colony of Massachusetts Bay and the Pequots in 1634.

BOSTON IN A HUBBUB.

On the morning next following this treaty, news arrived "that two or three hundred Narragansetts were waiting at a place called Neponset to kill the Pequot messengers on their way home."

Thereupon a few armed men were collected by an order from the governor; and they proceeded to Neponset with a message to come to Boston and have a talk.

But, on reaching Neponset, the white men found only two sagamores with about twenty warriors, who put in a disclaimer by saying that they were out on a hunting expedition, and had come thither simply to make their old friends at Neponset a visit.

THE COLONY TRIES TO PACIFY THE TRIBES.

The English now make the attempt to negotiate a peace between the Pequots and the Narragansetts.

SETTLEMENTS AMONG THE PEQUOTS.

To this end they offered the Narragansetts a part of the wampum which was to be paid by the Pequots; and, as appears, the Pequots had stipulated to furnish the governor with four hundred fathoms of that article, *extra*, for that very purpose.

The Narragansetts acceded to this proposition; and a treaty of peace was also concluded between them and the Pequots.

From this treaty, for the time being amounting to a sort of reconciliation on the one side and on the other, the English advanced to make settlements among the Pequots at Wethersfield and elsewhere; and there is a deed wherein it appears that within the two next years they had purchased of Sowheag the sachem, certain territory "measuring six miles in width north and south, and nine miles in length, of which six miles were on the west side of the river."

There is another deed, bearing date April 25, 1636, by which they obtained by purchase a tract on the east side of the Connecticut, lying between the Podunk and Seantic Rivers, and extending a day's march into the country.

CONSIDERATION OF THE DEED.

Its consideration was twenty cloth coats, fifteen fathoms of wampum, a part of which was to be paid at the time and a part when the next English *pinnace* came up the river.

This deed was signed by *Arramament* (sachem at Podunk), Sheat (sachem of Poquonnuc), Cogremosset of Poquonnuc, and eight others, who hitherto had claimed an interest in the lands.

TREATY NOT FULFILLED.

John W. De Forest, in his concise history of the Connecticut wars, printed in 1750, says, that the treaties between the colonial government and the Pequots were imperfectly observed on both sides; that *Sassacus* paid none of the wampum or other articles which he had promised; nor is there any proof that for two years after the treaty the colonists ever sent a vessel to the Pequot country to trade; that the only article which the English fulfilled was that of planting colonies in Connecticut; and the only article which the Pequots fulfilled was that of allowing them to do so without opposition.

TROUBLE WITH THE NARRAGANSETTS.

It was thus that matters went on under that treaty; and at length it happened, John Oldham of Dorchester, an energetic commander of a *pinnace*, in which he made trading voyages along the coast for the purpose of obtaining corn and other Indian articles of traffic was slain.

In the spring of 1636 he sailed up the Connecticut, having for a crew two boys and two Narragansetts to assist him in trade with the Pequots.

OLDHAM finished his dealings with the natives; but, pausing on his return at *Manisses* (Block Island), he was murdered by its Indian inhabitants July 20, 1636.

Upon this being known to another trader, *John Gallop*, who was voyaging along the eastern part of Long Island, he discovered *Oldham's pinnace*, having on board of it sixteen Indians, and a canoe, manned by other Indians, loaded with goods, putting off from the shore.

HE HAILS IT.

Gallop, running close to it, gave a hail in English; but, obtaining no answer, his suspicions were aroused by observing that the Indians were armed with guns. Immediately a sail was hoisted on board the pinnace. The wind and tide being off the island, their boat began to drive northward towards the Narragansett shore. Gallop then bore up as if to head them off, and occasionally fired at them with duckshot; upon which they all took shelter under the hatches. He then, standing off at a distance, made a run upon the *pinnace's* quarter with heavy force. Six Indians, frightened at the shock, jumped overboard, and were drowned while making for the shore.

He then made another rush upon the *pinnace* with his heavier vessel; and, no other Indians making their appearance, he used his muskets in firing through her sides.

Then six others of the plunderers leaped overboard, and were drowned.

The victors then (three men and two boys) boarded their prize. Two Indians came up on deck, surrendered, and were secured; but, as they made him trouble in securing them, he threw one of them into the sea. Two other Indians still remained under the hatches armed with swords, in such a position that they could not be killed or taken.

JOHN'S BODY.

The body of *John Oldham* was found beneath an old sail, his head split open, his arms and legs gashed as if the Indians had tried to amputate them, and his flesh still warm.

Gallop committed these remains to the sea, took the sails and remainder of the cargo on board their own craft, and then tried to tow the pinnace away with the two Indians still in it.

But the high wind and heavy sea drove the pinnace from them: they were obliged to loose her; and she drifted over against the Narragansett shore.

CHAPTER IX.

THE OLD NARRAGANSETTS.

With the English Harmonious usually. — An Eruption. — The Tribe proposes War. — Gov. Winthrop returns the Rattlesnake Skin, and avoids Trouble. — Canonicus and his Sachems. — Pequots suspected of Hostility. — An Expedition sent against them with Terrible Instructions. — Fleet lands. — The Indians run away. — English commit Depredations. — A Dread Warfare is at hand. — Murders ensue from the Tribes. — Men, Cows, &c., are killed. — Miantonomo and two Sons of Canonicus, and Twenty Others visited Boston in Kindness, and made an Alliance. — Tilly and Others murdered. — Uncas at the Saybrook Fort. — Battle on the Highlands at Mystic, led by Mason. — Underhill and Uncas and Wequash on the One Side, and the Sagamores of Sassacus on the Other. — Its Description. — Numbers Slain. — Sassacus in sight of his Dead Nation. — He seeks the Mohawks. — They murder him, and return his Scalp to the English.

CANONICUS for many years was their chief; and every thing, as between them and the English, seemed to move harmoniously at all times, with the exception of one or two instances of apparent warlike eruptions.

One of these causeless misunderstandings is described by *Edward Winslow* in his GOOD NEWS OF NEW ENGLAND, and is repeated by Mr. Drake the historian, as follows : —

In February, 1622, Canonicus sent into Plymouth by one of his men *a bundle of arrows*, bound with a rattlesnake-skin, and left them there, and retired. The Narragansetts were then many thousands strong. Tisquantum the interpreter, after the messenger had left, being called, told the English that the arrows lapped in a rattlesnake's skin was intended as a challenge for war.

Thereupon Gov. Winthrop took the rattlesnake's skin, filled it with powder and shot, and returned it to the old Narragansett, with a message of defiance, and at the same time invited him to a trial of strength.

The messenger, with his daring demand, produced the desired effect upon Canonicus, who, declining to receive the rattlesnake-skin, at once returned it.

And here, as we believe, the trouble ended. Canonicus had held, and still maintained, an influence over some of the Massachusetts sagamores, who were inclined to follow him.

We are told that in the war between Uncas and Miantonomo, two sons of Canonicus fought for Miantonomo, and that they were wounded at Sachem's Plain.

Poems were published of this chief, of which a few lines are here copied: —

THE PLOT AGAINST OLDHAM.

"A mighty prince of venerable age,
A peerless warrior, but of peace a friend;
His breast a treasury of maxims sage,
His arm a host to punish or defend."

The tribes of Canonicus from the beginning, as we have said, had maintained good faith with the Pilgrims. They had become more civilized, and had been better in their behavior, and more inclined to progress, than any other of the tribes within the sixteen years since they had entered into an allied treaty with the English.

But now an event has happened which makes *Canonicus*, that faithful old Sachem, sad. It was not the act of *Canonicus:* his sorrows arise from the perfidy of a few of his men, just as great quarrels usually commence. This old chief of the Narragansetts, seeing the situation, as avowed, forthwith sent Miantonomo his nephew, with seventeen canoes and two hundred men, to punish the murderers.

It was undoubtedly true that the plot at the murdering of Oldham was planned and perpetrated by his Narragansetts, because this captain had traded with their enemies, the Pequots. Canonicus, in view of this troublesome murder, had applied for aid and advice to Roger Williams, a clergyman in that vicinity. Accordingly Williams had prepared a letter in his behalf; and three Narragansetts were made the bearers of it as ambassadors to the governor at Boston. The plot had been formed, and the murder committed, by certain reckless savages on the island: as we have said, they had taken offence because Oldham had favored the Pequots with his trade.

The authorities at Boston finally sent the messengers back to Canonicus, expressing some suspicions which they had entertained upon this matter. They, however, demanded that Canonicus should surrender Oldham's two boys, whom the savages still held, and that he should inflict severe punishment upon the guilty tribes upon the island.

The boys accordingly were returned; and *Canonicus* and *Miantonomo* thereafterwards succeeded in convincing the governor that neither he nor his sagamores had any knowledge of, and that they had not had any participation in, the murder.

PEQUOTS SUSPECTED.

It came to light that some of the Pequots had harbored some of the murderers of Oldham; and by the Colony it was thought they had been partakers of guilt with the Narragansetts; and, in that time of faithless fear and excitement, hasty measures were adopted.

Although, by the treaty of 1634, the Pequots were to have paid the Colony four hundred fathoms of wampum, which was to have gone to the Narragansetts, they had not done it. Yet from that treaty they had behaved well towards the Colony, and could not be accused of having committed any outrage against the English, their property, or their allies. "Yet such were the suspicions against them, which were now aroused in this time of excitement, that the government at Boston resolved to demand of the Pequot nation six hundred additional fathoms of wampum, and some of their children as hostages for its delivery."

On Sept. 25, 1636, pursuant to orders from the governor and council, John Endicott of Boston was furnished with three small vessels and with ninety men, of which John Underhill and Nathaniel Turner were captains, and Jenyson and Davenport ensigns, and with instructions to invade Block Island, and, sparing "the women and children, put all the men to the sword." Endicott was commanded to go farther: he was to advance into the Pequot Country, obtain the "infidel murderers of Stone," together with a thousand fathoms of wampum, demand some of their children as hostages for the performance of these conditions, and, if the children were refused, to take them by force, and bring them to Boston.

The fleet was off, and landed on the island. The principal chiefs were away. No attack was made on that day. They made some random shots, by which it is supposed *one* Indian was killed; but the Indians at the smell of gunpowder ran away, as usual. On the following day Endicott and his force marched over the Island, but, finding no Indians there, " burned down their wigwams, destroyed their canoes, carried away some of their mats and baskets, shot their dogs, and laid waste about two hundred acres of corn."

They spent two days there, but found no more Indians. Thence Endicott with his force advanced to Saybrook. Lieut. *Gardner,* who commanded the fort there, expressed great surprise at the sending out of such an expedition, and appeared almost exasperated at the madness of such an unreasonable movement. Addressing the commander, says he, " You have come to raise a nest of wasps about your ears; and then you will flee away."

Gardner, however, upon reflection, and in obedience to orders, re-enforced the expedition with two shallops and twenty men.

They remained four days by reason of stress of weather; and then they advanced along the coast of the western Nehantics. As they passed, the Indians, at the sight of so many vessels, innocently and unsuspiciously came running to the shore in large numbers to inquire the object of their visit. "*What cheer?* Englishmen!" they shouted. "*What do you come for?*"

The craft kept steadily on, making no answer (for they seemed to have none to make). When arriving at the mouth of the Thames, and when, as it appeared, the white men would not answer, the Indians turned and began to cry, "*Are you angry, Englishmen? Will you kill us?*"

No answer was returned. The vessels silently passed down the river, cast anchor far from the shore; and the anxious Pequots sadly turned away.

Dread alarms reverberated through the wilderness that night; and next day the Pequots in that neighborhood were few. It being late in the season, the expedition was finally given up. By such a demonstration, that wicked, barbarous nation the Pequots were driven to desperation; and a reckless warfare again commenced. In the field, in the forest, on the highway, in the church, or in the cot, danger, like a pestilence at noonday or at night, to men, innocent women, and helpless children, followed all alike.

At Saybrook in October, 1636, five men, while haying in a meadow, were attacked; and one of them, by the name of Butterfield, was killed; and that meadow bears the dead man's name to this day.

About fourteen days afterwards, two men were taken in a cornfield two miles from Saybrook Fort. Within a mile of the fort six men were surrounded by two or three hundred Indians. Four escaped; two were taken: the two of course were slain. Advancing, they killed one cow, and shot arrows into others.

Oct. 21, the friendly *Miantonomo*, a Narragansett, with two sons of CANONICUS, came to Boston with twenty other Indians, to give notice to the English of the approaching dangers. Katashamakin also sought a conference with the governor; and giving notice of his purpose, a military company, being ordered, met him at Roxbury and escorted him into Boston.

Here at this time he made an alliance against the Pequots, agreeing with the English that neither party should make peace with the Pequots without consent of the other, and made it a duty to deliver up murderers, or to put them to death.

John Tilley about the same time was sailing down the Connecticut in a boat; and within about three miles of Saybrook Fort he shot at some game. The Pequots, hearing the report of his gun, overtook him, tortured and maimed him in the most brutal manner, and at length cut off his legs and arms, cruelly leaving him alive. He lingered about three days.

THE CONFLICT.

He was denominated "*a stout man*" by his tormentors. A man who at the same time was with Tilley was also killed.

On Feb. 22, 1636, several Englishmen, as they went out from Saybrook Fort, were decoyed into an ambush by the Pequots; and four of them were slain. The others with great difficulty made their escape.

At Wethersfield (same year) April 12, six men and three women were murdered; two young women were carried away; and one horse and twenty cows were killed.

Next, then, there was extraordinary alarm throughout these English plantations. Miantonomo had sent a notice to Boston that the Pequots had sent their women and children away to an Island.

Forty men were thereupon raised and sent to Narragansett, to join others to be raised by Miantonomo himself, with the design of falling in upon the Pequot warriors by a surprise, and *driving them out of the world*.

About this time Capt. Mason, with ninety men raised in Connecticut, had been sent away to make war against the Pequots. The famous *Uncas*, with a large body of his warriors, advanced with Mason; and on their march to Saybrook, May 15, 1637, they fell upon about thirty Pequots, killed seven of them, and placed their heads on the walls of the fort at Saybrook.

Immediately afterwards Capts. Mason and Underhill advanced to take one of the forts of the enemy, which was situated on a rise of ground, where Groton, Conn., now stands. The English and about five hundred allied Indians arrived there on the 25th of May, and surrounded the eminence before day on the morning of the 26th; and the battle was obstinate, furious, and bloody. Beforehand, however, the Mohegans and Narragansetts had begun in their talk to hesitate, thinking that the English would not stand their ground as against the Pequots led by so brave a sagamore as Sassacus.

Thereupon Mason and Underhill, who commanded the seventy-nine Englishmen, called up *Uncas*, who was to lead the Mohegans, and *Wequash*, a fugitive Pequot chief who had acted as a pilot, and who was to assist in the lead of the Narragansetts, and endeavored to excite them to bravery, urging them to follow the English; and then, the battle commencing, the Pequots swarmed out against them furiously. On the other hand, the allied Indians, although they kept at respectable distances from the front, maintained their ground, and did good service in heading off the fugitive Pequots, as the fight extended along the way for several miles.

THE PEQUOT SLAUGHTER. 153

The English had but seventy-seven men, which were divided into two companies, one led by Mason, and the other by Underhill. The hostile Pequots were all within their wigwam-fort, asleep. The barking of a dog was the first notice they had of the approach of the allied forces; yet none of them knew the cause of the alarm, until met at their gates by the foe.

The fort had two entrances at opposite points, into which each party of English were led, sword in hand. "*Wanux, Wanux!*" (English, English) was the wailing cry of the five hundred savages within the distracted wigwams of the fort.

The bow and the arrow, or even the tomahawk, were as nothing to them then. The English, rapiers in hand, backed up by the Mohegans and Narragansetts, from wigwam to wigwam, pursued and slaughtered them in every place. Men, women, and children, all were falling, one after another, without reservation or distinction. At length fire was set in the mats and other combustible material that covered the wigwams: it furiously spread over the whole fort; and the dead and dying were together consumed.

A part of the English had formed a circle around and on the outside of the fort; and they made it a business to shoot all those that attempted to fly. Some of them tried to ascend the pickets to escape the flames, but fell, being shot down. Upwards of five hundred Pequots perished in this battle. Two only of the English were killed; and about twenty of them were wounded. *Sassacus* himself was in another fort, and, being informed of the fate of his tribes, destroyed his habitation, and with about thirty others fled to the Mohawks; but the faithless Mohawks treacherously beheaded him, and made a return of his scalp to the English. Thus perished the Pequots; and thus ended the Pequot war, and almost the entire Pequot race. Yamoyden the poet celebrates this battle as follows: —

> "And Sassacus, now no more,
> Lord of a thousand bowmen, fled;
> And all the chiefs, his boast before,
> Were mingled with the unhonored dead.
> Sannap and sagamore were slain
> On Mystic's banks, in one red night:
> The once far-dreaded king in vain
> Sought safety in inglorious flight;
> And, reft of all his regal pride,
> By the fierce Maqua's hand he died."

At this terrible battle,* waged as it was by the English and their Indian allies on the one side, and by

---

* *Cotton Mather* says, that, while this Pequot battle at the fort was progressing, a party of three hundred of them from another place came up, and that they "acted like bears bereft of their whelps;"

the perfidious Pequots on the other, *Sassacus*, their great sachem, was away. Some eighty of his men also were away guarding another locality, who, as appears, subsequently came in, and rallied in the fight. Tragical indeed was that scene on the morrow. When the news of the loss of his nation fell upon the ears of Sassacus, and his eyes came to behold the ruins of his great wigwam fortress, together with the dead and mangled bodies of his slaughtered tribes, he with his thirty attendants appearing as the pitiful remnant of a powerful nation, the picture was indeed pitiful. The dead extended from the fort to distant swamps; and the whole loss to the Pequots, first and last, was nearly seven hundred. Mather says, " When they came to see the ashes of their friends mingled with the ashes of their fort, and the bodies of so many of their countrymen terribly 'barbikew'd,' where the English had been doing a good morning's work, they *howled*, they *roared*, they *stamped*, they *tore their hair ;* and, though they did not swear (for they knew not how), yet they cursed, and were the very pictures of so many *devils* in desperation." This was the last day of Sassacus on his old hunting-grounds in the val-

---

that they "combined a bloody fight for miles together ;" that they made a fort of every swamp in their way, until they became finally "discouraged, and gave over" at a place called Fairfield.

leys of the Connecticut, and along the beautiful Thames. His hand had been raised against every man's hand; his hostile nation had left its scars on the red, brawny faces of all the neighboring tribes: and now, while he stood there in sight of the horrors of that tragic morning, amid the mangled bodies of his tribes, and in the midst of the wailings which Mather has described, — whither, oh whither now should he fly? His thirty bereaved friends, the remnant of his mighty tribes, then filling the air with their lamentations, were powerless to aid, to comfort, or to tell him. The English were away; but, reeking with vengeance, they were as yet on the alert, and were yet seeking *his* blood. Where, to whom, should he fly? Like a wounded deer pursued by the hounds he leaped: he fled away for the Mohawks. The *Mohawks!* and they, too, were still bearing upon their bodies the same deep-cut scars which Sassacus himself had made; and oh, what madness! Nowhere else could he go. Forgetting his own bloody aggressions, and depending for his life upon an unforgiving, merciless Mohawk, *impetuous*, he flew away to him, still meditating vengeance, and whose hostile tribes on the borders of New York destroyed him, and then afterwards waged war upon Passaconaway. It was thus Sassacus fell.

The wrath of the English, and of their allied

Mohegans and Narragansetts, had swept over his nation like a pestilence; and then, like a fish at the net, and the bird caught in the snare, Sassacus perished at the hand of the Mohawks. The Mohawks (as if in fear of the English), when Sassacus came falling penitently into their open arms, murdered him in cool blood; and then with Mohawk ceremonies treacherously they transferred and transmitted his bleeding scalp to the English government at Boston.

Here ended the last sad lesson which may be taken from the history of this famous, belligerent, fated Sassacus, — a lesson among many, wherein the wrath of man has been permitted to prevail over his better passions, and where professed civilizations as well as barbarisms have been at fault, through which an entire nation perished in a night; and that original Pequot tribe of New England *fell*, never more to be seen.

However cruel the provocations, that urged the immediate necessity of destroying the Pequot race might be, yet the reader cannot but be surprised at the evident complacency of its leading enemy, Cotton Mather, in announcing the result of that murderous conflict, while he asserts that in a little more than an hour "*five or six hundred of these barbarians were dismissed from a world that was burdened with them.*"

He states that on that bloody night of May 20,

1637, not more than seven or eight persons of all that multitude of Pequots at the garrison escaped: these fled with Sassacus to the Mohawks.

Dwight, on this slaughter, concludes a poem thus: —

THE PEQUOTS.

"Undaunted, on their foes they fiercely flew,
  As fierce the dusky warriors crowd the fight;
  Despair inspires; dread combats strength renew;
  With groans and shouts they rage unknowing flight,
And close their sullen eyes in shades of endless night.

"Indulge, my native land, indulge the tear,
  That steals impassioned o'er a nation's doom:
  To me each twig from Adam's stock is near;
  And sorrows fall upon an Indian's tomb.

"And, oh! ye chiefs in yonder starry home,
  Accept the humble tribute of this rhyme:
  Your gallant deeds in Greece or haughty Rome,
  By Maro sung, or Homer's harp sublime,
Had charmed the world's wide round, and triumphed over time."

CHAPTER X.

MIANTONIMO.

Uncas excites Suspicions against him. — A Hearing is had at Boston. — Nothing is Proved. — Thence he and Miantonimo were in Conflict. — Another Hearing was had. — Uncas proved to be in the Wrong. — Council disbelieve the Witness. — The Witness murdered. — Uncas is waylaid and shot at. — He demands for it that Six of Sequassen's Men shall be delivered to him to be put to Death. — One is adjudged Sufficient. — Sequassen, as probably advised by Miantonimo, would not give him up. — Miantonimo threatens War against Uncas. — English do not object to it. — Uncas invades Sequassen. — Miantonimo then invades Uncas. — Uncas routs Miantonimo's Force by deceitful Strategy. — Miantonimo is taken Prisoner. — Imprisoned. — The Four Colonies, under Advice of Fifty Clergymen, authorize Uncas to murder him. — His Secret Execution. — Burial on Sachem Plain. — The Narragansetts visit his Grave. — Vengeance visits the Clergy of New England.

THE next war of much importance after the destruction of the Pequot nation was that of the Mohegans, commanded by *Uncas*, against the Narragansetts, led by the adroit, the ambitious, but the fated *Miantonimo*.

> "Two mighty chiefs, *one* cautious, wise, and old,
>   One young and strong and terrible in fight,
> All Narragansett and Coweset hold:
>   One lodge they build; one council-fire they light."
>
> Durfee.

In 1640 suspicions arose among the English chief magistrates at Boston that Miantonimo was brooding dissensions, and that he, as the leader of the Narragansetts, was endeavoring to excite the tribes to a general rebellion against the four colonies.

Miantonimo accordingly was summoned, and, appearing before the governor, claimed that his accusers should be held to appear at the same time, that they might meet him face to face; he averred that Uncas and the Mohegans had become his enemies, were busy in malicious slanders; and, demanding an investigation, he urged that his accusers, if found in the wrong, should be put to death.

Nothing of importance was proved against him; but from that time, of course, *Uncas* and *Miantonimo* were enemies; and one evening, while Uncas was passing from one wigwam to another, an arrow was shot at him by an unknown marksman. It went through his arm, inflicting a painful wound. It appeared soon afterwards that a young Pequot had a considerable quantity of wampum. This aroused suspicion. The Pequot, as if conscious of guilt, fled to the Narragansetts, and took refuge under and within the wigwams of Miantonimo.

Thereupon Uncas called the matter up; and Miantonimo was again called before the council at Boston; and the Pequot, being called there as a witness, went on to testify as to how at one time he was staying at Uncas's fort; how Uncas then and there had tampered with him, had tried to induce him to tell the English that Miantonimo had employed him to kill Uncas,; and how Uncas, as if to make this story effective, took a flint from his gun, and cut his own arm on two sides, leaving it as if an arrow had gone through it.

This story, not being believed by the English, operated in their minds against Miantonimo, who introduced him; and they at once decreed the Pequot to be delivered over to Uncas and his Mohegans, and by this intended to subject him to their vengeance.

Miantonimo, having induced this Pequot to attend this trial, claimed the right of returning him to his (the Pequot's) own hunting-ground, promising that upon arriving there he would deliver him up to Uncas. This was allowed; and the two parties separated. But for some reason the Pequot was not permitted to return home.

The friends and followers of Miantonimo knowing "that it would be a great gratification to their enemies the Mohegans, to wreak vengeance on this witness," and knowing that a dead man could tell no further tales, they, while on the way with him homeward, murdered him themselves.

Enmity existed between Sequassen, sachem of the tribes of "*the river country*," who was of Connecticut, and who was friendly to Miantonimo and to the Mohegans. Soon after the happening of that event, some of his Indians slew a leading Mohegan. They also waylaid Uncas, tried to poison him, and, while paddling his canoe at one time, shot arrows at him on the Connecticut. Of all this *Uncas* complained, and before the authorities at Hartford, Conn., claimed that for this murder and other trespasses he ought to have *six* of Sequassen's men, in order that he might put them to death.

The governor remonstrated against a demand which seemed to him to be so captious and unreasonable. Finally, he induced *Uncas* to be content if he could have the man who had committed the murder.

Inasmuch as the assassin was a friend and relative of Miantonimo, Sequassen, being called on to that end, refused to deliver him up, relying as to *this* upon Miantonimo and his Narragansetts for assistance in the maintenance of this purpose.

Thus the magistrates, failing in all attempts to produce a reconciliation, dismissed the two sachems (Uncas and Sequassen), but at the same time advised UNCAS to avenge his own grievances. UNCAS, immediately advancing to do so, invaded Sequassen's territory, killed seven or eight of his warriors, wounded thirteen others, burnt up his wigwams, and plundered wherever he went.

This news from Connecticut soon reached the Narragansetts; and Miantonimo thereupon began to meditate war. He sent a message to the Connecticut governor, complaining of the action of UNCAS against Sequassen and his allies, the Indians of Connecticut River. The governor refused to interfere in this matter. Miantonimo gave notice of what the Mohegans under UNCAS had done to the governor of Massachusetts, and earnestly inquired if the people of the bay would be offended if he should make war against the Mohegans, and obtained for a reply, "*that if* UNCAS *had done him or his friends any wrong, and had refused to grant satisfaction, the English would leave him to choose his own course.*"

By these complaints made to the English governors, this chief had complied with the terms of his treaty with them in 1638; and at once he accordingly proceeded to collect a large band of Narragansett warriors, and thence proceeded with secrecy and alacrity, to make invasions against the forts and hunting-grounds of the Mohegans.

Now, then, from the lofty hills of Norwich, the Mohegan watchers began to discover the hostile Narragansetts as they emerged " from the old forest, and crossed the river Shetucket above its junction with the Quinnibaug."

It was then the runners dashed away, as it is said, to carry the startling intelligence to *Uncas*, and to excite him to call out and to rally his warriors to the battle.

His fort was on the banks of the Thames, some five miles below; and it was there that the messengers probably found him.

Uncas rallied; and, from their various tents in the dark forest, they swarmed forth to advance upon the invading Narragansetts, then numbering, according to the best estimation, about six hundred warriors.

Uncas, then present on the field at Norwich with his tribes, numbered in all three hundred men. And there, in front of his men on the rise of ground upon " the *Great Plain*," *Uncas* cautioned his men, and made known to them the strategy by which he would win the battle against the veteran Miantonimo, and against his superiority of numbers.

In the mean time (as De Forest's history has it), the Narragansetts had crossed the fords of the Yantic, and were in loose ranks descending the declivities nearly opposite to the Mohegans.

Uncas despatched a messenger to Miantonimo, asking an interview. It being granted, the two commanders met for a conference between the two armies that then awaited the issue, all in breathless suspense, and all within bow-shot of their formidable deadly enemies, with eager eyes intent upon the movements of their two gallant sagamores.

The Narragansetts still waiting! — the Mohegan army listening and watching for the signal!

Uncas urges Miantonimo against the folly of wasting the precious lives of their warriors in a contest which might as well be settled by *themselves alone.*

"*Let* us *fight it out,*" said Uncas. "*If you kill me, my men shall be yours: if I kill you, your men shall be mine.*"

Miantonimo, although in person tall and strong, desiring rather to depend on his strength of numbers made immediate answer, —

"*My men came to fight; and they shall fight!*" Such an answer *Uncas* had of course expected. He at once fell upon the *ground.* His forces recognizing the signal, with bow in hand, quick as sight, they let fly three hundred arrows to the hearts of the Narragansetts.

"Uncas sprang up; and his warriors pealing forth the yell of battle, and brandishing their tomahawks, rushed forward with him" upon the staggering enemy.

The Narragansetts, panic-struck at the assault, made but feeble resistance, and were speedily put to flight.

The Mohegans followed them with impetuous fury, drove them through the shallows of the river, and chased them far into the forests beyond. All over that rude and hilly country (as tradition told it), the pursuers and pursued might be seen leaping over rocks and dashing through thickets, like wolves in the chase of timid deer.

Miantonimo fled with his followers; but his flight was impeded by an English corselet which he had put on to protect him in battle. Two of the Mohegans followed him closely, and still further prevented his escape by springing against him, and jostling him as he ran. They said they might have taken or killed him with their own hands; but this honor they were willing to reserve to their sachem.

The first of these men who followed the flying chieftain was a sagamore named *Tantaquigeon*, whose descendants were long held noble among the Mohegans, and whose renown for a long time was matter of boast among the Mohegans.

MIANTONIMO A PRISONER.

Uncas, a robust, muscular man, finally came up, and seized Miantonimo by the shoulder. The ill-fated sachem, as soon as he felt the hand of his enemy upon him, ceased his flight, and sat down upon the ground. From his closed lips not a word came to indicate his misery at heart.

Thirty of the Narragansetts had been slain; and many more were wounded. The rest, without an effort to wipe out their disgrace or to rescue their captive sachem, retreated to their own "prescribed dominions."

Miantonimo remained silent, although some of his own followers were brought up and tomahawked before his eyes.

Uncas was disappointed in not being able to draw out from him a single confession of weakness or fear.

"*Why do you not speak?*" said he. "*If you had taken me, I should have besought you for my life.*" But he obtained no answer.

This chief was carried in triumph to the fortress, and was there held. A truce was opened between the tribes, to remain while this prisoner remained there at the fort.

The Narragansetts sent their chief several packages of wampum while he remained imprisoned, which the prisoner gave away, some to Uncas, some to Uncas's wife, and some to his favorite counsellors.

The English in Rhode Island took sides in favor of this sachem. He had won their good-will; and they believed him mainly in the right. And one Samuel Gorton, a wild-headed enthusiast, yet kind-hearted, also beset Uncas to liberate him. Uncas refused, but finally referred the matter to his old friends the English of Connecticut, as to whether he should try still to hold him, release, or put him to death.

While the matters were maturing before the English authorities, it had been affirmed by the adherents of *Uncas* that Miantonimo had engaged the Mohawks to join him, and that they were then encamped within a day's journey of the frontiers, and were awaiting his liberation.

Then and thereupon the English record is finally made up as against old Miantonimo, who in his long lifetime had extended to the English settlers in New England so many favors, thus: —

"These things being duly weighed and considered, the commissioners apparently see that Uncas cannot be safe while Miantonimo lives; but that, either by secret treachery or open force, his life will be still in danger.

"Wherefore they think he may justly put such a false and

MURDER OF MIANTONIMO.

blood-thirsty enemy to death, but in his own jurisdiction, not in the English plantations; and *advising* that in the manner of his death all mercy and moderation be showed, contrary to the practice of the Indians, who exercise tortures and cruelty.

"And *Uncas* having hitherto shown himself a friend to the English, and in this craving of their advice, if the Narragansett Indians or others shall unjustly assault *Uncas* for his execution, upon notice and request the English promise to assist and protect him as far as they may against such violence."

Before dismissing the Narragansett deputies who had attended with earnest solicitation upon the trial, the commissioners induced them to subscribe to articles of agreement, as follows:—

"That they (the Narragansetts) would not make war upon *Uncas*, until after the next planting of corn; and even then, that they should give thirty days' notice to the English before commencing hostilities: also, that, if any of the Nayantick Pequots should make any assault upon *Uncas* or any of *his*, they would deliver them up to the English to be punished according to their demerits; and that they should not use any means to procure the Mohawks to come against *Uncas* during this truce."

MASSACRE OF MIANTONIMO.

The decision was kept an entire secret, lest the tribes should know of it, and arrest the commissioners while on their way home, to hold them as hostages for the redemption of Miantonimo; and all the preliminaries of killing him were written down, for the time being to be kept secret.

As soon as Eaton and other commissioners were far enough towards home to be out of reach of the tribes, then *Uncas,* attended by his brother *Wawequa,* with a select band of warriors, was to take the prisoner from the jail in Hartford, which they accordingly did. And, pursuant to instructions, they travelled back through the forest with the old, war-worn sachem; and, when they came to the plain where the battle was fought, *Wawequa,* stepping behind Miantonimo, split him down with a hatchet; and there they murdered him.

What the names of those reverend Englishmen were, referred to in the following page, does not appear in the annals which I am now consulting, and that too, perhaps, for the best of reasons.

It, however, does appear, that, while the flesh of Miantonimo was yet warm at his death, Uncas cut a large piece from his shoulder, and ate it down with savage exultation, saying, "*It is the sweetest meat I ever ate. It makes me strong!*"

They buried him there on Sachem's Plain. A friend piled up a heap of stones there; and, for a hundred years, every Narragansett that passed that way turned, in his sadness, and added one stone to the pile.

That battle-field still retains the name of Sachem's Plain.

This trial and murder by referees was had at Boston, Sept. 17, 1643.

The commission before whom this venerable sachem's fate was determined consisted of the following members, as the representatives of the four colonies, to wit, —

John Winthrop, Thomas Dudley,	} Massachusetts.	George Fenwick, Edward Hopkins,	} Connecticut.
Edward Winslow, William Collier,	} Plymouth.	Theophilus Eaton, Thomas Gregson,	} New Haven.

In the startling, extraordinary proceedings and decision of the commissioners above named, it is perhaps to their credit, that they could not make up their minds to spill the blood of the gallant old MIANTONIMO, until they had summoned to their assistance a train of fifty clergymen, who from their number selected five who were subtle enough to become the scape-goats to carry off the sins of white men in seeking the blood of one who, during a long and painful life, had with extraordinary good-will and sagacity invariably proved the friend, and who, in that hour of trial, with no guilt upon his garments, had thrown himself into their arms for protection. That the Mohawks, having a deadly hate to the Pequot *Sassacus*, when he thus imploringly threw himself upon them, murdered him, was terrible; but when a company of white men, with religion and civilization uppermost upon their tongues, will condescend to make merchandise of innocent blood, *not* through prejudice, mistake, or malice, but through an inordinate desire to obtain a political advantage, or to seek dominion through blood in a manner foreign to a fair, open warfare, the humane heart is made pale and *pitiful:* it falls sick in *sight* of it.

The injustice of this massacre of *Miantonimo* must have been felt at the time in every vein of all New England, while it foreshadowed what deeds of blood white men could be led to seek and sanction. At the same time it must have created an abiding distrust in the hearts of red men *never to be obliterated.* It proclaimed a precedent which, in the advancing years, daily and nightly brought premature death to scores of the reverend clergy of New England, however perfect and pure their lives, or however kind and circumspect their demeanor towards the tribes. Alas! how, in sight of the unjust slaughter of *Miantonimo,* can we wonder at the record which history discloses for the hundred years then next ensuing, wherein it appears, all the way long, more clergymen fell in New England by the blade of the tomahawk, according to their numbers, than of any other class of mortals?

CHAPTER XI.

INDIAN WARS. — NATIVE PEACE-MAKERS.

Dominion of Passaconaway. — His Oration. — Eliot at Pawtucket Falls. — The Great Feast. — Wonalancet of Wamesit, peaceful. — Ninegret's Dominions. — The English distrust him. — He offends the Tribes of Long Island. — His Address to the English Magistrates. — Cotton Mather against Barbarism. — His Opinion of the Pequots.

AS we have already seen, one of the most powerful tribes in New England were the Penacooks, and next to them, as allies, were the Pawtuckets and Penobscots. The strongest and most conspicuous chief of all the tribes in the East was Passaconaway. His dominion under, after, and from Massasoit, extended over a very large part of New England.

Nearly all the serious difficulties that arose among his people were from time to time submitted to his consideration and decision.

His territory extended from the sea to the mountains, and from the Penobscot to the Merrimack River. His places of residence were at Pawtucket, Piscataqua, and at Penacook. Thomas Morton, in his New-England Canaan, writes of him thus:—

"Papsiquimo, the sachem or sagamore of the territories near Merrimack River, is a man of the best note and estimation in all these parts; and (as my countryman, Mr. Wood, declares in his prospectus), a great necromancer." We infer, from an account of him in Winthrop's journal, that Passaconaway was a clever juggler, as well as warrior.

In full belief of his supernatural powers, his tribes were held in awe of him, and their destinies were controlled in a great degree by this, as well as by his wise councils. They believed he could make a dry leaf turn green; that he could make water burn, and then make it turn to ice; that he could hold the rattlesnake in his hands without danger of hurt or harm.

In 1642 a suspicion arose among the English that a conspiracy was being formed by the Indians to crush out the white man. Thereupon men were sent out to arrest some of the principal chiefs, and forty of them were directed to arrest Passaconaway, but he escaped by reason of an intervening storm. His son, Wonalancet, not being so fortunate, was taken, but his squaw escaped. As Winthrop relates it, they barbarously and insultingly led Wonalancet away by a rope ; that he loosened the rope and escaped from them, but was finally retaken.

For such a wrong Passaconaway was afterwards distrustful of his English neighbors. For this, in 1647, he refused to see his friend Eliot, while both were giving attendance to the fishing season at Pawtucket Falls. Being fearful that the English would kill him, he regarded their religion, which seemed to tolerate such invasions upon the rights of the red man, to be unworthy of his attention.

But in 1648, when Eliot again visited Pawtucket Falls at the fishing season, Passaconaway was then pleased to hear his preaching. To the assembled Indians, Eliot then preached from this

TEXT.

"*From the rising of the sun, even to the going down of the same, my name shall be great among the Gentiles; and in every place incense shall be offered unto my name, and a pure offering; for my name shall be great among the heathen, saith the Lord of hosts.*" — MAL. i. 11.

The Indians paid respectful attention, and, after the discourse was closed, proposed many questions. At length Passaconaway arose, amid the most profound attention, and announced his belief in the God of the English. Says Eliot, "He said he had never heard of God before as he now doth; that he would consider the matter, and would persuade his sons to do the same," pointing to two of them who were present. Passaconaway was doubtless sincere in his belief, and, as it appears, so continued until his death.

We have but little else of this chief until 1660, when he had become old. He was at Pawtucket Falls (now Lowell), on the Merrimack, at a great assemblage of Indians, where, as Capt. Gookin says, they had a great feast. The old sagamore then and there made a farewell address to his tribes. His raiment was plain, but somewhat gaudy and beautiful. He was full of sorrow, being deeply affected; his utterances were tremulous from the storms of a long life, yet musical. Standing erect before that assembled multitude, he delivered this

ORATION.

"Hearken to the words of your father! I am an old oak, that has withstood the storms of more than a hundred winters. Leaves and branches have been stripped from me by the winds and frosts. My eyes are dim; my limbs totter; I must soon fall. When young, no one could bury the hatchet in a sapling before me. My arrows could pierce the deer at a hundred rods. No wigwam had so many furs, no pole had so many scalp-locks as Passaconaway's. Then I delighted in war. The whoop of the Penacooks was heard on the Mohawk,* and no voice so loud as Passaconaway's. The scalps upon the pole in my wigwam told the story of Mohawk suffering. The English came; they seized the lands; they followed upon my footpath. I made war on them; but they fought with fire and thunder. My young men were swept down before me when no one was near them. I tried sorcery against them, but they still increased, and prevailed over me and mine; I gave place to them, and retired to my beautiful island, Naticook. I, that can take the rattlesnake in my palm as I would a worm without harm, — I, that have had communication with the Great Spirit, dreaming and awake, — I am powerless before the pale-faces. These meadows they shall turn with the plow; these forests shall fall by the axe; the pale-faces shall live upon your hunting-grounds, and make their villages upon your fishing-places. The Great Spirit says this, and it must be so. We are

* The Mohawk tribes dwelt on and about the eastern borders of New York.

few and powerless before them. We must bend before the storm; peace with the white man is the command of the Great Spirit, and the wish — the last wish — of Passaconaway." *   Soon after this, his mantle fell upon his son Wonalancet, who continued sagamore of the Penacooks for several years, yet he was always at peace with the English.

WONALANCET.

This Penacock sachem was the son of Passaconaway, succeeded him, and was chief over the dominions of his deceased father, and dwelt mostly at Wamesit, now Lowell, on the beautiful Merrimack, from 1660 to 1677.

Lowell is Queen, her history recalls
The might and memories of Pawtucket Falls,
Where lived the tribes, to proud progression blind,
Science and art, with enterprise combined,
Prove true to tell how moves the world apace
At the will and wisdom of a Saxon race.

On the 7th of September, 1675, the authorities of Boston, through Lieut. Thomas Henchman of Chelmsford, despatched an order, to be borne in company with two suitable Indians of Wamesit to this sachem, of which the following is a copy: —

* Passaconaway is said to have lived to the age of one hundred and twenty years.

"This our writing or safe conduct doth declare that the Governor and Council of Massachusetts do give you and every of you, provided you exceed not six persons, free liberty of coming unto, and returning in safety from, the house of Lieut. T. Henchman at Naamkeake, and there to treat with Capt. *Daniel Gookin* and Mr. *John Eliot*, whom you know, and whom we will fully empower to treat and conclude with you upon such meet terms and articles of friendship, amity, and subjection, as were formerly made and concluded between the English and old *Passaconaway*, your father, and his sons and people, and for this end, we have sent these messengers [   ] to convey these unto you, and to bring your answer, whom we desire you to treat kindly, and to despatch them back to us with your answer. Dated in Boston, 1st October, 1675.

JOHN LEVERETT, *Governor.*
"EDWARD RAWSON, *Secretary.*"

The messengers did not find Wonalancet: as it appeared, he had retired into the wilderness, in the Valley of the Connecticut, and did not return until the next summer.

He then returned, having with him a party of Nipmucks, Sagamore Sam, One-Eyed John, and others who had been hostile to the English, but who now sought pardon and aid through the good faith of Wonalancet.

Previous to the 19th of September, 1677, this sachem sold out all his titles to lands in New Hampshire and Massachusetts not previously conveyed, and then left the pale faces, and the graves of his fathers, and sought a distant home in the dense forest, where no intruder could come to disturb the peace and quiet of his old age.

The Pawtuckets, after his departure, gradually vanished away, through the overpowering numbers and influence of their white neighbors, who, as it seemed, continually intruded upon their hunting-grounds and otherwise became more and more offensive.

This sachem once had occasion to be at Dover, — we shall hear of him again there, prior to his departure. He had a fort, while here, at Wamesit, Lowell, on a beautiful rise of ground near its cemetary, now known and celebrated as "FORT HILL."

NINEGRET.

This influential Sachem was a Neantick, usually friendly to the Narragansetts, and was a successor of Miantonimo, of whom we discoursed in another chapter.

He claimed dominion over a part of the Indians on Long Island (but *Ascassasotick* had the immediate control of them), as well as over the old Narragansetts. Yet the winter of 1652–53 he spent with the Dutch in New York.

This caused suspicions in the minds of the English

authorities, they being unfriendly to the Dutch; and from this a meeting was held in Boston, in April of that year, upon the suspicion that the Narragansetts were uniting with the Dutch, being, as they supposed, bent on mischief.

To test the correctness of this suspicion, a committee was sent to Ninegret, with interrogatories propounded as follows to each of the following chiefs, *Mexam, Pessacus,* and *Ninegret.*

1. Whether the Dutch had engaged them to fight against the English?

2. Whether the Dutch governor did not indorse such conspiracy?

3. Whether they had not received arms and munitions of war from the Dutch?

4. What other Indians are engaged in the plot?

5. Whether, contrary to their engagement, they were resolved to fight against the English?

6. If they are so resolved, what they think the English will do?

7. Whether were their grounds against the English?

8. Similar to the *first?*

9. What were their grounds of war against the English?

10. Whether they had not better come or send messengers to treat with the English?

11. Whether they had hired the Mohawks to help them?

Each answered in their order.

NINEGRET, addressing them in reply, says, —

"You are kindly welcome to us, and I kindly thank the Sachems of Massachusetts that they should think of me as one of the Sachems worthy to be inquired of concerning this matter.

"Had any of the other Sachems been at the Dutch I should have feared their folly might have done some hurt, one way or other; but they have not been there. I am the man. 1 have been there myself. I alone am answerable for what I have done. And as I have already declared, I do utterly deny and protest that I know of no such plot as has been apprehended. What is the story of these great rumors that I hear at Pocatoke, that I should be cut off, and that the English had a quarrel against me.

"I know of no such cause at all, for my part. Is it because I went there to take physic for my health? or what is the cause? I found no such entertainment from the Dutch governor, when I was there, as to give me any encouragement to stir me up to such a league against the English, my friends.

"It was winter time, and I stood a great part of a winter day, knocking at the governor's door, and he would neither open it, nor suffer others to open it, to let me in. I was not wont to find such carriage from the English, my friends."

All this was said and done, and much more, evincing an over zeal; yet such an inquisition was of no avail to the English. No plot was discovered.

Afterwards, in 1654, Rhode Island communicated to Massachusetts "that last summer NINEGRET, without any cause, had fallen upon the Long Island Indians, our friends and tributaries;" that he had killed many of them, had taken others prisoners, and would not restore them.

That *this* summer he had made two other assaults upon them, " in one whereof he killed a man and woman that lived upon the land of the English, and within one of their townships, and another Indian that kept the cows of the English," that he had drawn many of the foreign Indians down from the Connecticut and Hudson Rivers who rendezvoused upon Winthrop's Island, where they killed some of his cattle.

This war of murders commenced in 1653, and continued several years.

But there were other wars of murder going on elsewhere, and at other various times. Some of *these* Cotton Mather, that indomitable leading New England divine, refers to in a brief summary, which I copy in this place,—

REV. COTTON MATHER SAYS:

"In the year 1634 these terrible savages [Pequots] killed one Capt. Stone, and Capt. Norton, with six men more, in a bark sailing up Connecticut River, and sunk her.

"In the year 1635 a bark sailing from Massachusetts bay to Virginia, being by a tempest cast away at

Long Island, the same terrible salvages killed several of the shipwrecked Englishmen.

"In the year 1636, at Black Island, coming aboard a vessel to trade, they murdered the master (2 Magnalia, p. 480), and another coming that way found that they had made themselves masters of a bark, which occasioned the sending of one hundred and twenty soldiers thither, under the command of Capt. Endicott, Capt. Underhill, and Capt. Turner, by the governor and council of Boston, upon whom, at the then landing, the Indians violently shot, and so ran away where no English could come at them. Travelling further up the Pequot country the Pequots refused, upon a conference, to surrender the murderers harbored among them, which were then demanded; whereupon a skirmish ensued, in which, after the death of one of their men, the Indians fled, but the English destroyed their corn and their huts, and so returned."

From this many lives were lost from time to time in various ways, and Mather says, —

"These parts were then covered with nations of barbarous Indians, and infidels, in whom the *prince of the power of the air did work as a spirit;* nor could it be expected that nations of wretches, whose whole religion was the most explicit sort of *devil worship*, should not be instigated by the Devil to engage in some early and bloody action, for the extinction of a plantation so contrary to his interests as that of *New England.*

"Of these nations there was none more fierce, more warlike, more potent, or of greater terror unto their neighbors, than that of the PEQUOTS; but their being so much a *terror* to their neighbors, and especially to the *Narragansetts* on the east side of them, and the *Monhegans* on the *West,* upon whom they had committed many barbarous outrages, produced such a division in the kingdom of Satan against itself, as was very serviceable to that of our Lord."

After repeating many other enormities perpetrated by the *Pequots*, Mather continues, "Unto all which there was annexed the slaughter of nine men, with the taking of *two maids,* by this horrid enemy lying in ambush for them as they went into the fields of *Weathersfield.* So that the infant colonies of *New England,* finding themselves necessitated unto the crushing of serpents, while they were but yet in cradle, unanimously resolved, that, with the assistance of Heaven, they would *root this nest of serpents out of the world.*"

I will close this chapter with one or two brief anecdotes: —

"A SERIOUS QUESTION. — About 1794 an officer

presented a western *chief* with a *medal*, on the one side of which was represented *Gen. Washington, sword in hand*, and on the other an Indian in the act of burying the hatchet.

"The chief, carefully looking the medal over, earnestly inquired, 'Why don't the president *bury his sword* also?'"

"Self-esteem. — A white man, meeting an Indian, accosted him as *brother.* The red man, with much expression of meaning in his countenance, inquired *how they came to be brothers.* '*By the way of Adam* I suppose,' said the white man. The Indian added, '*Me thank him great Spirit, we no nearer brothers!*'"

"Comic. — An Indian having been found frozen to death, an inquest of his countrymen was convened to determine by what means he came to such a death. Upon a full hearing, they returned the following
"*Verdict.*
"'*Death from the freezing of a great quantity of water inside of him,*' which, as they averred, he had taken instead of rum."

CHAPTER XII.

THE TRIBES AGAINST THE DUTCH.

Union of the Four Colonies. — Trouble with the Narragansetts prevented. — The Dutch of New Netherlands and Indians confederated against the Colonies. — It comes to an End. — War. — The Narragansetts and Nianticks pursue the Montaokes. — The Colonies advance and settle this Matter. — Foreigners induce Conflicts. — War. — Dutch against the Tribes. — Mohawks against the Hudson Tribes. — Dutch Battle with the Tribes. — One Hundred Indians slain. — Fifteen Hundred Indians organize into *Eleven Clans*, and beset the Dutch on the Connecticut and Hudson. — Dutch against Mayn and Mayano's Tribes. — Their Battle. — Eighty Indians slain. — Their Village consumed. — King Philip. — His Biography. — Intends War. — Individual Intrusions. — Sassamon murdered. — Indictment. — Trial of the Murderers. — Philip in Court. — Three Indians are hanged by the English. — War is threatened.

AFTER the extermination of the Pequot nation, there were now and then, as usual, occasional eruptions between the various tribes and the English, growing out of trespasses committed through individual recklessness on the one side and on the other, resulting sometimes in terrible retaliations in trespasses, conflagrations, and bloodshed. But in the year 1643, March 19, a union, offensive and defensive, was formed of the four united colonies of New England; which colonies were to furnish proportionate forces, in any event of necessity, as follows:—

The Massachusetts colony one hundred men; and the Plymouth, Hartford, and New Haven, *each*, forty-five men.

In 1645 and 1646 the Narragansetts, by reason of certain misunderstandings, threatened insurrection, and made some trouble for the English, but were soon brought to amicable quietude by the leaders of the colonies.

WAR ON LONG ISLAND.

In 1653 the DUTCH of New Netherlands undertook a confederacy with the INDIANS, for the purpose of cutting off and destroying all the English settlements in New England; but, by an early declaration of peace between England and Holland, that desperate, diabolical scheme was defeated at the threshold. The year 1654 inaugurated a war, for the most part between the tribes themselves; yet, more or less, it affected the peace and quietude of the individual colonies. In *this* the *Narragansetts* and *Nianticks* had waged war, and were pursuing the *Montaoke* Indians in and about Long Island.

FRUITS OF FOREIGN WARS.

Thereupon the united colonies fitted out two hundred and seventy foot, and forty horsemen, and, advancing to the front, soon brought all these conflicting powers to a final settlement.

FOREIGNERS INDUCE CONFLICTS.

It will be seen, as we advance in these annals, that the wars in New England were, in the main, the offshoots of the conflicting powers of foreign countries. For instance, whenever France and England declared war, that event was but the signal to the French Jesuits in Canada to incite and encourage the tribes to annoy, to murder, and destroy the English population on this side of the great waters. So that each and every declaration of war in Europe, wherein England was a party, covered her colonies here, as with a *cloud;* and, sad to tell, the sound of a war-trump there was but a death-knell to the women and children of New England.

At length the French with England disagree,
Which now portends what carnage hence shall be,
What man's estate must prove, — a varied life,
From quiet peace proceeds terrific strife;
From plenty dearth, from faith and virtue, sin,
From health disease, that wages war within.

As early as 1642, a war began to be threatened between the Dutch settlers of New Amsterdam and their neighboring tribes. Dutch traders, having induced an Indian to become intoxicated, robbed him of a valuable dress of beaver skins. In retaliation for this robery, an Indian warrior killed *two white men*, and then escaped to another distant tribe. A demand was made by the Dutch governor (Kieft) that the murderer might be given up; which, being refused under a false pretence that he could not be found, and the governor forgetting his civilization, revenged himself by an act of cruelty. Then, at some time that winter, two tribes on the Hudson were surprised by the Mohawks; seventy of their warriors perished, and many prisoners were carried into captivity. The survivors of these tribes, several hundreds of them, came for protection to New Amsterdam, there to dwell as hunters in that vicinity.

Keith, seeing their sufferings, at first gave them aid by furnishing them with corn; but at length, getting offended with them, and remembering the old conflict, he and his councillors agreeing together, sent a band of soldiers against them, surprised them at midnight, and put to death more than a hundred of them in cool blood.

This was an act done under the laws of civilization, probably with high professions of humanity, if not of religion; but pause for a moment, and see the result.

The Indians on the Hudson arose at once to revenge this cruel treachery, the tribes on Long Island uniting with them. They formed a confederacy of *eleven clans,* in all more than fifteen hundred warriors; and fire and the tomahawk visited every Dutch settlement on Long Island, Manhattan, and along the Connecticut and Hudson Rivers.

Desolation followed the Dutch and English, also, along the Connecticut coast as far as East Stamford. The pretended prophetess, Anne Hutchinson, who had taken up her residence here, although she had escaped her persecutors in Massachusetts, fell among their other victims. Until the last moment, it is said, the Indians came to these houses apparently friendly; and then, in an unexpected moment, the hatchet fell, and seventeen perished in the same massacre. Horses were driven into the barns when they were on fire, that they also might be consumed.

NEW AMSTERDAM. — THE DUTCH AGAINST MAJOR MAYANO'S TRIBES.

These tribes were as hostile as its sachem, Mayano, had been known to be; and in February, 1644, after certain preliminaries had transpired, one hundred and thirty men were raised and sent off for Greenwich, Conn., under the command of *Underhill* and *Vandyck.*

Underhill had fought in the Pequot war, and also had done service in an expedition on Long Island, and had but recently, at the head of twenty-five men, surprised a small Indian village, " killed eighteen or twenty of the inhabitants, and had taken the rest, an old man with some women and children, prisoners. These commanders, with one hundred and twenty men, then embarked, and on the same evening landed at Stamford; but a snow-storm detained them nearly all night. Next morning they advanced, marching all day: at eight in the evening they came to two rivers, one of which was two hundred feet wide, and three feet deep. There they halted to rest the men, and prepare for the conflict. They again advanced at ten o'clock; the sky had become clear, and a full moon cast its light upon the snow. And now they came in sight of *three long rows of wigwams*, standing near a rise of ground which protected them from the northeast gales. They called it an Indian village. The Indian inhabitants had obtained notice, and were on the alert. But the *Dutch* surrounded the village, allowing none to escape. Gallantly, however, the Indians charged, with the intent of breaking the Dutch lines; yet twelve of the foremost were taken prisoners, and the others were driven back. A fire of musketry was opened upon them by the Dutch. The conflict was bloody and furious for an hour; and then the Indians fled back to their fortified wigwam, leaving upon the cold, down-trodden snow eighty of their valiant number dead and dying.

Then (as at Fort Mystic against the Pequots), they set fire to their village, into which they were driven by the sabres and musketry of the Dutch, and there they perished, men, women and children. Five hundred fell in that battle: eight or ten only of the tribes escaped.

The Dutch forces built large fires, and camped down for the remainder of the night. Next morning they returned, arriving at the English settlements at Stamford. And from that day all the Dutch chroniclers daily discoursed and rejoiced that "*the Lord had collected the most of these enemies,*" thus to be slain, and that of the Dutch soldiery on their way home, "*the Lord endued the wounded with extraordinary strength.*" Thus ended the Dutch war.

PHILIP'S WAR.

Massasoit, the chief of thirty tribes, had, as we have seen, two sons, Wamsutta and Pometacon: the one (by the governor from the English court at Plymouth) took the name of Alexander, the other they called Philip.

Alexander, soon after the death of his father in 1622, died. Philip then became sachem of the Wampanoags. He resided at Pakanoket, now within the town of Bristol, in the State of Rhode Island, at a place called Mount Hope. It is an elevation of land about two hundred feet in height, and was the ancient dwelling-place of his fathers. The view from its summit, even in this day of change, is said to be beautifully picturesque, and full of inspiration.

Philip, after the death of his father, in the winter of 1661–2, and of his brother, now being king of the tribes, entertained the idea that the English intended, by their proceedings, to crush out his own native race, and to take this domain entirely and exclusively to themselves. And although he tried to dissemble, yet the startling purpose of his heart to make war against them could not long remain concealed nor mistaken; for, as soon as his hostile intentions were suspected by his sagamores, then it began to be foreshadowed by murders and unprovoked trespasses. Yet Philip and his sagamores did not themselves remain unprovoked; and of their provocations we will give one or two instances. Squando, one of his allied chiefs, who dwelt on the Saco, had a squaw with an infant passing down the river in a canoe;

and meeting some sailors, who had heard that a pappoose at any age would swim, with a view to try that question, the sailors recklessly overset their canoe. The squaw, diving to the bottom, brought up her drowning infant, and saved its life; but alas! by reason of this exposure, soon afterwards it sickened and died.

Other provocations were constantly on foot in the form of trespasses on the Indian hunting-grounds, and in various other ways, wherein their primeval rights and titles were often, *too often*, ignored or denied.

Thus Squando, as well as Philip, was provoked; and the seeds of discontent, hatred, and jealousy, falling in every direction, began to swell and take root.

The design of the leading colonists to usurp jurisdiction over all this New-England domain had then from all their actions become quite apparent; and trespasses, arsons, robberies, and murders presently became common in Maine, Rhode Island, and elsewhere all along the English settlements.

In the month of September, 1675, a party of Indians advanced upon the plantations at Piscataqua, and there at Dover, where Durham now is, killed two men, burned down two dwelling-houses belonging to the two Chesleys, and carried away two captives.

Philip, to the vigilant colonies, all this time still denied that he intended to make war. His deadly intent, however, soon leaked out, through Sassamon, an Indian graduate from Harvard, who had been an itinerant preacher among the Mohegans in Connecticut, and who latterly had been acting as an interpreter between Philip's native tribes, and the English New-England settlers. This Sassamon, as now Philip had heard, had given his enemies to understand that Philip was instigating an insurrection.

Soon, then, in the spring of 1674, it happened Sassamon was missing, — was supposed to have been murdered. Search was made for the body, and it was found in Assawomset Pond in Middleborough. His hat and gun were found near the opening in the ice, through which he had been dropped, supposed to have been thus left in sight, to indicate a suicide. But by marks upon the body, and by the fact that his neck was broken, murder itself became apparent.

The English took this matter in hand: three Indians, to wit *Tobias*, and his son Wampapaquam, and Mattashunannamo, in the June then next, were indicted. The indictment contained the following count: —

"*For that being accused, that they did with joint consent upon the 29 of January, anno* 1674 (1675 *new style*), *att a place called Assa-*

wamsett pond, *wilfully and of sett purpose, and of malice, forethought, and by force and armes murder John Sassamon, another Indian, by laying violent hands on him, and striking him, or twisting his necke until he was dead; and to hyde and conceale this theire said murder att the tyme and place aforesaid, did cast his dead body through a hole of the ice into the said pond."*

The twelve jurymen, as empannelled, were Englishmen. We give their names, as follows: —

Wm. Sabine, Wm. Crocker, Edward Sturgis, Wm. Brookes, Nath. Winslow, John Wadsworth, Andrew Ringe, Robert Vixon, John Done, Jona. Bangs, Jona. Shaw, and Benja. Higgins.

A trial was had. The record then goes on to state, —

"Itt was judged very expedient by the court, that, together with this English jury aboue named, some of the *most indifferentest, grauest, and sage Indians* should be admitted to be with the said jury, and to healp to consult and aduice with, of, and concerning the premises: there names are as followeth, viz., one called by an English name, *Hope*, and *Maskippague, Hannoo, George Wampye,* and *Acanootus*: these fully concurred with the jury in theire verdict."

JOSIAH WINSLOW was then governor of the Plymouth colony; and under his lead, as it appears, these murderers were sought out, apprehended, tried, and hanged. This seems to have been the first *great* capital trial which was had here in New England by an English court.

And it seems that from that day Philip became more and more exasperated, denying that the English of right had any thing to do with *his* men, this being his own domain; and thenceforth rallied his tribes with dread revenge.

In " My Merrimack," page 29, with measured language, glancing at the above, as follows, I tried to paint a portrait of

PHILIP IN COURT.

Next follows war. Dread anarchy appears
As if to blast the crowning thrift of years;
At death of Massasoit, Philip succeeds
As king, and hostile to the whites, proceeds
To flagrant deeds; and first of all in time,
A native priest suspected of no crime,
But to have broached a secret plot, is slain
By murderous hand. On Philip rests this stain
Of blood; and justice stern but waits to draw
Her penal sword by force of English law
Against the natives. 'Tis not long withheld;
By strong indictment seized, arraigned, and held,
Tobias and confederates are tried
By petit-jury, white and red allied,

Whose doubtful jurisdiction Philip pleads,
And to address the forum thus proceeds : —
" What right, what law, these prisoners to arraign
Have Englishmen in this my own domain?
What lease of venue from allotted lines
To make invasion and adjudge of crimes?
Why seek the Indian's life in guile forlorn ;
Of these three men of native mothers born;
Who, one and all, with Sassamon, the slain,
Were my liege subjects, bound by laws, the same
Which governed tribes a thousand years ago,
But which evaded brings an endless woe?
What mind, what project, prompts your boundless
    sway,
But hence to drive the red man far away
From this fair land, his birthright and his wealth,
And hold these regions vast through royal stealth,
With flagrant wrong the tribes will ne'er concur,
And to your bold intrusion I demur!
My subjects here an English court may try ;
By spurious judgments, they may fall and die ;
Yet vengeance dread shall point the red man's steel,
And to the God of battles I'll appeal."
Philip withdrew, and ne'er returned again ;
His truthful talk was uttered but in vain.
The prisoners held, and thus condemned to die,
Brought darkness gathering o'er the western sky.

"The bloody sunset," and the forked light
That broke the curtain of that fearful night,
Awaking English matrons, 'mid alarms,
To hug sweet infants with tenacious arms,
Foretold gross carnage of successive years
And devastation in a land of tears.
True to his word, which prudence thus defied,
Philip the Pilgrims fought; and, fighting, died,
With countless victims by the self-same blade,
Which mutual madness had in folly made.

Let us now return briefly to advert to a few things which from time to time had previously happened.

Lands which Philip had inherited of his fathers had been purchased of him by individual Englishmen, as follows:—

In 1662 the English of Dedham purchased of Philip the territory now held within the lines of *Wrentham*, at the cost of £24. 10s.

In 1668 Constant Southworth and others purchased of him all the meadow lands from Dartmouth to Matapoisett, at the cost of £15.

Thomas Weld bought all his land, lying and being between the River Wanascottaquett and Cawatoquissetts, being a tract two miles long, and one mile wide. TOM, PHILIP's counsellor, and *Nannuntnew*, witnessed the deed. Consideration, £10 sterling.

DEATH OF KING PHILIP.

Same year the Englishmen buy of him certain lands which are now included within the lines of Swansey; and in the following year they induce a sale from him of Memenuckquage and Towanset Neck, supposed now to be a part of Swansey.

Next year they purchased of him, at the cost of £20, five hundred acres, which now also is a part of Swansey.

About the same time Philip presented a plan of lands, which the venerable historian, S. G. Drake, copies in his elaborate history of North American Indians, to the English court i. Plymouth, with a kind proposition, and with words of explanation, as follows:—

"*This may inform the honoured court, that I, Philip, am willing to sell the land within this draught;—but the Indians that are upon it may live upon it still,—but the land that is (Waste) may be sould, and Wattachpoo is of the same minde.*

"*I have sed downe all the principal names of the land wee are willing should bee sould.*

"PHILIP *P* his mark.

"From PACANANKETT.
the 24 of the 12 Mo. 1668."

In 1669, for £10, Philip sold to John Cook an island near the town *Nokatay.*

Also for £13 he sold a considerable tract, now within the boundaries of Middleborough. In 1671 he, with Monyocam, for £5, sold to Hugh Cole of

Swansey, lands lying near *Acashewah* in Dartmouth.

In 1672 Philip sold to *Wm. Brenton* and others of Taunton, a tract, south of that town, for £143, which contained twelve square miles.

Also to *Constant Southworth*, another tract of four square miles.

Thus we have given the dates, &c., of a few of the sales which were made in this part of New England, by this then most wealthy and renowned sachem; and the reader will perceive the position in which he had stood in the world anterior to the fatal day when he fell.

The English sought him to obtain his lands, and as speedily to divest him and his race of any and all power in the administration of the government of New England.

Their constant importunities had induced Philip and his confederates to do and concede, for the sake of peace, many things which otherwise they, in all probability, never would have done.

Listen for a moment to "Mr. Morton," who wrote anterior to this conflict, when Philip's garments, as yet, remained unstained of blood. In the year 1662, he observes,—

" *This year upon occasion of some suspicion of some plot intended by the Indians against the English, Philip, the sachem of Pokanoket,* otherwise called *Metacom*, made his appearance at the court held at Plymouth, August 6, did earnestly desire the continuance of that amity and friendship that hath formerly been between the Governor of Plymouth and his deceased father and brother."

The court thereupon presented certain articles of mutual agreement, in writing, on which signatures were given as follows: —

"The mark of *P* Philip Sachem
of Pocanaket
The mark of ∠] Vucumpowet
unkell to the abovesaid Sachem.

"*Witnesses:*"

John Sassamon

The mark of *M* Francis, Sachem of Nanset
The mark *D.I.* of Nimrod, alias Pumpasa
The mark *V* of Punckquaneck
The mark *S* of Aquetequesh."

There were misunderstandings also in 1671, between Philip and the English, but which at that time were adjusted; for which, in this, we have no space.

Weetamoo.

This squaw sachem resided at Pocasset. Her husband Petunaet, seeking out the distinguished Capt. Church, crossed over to him in a canoe from Philip's head-quarters at Mount Hope. It was then that Church obtained from him the confirmation that Philip was making preparation for open war.

At this time Weetamoo was at her camp on a high hill to the north of Howland's Ferry, and not far from the Pocasset shore. Her husband invited Church to make her a visit. Church found her in a melancholy mood, as she said all her men had left her, being absent at Philip's war-dance; and she talked, perhaps too freely, of Philip and of his intentions. Church, on his return to Plymouth, reported this squaw sachem as being secured to the English; but in the mean time, Philip having reclaimed her, she afterwards advanced to the conflict with him, and finally perished, fighting heroically against the English in behalf of her own falling race.

" I will go to my tent, and lie down in despair;
I will paint me with black, and will sever my hair :
I will sit on the shore where the hurricane blows,
And reveal to the God of the tempest my woes;
I will weep for a season on bitterness fed,
For my kindred are gone to the mounds of the dead :
But they died not by hunger, or wasting decay;
The steel of the white man hath swept them away.'

CHAPTER XIII.

LAWS OF THE NATIVE NATIONS.

Impending Dangers. — Insurrections. — Philip is in Arms. — The Colonies, troubled, are moving. — The Clergy do not seek to prevent War. — Warriors send their Women and Children away. — Depredations at Swansey. — Slaughter there. — Plymouth Governor applies to the Massachusetts Colony. — They try to dissuade Philip. — Messengers dare not approach him. — Forces sent to Swansey. — Hammond is killed. — Five or Six Indians killed. — Philip's Councillor slain. — July 4, Capts. Mosely and Page obtain a Treaty with the Narragansetts. — The Articles as signed. — War begins. — Capts. Church and Fuller with Forces move to Pocasset. — They form Two Companies. — Fuller goes Seaward. — Finds too many Indians. — Indians pursue Church Seaward. — He kills Fifteen. — Fuller and Church return to Rhode Island. — Taunton secures her Families into Eight Garrisons. — English advance to the Swamp. — Five of them killed from an Ambush. — Their Hundred Wigwams deserted. — Five or Six Farmers killed in Mendham. — Force sent there. — Deserted. — Burned down. — Henchman tries to starve out Philip. — Philip with his Warriors escapes to the Nipmuck Country. — Rehoboth Men. — Mohegans and Henchman Pursue him. — The two former Forces kill Thirty of Philip's Men. — He is not reached. — Insurrections in Connecticut. — Two Englishmen slain at Brookfield. — Mosely is sent to Penacook. — Wonalancet Neutral. — Hutchinson and Wheeler are to obtain a Treaty. — Hutchinson and Seven others are murdered by Nipmucks.

IN the preceding chapter we have noticed some of the foreboding incidents which inaugurated that general uprising of the tribes on the one hand, and of the English planters on the other, in that terrible struggle of barbarians against a professed civilization, each contending with bloody cruelties, for a national existence.

At first the laws of the tribes for a long period had been ignored; and the English statutes had been enforced against three of Philip's men for the murder of one of his own race: and from this and other real or supposed encroachments, long and constantly continued, Philip and his sagamores could but see in prospect the fearful fate of their race. In truth, an unmistakable, ominous hand had for a long time been " writing upon the wall."

And now the public mind had begun to be agitated with anxious fears and forebodings. The colonial leaders were constantly sending from Boston emissaries to the tribes in Connecticut, and to the eastward on the Saco and Kennebeck, disarming them, and securing pledges of good faith, and of course thereby making at every step hostility still the more acrimonious, yet obtaining promises often obtained but almost as often violated. Everywhere among the planters, as well as among the natives, "*loud rumor*" *spoke;* and it spoke of blood, carnage, and despair.

The New-England clergy, for the most part, led by such men as that indomitable Cotton Mather, laid aside their prayer-books, and with carnal weapons went in for a total extermination of the native nations of New England.

The tribes could not have been unmindful of the destruction of the Pequot nation and of the murder of the valiant Miantonimo the Englishman's friend, slain in cool blood at their own hands. They well knew that the leaders in such barbarisms sought but little else than destruction of the tribes for the purpose of obtaining political advantages and a national supremacy.

To the end of disarming the New-England tribes, hostile or otherwise, commissioners, having been appointed, were constantly on the alert in Massachusetts, Connecticut, and Maine, or wherever in New England they might be found.

Of the Narragansetts it was reported "that the elder people were inclined to peace, and that the old sachems expressed a desire that all controversy might be brought to an end; but the commissioners volunteer an opinion that their intent is as treacherous as ever, and that they intend in the spring to invade the plantations all at once, and that their pretences for peace are all a mere sham."

At an early day Uncas, the old opponent of Miantonimo, and the representative of the Mohegan tribes of Connecticut, was ordered to appear at Boston, and by surrendering his fire-arms give additional assurance of his good faith towards the Colonies. Thereupon Oweneco the eldest son of Uncas, attended by fifty warriors, made his appearance at headquarters, and returned with them their fire-arms. The two younger sachems were held to remain in Cambridge as hostages, while *Oweneco* and his warriors marched with the English forces in pursuit of Philip.

The Pequot race, who had been nearly annihilated in 1637, had accumulated, from scattered fragments, and from natural health and increase, to another distinct tribe, and (in *this* Philip's war) together with the Mohegans under Oweneco, continued true, and sustained the English throughout this conflict, as in the sequel it will appear. Other Connecticut tribes remained neutral, except the Poduncks of East Windsor and East Hartford, of nearly two hundred, and the Nipmucks of Windham County of about sixty warriors, who turned away, and sooner or later went into the fight for Philip.

It appears that in June, 1675, during all the time the murderers were on trial, whom we have noted in the preceding chapter, Philip had a *posse* of armed warriors on the march up and down near the court-house at Plymouth, and ever afterwards kept his men about him in arms, and still continued to enlist recruits from distant tribes then and afterwards.

The English at Plymouth, knowing this, ordered a

military watch in all the towns, hoping that Philip, not finding himself arrested by the court, might become appeased, and that this war-cloud might vanish away.

But the facts proved otherwise. His strength daily increased by the flocking of the tribes to him; and his women and children were continually being sent to the care of the Narragansetts.

Then the English at Swansey, a town adjoining Philip's country, were daily menaced by the doings of Philip, intent on war and bloodshed; and the savages, emboldened, began to kill their cattle and pillage their houses. At length an Englishman shot at one of these intruders, wounded, but did not kill him; upon which the Indians began to kill the English wherever they could find them; so that on the 24th of June, 1675, the alarm of war was sounded throughout the Plymouth colony, eight or nine of the English having been slain in and about Swansey, on the same day. They killed three of these men in the highway, and six men in and about a dwelling-house in another part of the town.

Upon that, on the 14th July, 1675, an amicable letter was sent to Philip by a magistrate from the Plymouth Colony, requesting him to desist; but no answer was returned.

The governor and council of Plymouth sent what

forces they had to secure the towns thereabouts, despatched messengers to the governor and council of Massachusetts, and solicited assistance, and also sent two messengers to Philip to ascertain whether he could or could not be diverted from his bloody purpose by mediation the same as an arrangement had been made previously in 1671. But the messengers, upon seeing the dead which lay in the way, did not dare approach him, and, discouraged, returned speedily to Boston.

Massachusetts forces were immediately fitted out; and others were ordered to follow.

First, a foot company under Capt. Daniel Henchman, and a troop of horse under Capt. Prentice, bound from Boston to Mount Hope.

On the 20th these companies advanced to Swansey, and were quartered at Miles's house, minister of that town, within a quarter of a mile of the bridge that led into Philip's lands; arrived a little before nightfall, passed over the bridge, into the enemy's territories, where they found eight or ten Indians, who fired upon them from the bushes, killing Hammond and wounding Belcher, his horse also being killed. The eighty-seven English fired upon the Indians, killing five or six of them as they escaped into the swamps.

They were thus driven from Mount Hope; and all

escaped into the wilderness and were nowhere to be found.

Lieut. Oaks with another force, pursuing the savages, slew four or five others: among them was Thebe, a sachem of Mount Hope; another of the slain was a chief counsellor of Philip; the lieutenant lost one of his number, a soldier by the name of John Druce. Capts. Mosely and Page were there with their dragoons; and while they thus pursued Philip in various directions they received orders from Boston, July 4, 1675, to pass into Narragansett, and make a treaty with the sachems there. They marched there, remained four days, and made their treaty. Hostages were given by the Narragansetts to enforce the performance of their treaty.

Treaty.

Articles, covenants, and agreements had, made, and concluded by and between Major Thomas Savage, Capt. Edward Hutchinson, and Mr. Joseph Dudley, in behalf of the government of the Massachusetts Colony, and Major Warto, Winthrop, and Richard Smith, on behalf of Connecticut Colony, the one party; and Agamand, Wampsh *alias* Corman, Taitson, Tawageson, councillors and attorneys to Canonicus, Ninigret, Matababug, old Quen Quaipen, Quananshet, and Pomham, the six present sachems of the whole Narragansett Country, on the other party: referring to several differences and troubles lately risen between them, and for a final conclusion of settled peace and amity between the said sachems, their heirs and successors forever, and the governor of the said Massachusetts and Connecticut, and their successors in said governments forever.

I. That all and every of the said sachems shall from time to time carefully seize, and, living or dead, deliver unto one or other of the above-said governments all and every of Sachem Philip's subjects whatsoever that shall come or be found within the precinct of any other lands; and that with greatest diligence and faithfulness.

II. That they shall with their utmost ability use all acts of hostility against the said Philip and his subjects, entering his lands, or any other lands of the English to kill and destroy the said enemy, until a cessation from war with the said enemy be concluded by both the above-said Colonies.

III. That the said sachems, by themselves and their agents, shall carefully search out and deliver all stolen goods whatsoever taken by any of their subjects from any of the English, whether formerly or lately, and shall make full satisfaction for all wrongs or injuries done to the estate of any of the subjects of the several colonies, according to the judgment of indifferent men, in case of dissatisfaction between the offenders and the offended parties, or deliver the offenders.

IV. That all preparations for war or acts of hostility against any of the English subjects shall forever for the future cease; together with all manner of thefts, pilferings, killing of cattle, or any manner of breach of peace whatsoever shall with utmost care be prevented; and instead thereof their strength to be used as a guard round about the Narragansett Country for the English inhabitants' safety and security.

V. In token of the above-said sachems' reality in this treaty and conclusion, and for the security of the several English governments and subjects, they do freely deliver unto the above-said gentlemen, in behalf of the above-said colonies, John *Wabequab*, *Weothint*, *Pewkes*, *Wanew*, four of their near kinsmen and choice friends, to be and remain as hostages in several places of the English jurisdictions at the appointment of the honorable governors of the above-said colonies, there to be civilly treated, not as prisoners, but otherwise at their honors' discretion, until the above-said articles are fully accomplished to the satisfaction of the several governments; the departure of any of them in the mean time to be accounted breach of the peace and of these present articles.

VI. The said gentlemen, in behalf of the governments to which they do belong, do engage to every the said sachems and their subjects, that, if they or any of them shall seize and bring into either of the above-said English governments, or to Mr. Smith, inhabitant of Narragansett, Philip Sachem alive, he or they so delivering shall receive for their pains forty trucking cloth coats: in case they bring his head, they shall have twenty like good coats paid them. For every living subject of said Philip's so delivered, the deliverer shall receive two coats, and for every head two coats, and for every head one coat as a gratuity for their service, herein making it appear to satisfaction that the heads or persons are belonging to the enemy, and that they are of their seizure.

VII. The said sachems do renew and confirm unto the English inhabitants or others all former grants, sales, bargains, or conveyances of lands, meadows, timber, grass, stones, or whatever else the English have heretofore bought or quietly possessed and enjoyed, to be unto them and their heirs and assigns forever;

as also all former articles made with the confederate Colonies.

Lastly. The said councillors and attorneys do premeditately, seriously, and upon good advice, covenant, conclude, and agree all above said solemnly, and call God to witness they are and shall remain true friends to the English governments, and perform the above-said articles punctually, using their utmost endeavor, care, and faithfulness therein.

In witness whereof they have set their hands and seals,

PETAQUAMSCOT, July 15, 1675.

Signed, sealed and delivered in the presence of us underwritten, being carefully interpreted to the said Indians before sealing.

Daniel Henchman,	TAWAGASON, his *C.* mark.
Thomas Prentice,	TAYTSON, his *D.* mark.
Nicholas Paige,	AGAMOUG, his *T.* mark.
Joseph Stanton, Interp.	
Henry Hawlaws,	WAMPSH
Pecos Burkow,	*alias* } his *X* mark.
Job Neff,	CORMAN,

The four colonies, as appears, were alarmed almost to desperation ; and, while this treaty with the Narragansetts was progressing, the English everywhere else were advancing to the various posts of danger, many of them commissioned to make treaties or alliances with the afflicted, troublesome tribes, all now more or less on the alert at the sound of the soul-trying, terrific war-whoop, and all charged to ferret out and destroy Philip and his bloody warriors then ambushed with a strong force in some New-England swamp (no Englishman knew where). Accordingly, Capts. Church and Fuller were despatched to Pocasset with a force of fifty soldiers, advanced, seeking the enemy, and trying to make peace or treaty of peace with the Pocassets. That day they traversed Pocasset Neck; and they watched all that night in a deserted house which they found there, but, sad to relate, they heard no tidings of Indians.

They then divided their company. Fuller took towards the sea, had a skirmish wherein one of his men was wounded; but, ascertaining that there were more Indians in that neighborhood than would answer his purpose to find, they turned back, and a sloop of war took them all to Rhode Island in entire safety.

Capt. Church with his force marched farther into the neck of Pocasset, and, coming near a field, discovered two Indians among the standing peas. Hearing them shout, a tribe in great numbers sprang up, and chased him and his fifteen attendants far away to the seaside; and there they too, without loss of life, found a sloop, " The Golden Gate," that took them to Rhode Island all in safety. It is recorded, that, on this retreat to the sea-shore, this gallant captain used up all of his ammunition, and killed at least fifteen from the tribes that pursued him.

Capt. Church soon returned to Massachusetts, took more soldiers, and advanced to Pocasset again, and there again, in a skirmish with the enemy, killed fourteen or fifteen of them; and at this time he ascertained that Philip had betaken himself and tribes to the swamps not far away.

Capt. Cudworth in the mean time operated with his forces in killing Indians nearer at home.

Thus did the Plymouth Colony busy itself during the negotiations with the Narragansetts. Then, on Friday, July 15, the same day when the Plymouth treaty was completed, the Massachusetts forces marched to Rehoboth; but, hearing of no Indians nearer than the great swamp of Pocasset, eighteen miles from Taunton, they the next day advanced twelve miles· to Metapoiset, midway between Taunton Bay and Mount Hope: thence, July 17, after a march of twenty miles, they arrived at Taunton, where the people generally had assembled and had secured their families within eight garrisons.

On the eighteenth of July our forces again advanced eighteen miles to the swamp, and, being joined by Plymouth soldiers, entered the thicket, and

PHILIP ESCAPES. 217

were fired upon by the Indians in ambush. Five of the foremost Englishmen were killed; seven were wounded: and then again there were no Indians to be seen.

Three hundred wigwams, made there of green bark, so that they would not burn, were entirely deserted. A God-forsaken, decrepit old Indian was found in and about them. He confessed that Philip had lately lodged there, but said Philip and his tribes were in parts unknown to *him*.

For some time they travelled about, searching the swamp; but no further trace was found of Philip.

Night now coming on, and a retreat being sounded, they buried their dead; and then most of the Massachusetts were drawn off, leaving Capt. Henchman with one hundred men, together with the Plymouth forces, to pursue Philip and his hosts from this locality.

Under this arrangement Major *Savage*, Capt. *Page*, and Capt. *Mosely*, with their companies, returned, and reported to their authorities in Boston.

And then Capt. *Prentice* with his *troop* of horse was ordered towards Mendham, where some of Philip's Indians had entered a field and had killed five or six men at their labor, and soon as done had taken flight to the wilderness. He advanced; but that little village of Mendon was soon found to have been entirely deserted; and its hitherto peaceful cots had now all been turned to ashes. "Benjamin was not, and Simeon was not;" and "the bowl" had been "broken at the fountain."

Captain Henchman, who had been left with strong forces at Pocasset, thence to pursue Philip, not desiring to beard the beast in his den, knowing the danger and folly of entering the dismal woods deep in its miry bogs, blindfolded by the boughs of trees, to be ambushed and shot down by unseen tribes, whose foot-paths in flight were plain and smooth to the savages, but dark and deadly to an Englishman, resolved to starve them out. Accordingly he built there a fort, as it were, to beleaguer the enemy, and prevent his escape from the swamp, where he was then known or supposed to be, and where, as he hoped, he would hold him fast within his surroundings.

Philip, of course not being ignorant of what was going on without, and perceiving himself doomed if he remained, late in July started with one or two hundred of his best fighting men, advancing towards an arm of the sea that bordered there, and, taking the advantage of a low tide, built rafts of timber in the night-time, and ere the day broke with all his company escaped in the wilderness away into the country of the Nipmucks, while yet his enemies

PHILIP SEEKS THE NIPMUCKS.

still remained in camp on an opposite side of the great swamp.

Philip left behind him a hundred or more of his women and children, whom he could but leave to the mercy of the English, and to the God of his fathers.

His way into the Nipmuck territory was beset with many an ambuscade of English forces, then vigilant, seeking his blood. He was first discovered near Rehoboth, where its inhabitants with a party of Mohegans (then on their way from their visit to Boston) started in considerable force to apprise Henchman of Philip's flight; but, meeting an English force in direct pursuit of the enemy, they fell into the same ranks, and advanced. The news of all this in the mean time had reached Henchman, who, as soon as he could cross over with six files of men rowing hard the most of a day, arrived at Providence, and thence also advanced in pursuit of Philip of Pokanoket.

In the mean time the Mohegans, with the men of Rehoboth, had fallen at night upon the enemy's trail, overtook him, killed about thirty of them, and took a considerable of plunder without much loss.

The men of Rehoboth that night, having left their horses three miles in the rear, returned the next morning; and the Mohegans wheeled in, and again agreed to advance forward with Henchman, in pursuit of the king and his tribes, towards *Nepsatchet*, then thirty miles distant. To that end Henchman supplied provisions to the Mohegans; and to the same end Capt. Edmunds and Lieut. Brown of Providence had supplied Henchman.

But the pursuit, as appears, from no good reason, was not then followed for any great distance or extent. Henchman followed him until his provisions failed: then he and his Englishmen, as well as the Mohegans, severally faced about and returned home.

Philip escaped away to the westward, kindling and fanning the flames of war in all the western plantations of the Massachusetts Colony, wherever he went: so that both westward and eastward Philip's war was now beginning to wax warm, and in the fury of its flame had begun to rage within the two colonies of Connecticut.

While these events were progressing within the Plymouth Colony, the commissioners of the other three Colonies were constantly consulting, advising, inventing, and forwarding means and measures to prevent, as far as possible, the hateful horrors of an impending barbarous, savage war.

By the treaty which we have copied, the Narragansetts were kept from waging war in conjunction with the tribes of Philip; and thus the inland plantations of the English, for the present at least, had been saved.

Henchman returned to Boston; and after a while his force was disbanded.

Capt. Mosely then, with his force, was ordered from there to Quaboag (Brookfield), with other captains, to protect its inhabitants, and "*to seek after the enemy in those woods.*" None for a long time being found there, they came down to Lancaster, where on Sunday, the 22d of August, a man, his wife, and two children had been slain, and where a young man, while keeping his father's sheep, had been shot at by an Indian at Marlborough.

There was an Indian fort here. Mosely demanded and took their guns. Suspecting evil in eleven of them, he took and sent them to Boston, as if they had had something to do in the slaughter of the four men and the shooting at the young shepherd. But these prisoners when tried were all acquitted.

Presently also Capt. Mosely, with a company of soldiers, was sent from Boston up the Merrimack River to Penacook (Concord, N. H.), but found no Indians. Wonalancet, the sachem of that valley, whose residence was at Wamesit (Lowell), together with his tribes, having no heart for bloodshed for either of the belligerent nations, turning aside to remain neutral, had wandered back into the dark, dense forest.

Thence Mosely was sent westward to Hadley, to

put a stop, if possible, to depredations and murders which Philip's men were making in that direction both by fire and by sword.

The authorities at Boston at this time stood greatly in fear of the Nipmuck nation, located as they were between the great Merrimack and Connecticut Rivers, and sent up there a committee to make inquiries, who on their return reported "*that they found the said Indians wavering, — the young men very surly and insolent, the elder ones showing some inclination to maintain the wonted peace.*"

On July 28, 1675, Capt. Wheeler was sent from Boston with a company of twenty horse, to assist Capt. Hutchinson at Quaboag (Brookfield, Mass.), for the purpose of obtaining, if possible, a treaty of peace. They arrived there, and obtained the promise of an amicable arrangement. The day (Aug. 2) was set for the negotiation to be signed or completed: whereupon, on that day some of the principal men of the town, unarmed, rode along with said Hutchinson and Wheeler to the place appointed; but, finding no Indians had arrived, they, suspecting nothing, passed over to the chief town of the tribes, some three or four miles beyond, where they were assailed from an ambush, eight of them being shot down. Capt. Hutchinson was among the slain.

Such, indeed, was the result of trying to obtain a treaty of peace in the land of the Nipmucks.

CHAPTER XIV.

BATTLE OF BLOODY BROOK.

A Massacre. — Deerfield is surprised and sacked. — Sam and Netramp executed. — Capts. Beers and Lothrop. — Hostile Indians westward. — Neutral Indians suspected, and fly. — Twenty-six of them slain. — Beers and Twenty Men are slain. — Garrisons. — Lothrop and Essex Men slain. — Treat arrives, joins Mosely to bury the Dead. — Story of a Wounded Soldier. — Mosely's Skirmish. — He drives them to their Swamps. — Cooper at Springfield. — Is assailed by Savages. — Treat comes out from Westfield. — Thirty-two Houses destroyed. — Capts. Mosely, Poole, and Appleton are assailed. — Seven of their Men killed. — Parties in the Woods. — They wander towards the Narragansetts. — Hassemenesit visited by Henchman. — Indians vanish. — Found Wigwams. — Heard of Indians farther away, — Twenty-two Men on Horses. — Their Commander is killed. — Towns are fortified. — Scouts of Indians all about. — Tribes vanish towards Dutch River, and to the Narragansett Country. — Philip concentrates. — The Colonies deliberate. — Advance upon the Narragansetts. — Battle of Pettyquanscot Swamp.

IN the preceding chapter it already appears that Capts. Hutchinson and Wheeler had been sent from Boston to negotiate a treaty with the Nipmucks at Meminimisset (Brookfield); and that Capt. Hutchinson and others, in passing into that Indian village, known to be there, as he was, for the purpose of peace, were fired upon by two or three hundred Indians from an ambuscade near a swamp, and were slain, and Capt. Wheeler wounded.

From that the Indians flocked into the village, setting fire to all the dwelling-houses and other buildings save the one in which the people had garrisoned themselves, and which they tried also to burn.

For nearly two days they tried to destroy the garrison-house, in which about seventy of the inhabitants had taken refuge, but failed.

Major Willard, with forty-eight dragoons, and Capt. Parker of Groton, with forty-six more, on the second day then from Boston came to their relief, fired upon the Indians; and the tribes as of course took to their dens in the woods and swamps.

In this raid many houses were burned, cattle were killed, and other trespasses committed. In the mean time Capt. Watts and Lieut. Cooper arrived with re-enforcements from Springfield, in all eighty Englishmen and Indians.

These Indians, as usual, moved in small parties, and were led by several sachems, among whom were *Sam*, sachem of Weshacum, and Netaump, who were afterwards captured, and were executed in Boston.

Then Capt. Lothrop and Capt. Beers were sent up

there; and Major Willard with several companies of armed men were sent into the Nipmuck country to head off any attempt on the part of Indians to take concert of action with King Philip; but to little purpose. These re-enforcements traversed the woods in various directions for many miles; but the tribes had fled.

DEERFIELD.

The hostile Indians generally wandered westward; and very soon a considerable force of them became concentrated at *Deerfield*, *Swamscot*, and *Squakeag*, places of plantations newly started.

At Hadley also the apparently neutral Indians began to be suspected, as they inclined to make noises while on the pursuit of Philip's force; by reason of which they were called upon to deliver up their arms; yet they refused, and fled like sheep. Lothrop and Beers pursued and overtook them about ten miles above Hatfield, at Sugarloaf Hill, killed twenty-six of them, but lost ten of their soldiers. The other fugitives fled away, and joined Philip.

On the first of September, 1675, the tribes beset Deerfield, killed one man, and laid most of the town in ashes.

SQUAKEAG.

Two or three days afterwards they fell in upon Squakeag, another new plantation fifteen miles higher up the river, where they killed nine or ten of the inhabitants, falling as they did before getting sheltered within the garrison-house.

CAPTAIN BEERS SLAIN.

The next day Capt. Beers, with his force, on the way near by, was suddenly surprised in a thicket by the swamp-side, fought valiantly, yet he and twenty of his men were killed; and the remainder of his men returned back to Hadley.

Here the heads of some of the slain were pinioned on poles; and one or two were afterwards found with a chain hooked into the under jaw, and suspended upon the limbs of a tree.

Major Treat and Capt. Appleton, with a hundred men, visited the place after the slaughter, and brought the families garrisoned there away, leaving the place deserted of the English.

GARRISONS.

Northampton, Hatfield, Deerfield, and other towns, were now ordered to be more securely garrisoned; Hadley being made their headquarters.

LOTHROP AND HIS MEN. 227

The corn at Deerfield, three thousand bushels, standing in stacks, was accordingly carried to Hadley.

LOTHROP AND HIS MEN SLAIN.

Capt. Lothrop with eighty or ninety men was left to guard the corn and other goods.

On the 18th of September, 1675, while marching along with their carts of corn, apprehending no danger, they were almost all cut off. He, with most of his men, was killed, some of them teamsters: no more than eight or ten escaped.

The soldiers slain were the choice young men of Essex County, leaving many a sad heart at home to mourn their sad, their early departure from earth.

The Indians here numbered seven hundred.

Subsequently in 1835, at this battle-ground in Deerfield, on the one hundred and sixtieth aniversary of the slaughter of Lothrop and his gallant young men of Essex, their bones were hunted out like the bones of Joseph in Israel, by the yeomanry who then came forth to the number of six thousand, and there at Bloody Brook advanced to erect a stately monument, six feet square, and twenty feet high. There under the cool shade of a walnut tree, the distinguished orator (Everett) as he was wont, eloquently discoursed to them of the past, of the present, and of the world to come.

Thanks to the inhabitants of Deerfield, who by *this*, have contributed so much to the valor of young men!

Those eighty young heroes of Essex, who had volunteered in behalf of civilization, will never grow old; nor will their memories (always green in every New-England heart) grow cold, or fade in the sunlight of the advancing ages.

STORY OF ROBERT DUTCH.

Major Treat had been directed to join Mosely at this point, who had previously started another way with about one hundred soldiers, Indians and English. They met, and buried the dead.

They found upon the battle-ground a soldier of the day before, Robert Dutch of Ipswich, who had fallen by a bullet in the head and by the weight of a hatchet, and had been stripped of his clothing, and left for dead. Yet he crept his way to these undertakers, and was a live wonder in the midst of the silent-dead, having survived through that dreary night to hail the light of another day; and they say lived to a good old age.

This victory greatly encouraged Philip and his tribes. Yet it was stated as coming from the enemy that on that battle-day with Lothrop they lost in all ninety-six men.

Soon after Lothrop's battle, Mosely came up while the tribes were still pillaging the dead, gave them battle, charged upon them; and his lieutenants, Perez, Savage, and Pickering, assisting in his command, drove the savages headlong into the swamp.

THE IMPENDING CRISIS.

The Springfield Indians had joined Philip; and in the midst of great precaution, by treaties, pledges, and hostages, obtained on the part of Springfield, Philip's Indians had resolved to burn and destroy it. To this end they cunningly enticed away the hostages from Hartford, and secretly received three hundred of Philip's Indians into their fort as re-enforcements, undiscovered of the English. All remained quiet, until at once the startling fact was revealed in tidings by post from below Springfield, that Lieut. Cooper had advanced there to ascertain the truth of the message, when forth came the bloody monsters, at once firing upon him, hit him several times; yet he reached the next garrison-house. They killed his attendants, and, advancing, fired the town in all of its parts outside of the garrisons.

As it happened, the inhabitants had taken alarm over night, and many of them had disappeared, or they would have been totally destroyed. Major Treat had come from Westfield in season for their rescue, although he had not sufficient boats to transport his men. Also Major Pinchen and Capt. Appleton came with their forces; and, although thirty-two houses had been destroyed, the remainder of the town was saved. The valuable library belonging to the minister of the town, Rev. Peletiah Clover, was among the property consumed.

BATTLES AT HADLEY, NORWOTTUCK.

The 1st of September, 1675, was a day of fasting and prayer in Hadley; and at church the Indians fell in upon them. The people took to their arms, which they had at church, confronted the invaders; but their numbers, greatly disproportioned, eventually were forced to falter; and they gave way. At this moment an old hoary-headed veteran, " *Goffe*," appeared in their midst, with his frosty locks moving in the breeze, with a firm, steadfast voice re-animating their spirits, led them on to another onset, and drove the heartless savages out of town.

NORWOTTUCK.

And then on Oct. 19, 1675, Capt. Treat being at North Hampton, Capts. Mosely, Poole, and Appleton advanced to Hadley, when all at once seven hundred of the enemy invaded the town in every direction, killing two or three of the scouts of citizens, and seven of Mosely's men; but they soon found it to be warm, dangerous work. Appleton's sergeant was mortally wounded. Night came on: many were seen to fall, some run into the river, while flying in various directions.

Sunday. — After their defeat at Hatfield, straggling parties of them were seen about North Hampton, Westfield, and Springfield.

In a short time afterwards they set fire to some barns and outhouses, and then vanished away into the wilderness. Winter setting in, they now wandered away into the Narrangansett Country; yet it was not known to the English where Philip was.

HASSAMENESET.

In 1675, Nov. 1, Capt. Henchman was sent from Boston to beset the Indians at this place. Advancing, he on the third day came in sight of Indian fires; but there were no Indians to be found. On the fourth day they hunted along among the plantations, and found a miller-boy who had been previously taken by the Indians from Marlborough: the Indians, upon seeing the belligerent intruders, fled, leaving every thing behind them. Henchman with his men advanced on toward Marlborough, but found no Indians. He then proceeded to Poppachuog: from there the tribes had fled. He then came back to Mendham to examine into affairs there, heard of wigwams about ten miles away, and marched onward in that direction. He was joined there by Capt. Philip Curtice.

Early next morning they espied a wigwam where the enemy had camped over night. Some Indians, as they ascertained, had been following them.

Hearing that there were Indians still farther on, the captain, with Curtice and his lieutenant, upon consultation mounted twenty-two men upon horses, who advanced into the woods ten miles, and found some wigwams. But the leader, upon looking back, found that he had but five men in the place of the twenty-two. He, however, assaulted the wigwam. The tribe, returning the fire, shot the lieutenant and one of his men; and all the rest of his force ran away.

The next day our people went up there: the Indians had left. They buried the two men, and then again returned to their quarters to Mendham.

On the way they destroyed two hundred bushels of corn, as they could not well save it.

INDIANS AT SPRINGFIELD AND VICINITY.

The Indians at this time had been driven away from Hadley; and the people round about there barricaded their villages and towns by setting up palisadoes of cleft wood about three feet in length to break the force of sudden assaults by the Indians, which proved advantageous in their defence against the invaders. Although in the spring at North Hampton, the enemy succeeded in breaking through one of these fortifications, generally the invention answered a good purpose.

At Springfield and other places about there, small parties of Indians were often seen in the woods, skulking about like demons, exciting the terrors of the white man, as they often devastated his lonely cot, destroyed his cattle, or murdered his women and children.

For instance: at Long Meadow a half a score of them beset a cottage remote from the village; but, being at once fired upon by our Englishmen, they fled towards Windsor and escaped.

A Springfield man, while visiting his deserted house, to look after his corn deposited there, was shot; and then his house was burned down by some of the same tribe.

Soon afterwards the tribes withdrew, some towards

the Dutch River, but most of them to the Narragansett Fort; these tribes having for the most part joined Philip, although old Ninegret, their chief, now in his dotage, had inclined otherwise.

After *this* the soldiers remained for a while at Hatfield, and then were called back to their headquarters at Boston.

THE COLONIES DELIBERATE.

Winter was now approaching; and the COMMISSIONERS of the four united Colonies took council together as to what should next be done. For now they saw Philip in great force of many hundreds concentrated; that during the winter, if left alone, more and more of the tribes would take courage, and follow at his command; that in the spring, leaving the swamps, the tribes would be likely to devastate the settlements of New England everywhere. They well weighed the effect which a cold, sharp New-England winter would have on an army waiting and bivouacked on a bleak field, — of its length, of the depths of the snow, of the difficulty of affording the men relief or supplies.

They reasoned, that, if Philip were let alone all that time, it would be impossible to cope with him successfully on the approach of spring and summer, when the advantages would turn in his favor; that the English soldiers, in squads and in companies, would be likely to fall one after another, as might well be seen from the experience of the past.

They further considered that the Narragansetts, numerous as they were, best disciplined, best clothed, having the best manners, of all the tribes, now remembering the fate of their dear old Miantonimo, the embers of whose ashes were alive, still burning and firing their hearts the same as they did forty years previously on Sachem Plain, — they knew that they had broken out from the network of the Colonies, and had become their deadly foes in their adhesion to Philip's army.

Thereupon the commissioners agreed to raise an army of a thousand men, to be gathered from the several Colonies as soon as might be, in time not to exceed the 10th of December of that year (1675); that the Narragansetts had violated every article of their treaty, lately renewed, in *this*, that they had not delivered up the Englishmen's enemies that had sheltered themselves in their midst, and had been supplying them with sustenance; that many of their young men were at least suspected of being in open arms with Philip's forces, some of them having been found among his wounded in the wigwams, and elsewhere to be healed of their injuries at home; that some of the Englishmen's guns, lost in the battle at Deerfield, were found in their fort, left there by Narragansett hands when it was fired and consumed: by reason of all which, the Colonial Commissioners having this matter in charge ordered the raising of an army of a thousand fighting men to be enlisted out of all the Colonies; of which the share of the Massachusetts Colony was to be five hundred and twenty-seven: the rest were to be supplied out of the Plymouth and Connecticut Colonies.

Accordingly the one thousand men, together with volunteers from the friendly tribes, were in due time forthcoming. A commission was granted to Josiah Winslow, Esq., then governor of the Plymouth Colony, a man of courage and prudence, as commander-in-chief. Thus under his command were six companies, led severally by Capt. Mosely, Capt. Gardner, Capt. Davenport, Capt. Oliver.

Also five companies from Connecticut under Major Treat, to be led severally by Capt. Siely, Capt. Gallop, Capt. Mason, Capt. Watts, and Capt. Marshall.

Also two companies from Plymouth, to be led by Major Bradford and Capt. Gorham. Samuel Appleton was in command as major of the Massachusetts forces.

The Massachusetts force as raised numbered four hundred and sixty-five men, besides a troop of horse commanded by Capt. Thomas Prentice, which were delivered to the general in command at Dedham, Dec. 9, 1675.

On that night they marched to Woodcock's, about twenty-seven miles from Dedham, and on the next night they had arrived at Seaconk. Thence Capt. Mosely and his company with Mr. Smith proceeded onward, and the next day were ferried over the water to Providence.

WICKFORD.

On the 12th, after passing over Patuxet River, they marched through Powham's Country, and at night joined in with Capt. Mosely and his force at their destined headquarters in Wickford.

On his way Capt. *Mosely* had surprised thirty-six Indians; took one by the name of Peter, and brought him along with him as a guide, who in the end proved useful.

On the 14th, two days afterwards, a scout was sent out under Sergeant *Bennet*, who killed one Indian and one squaw, and brought in four others. Afterwards the whole company moved into the wilderness, where they burned a hundred and fifty wigwams, killed seven Indians, and brought in at night eight prisoners.

STONEWALL JOHN.

On the following day this Indian came into camp as if from the sachems, expressing a desire for peace, yet full of doubts whether the English would dare engage so formidable an enemy as King Philip. At length this fellow started homeward; and the crew that attended him falling in with some of Capt. *Gardner's* men, who were wandering about without orders, slew his sergeant and one or two more, and also two of Capt. Oliver's men. Others came up, fired several times at Capt. Mosely, doing him no harm; but some of his men, charging upon the savages, killed one of them and the rest fled.

BULL'S GARRISON.

Next day news came that Jerry Bull's garrison-house had been burnt at Pettyquamscot by the tribes, that ten Englishmen and five women and children had been killed, two only having escaped from it.

On the following day news also came from Pettyquamscot that the Connecticut forces had arrived there on behalf of the English with *three hundred Mohegans* "*ready fixed*" to give battle against the Narragansetts, and that they had already slain five or six of them, and had taken as many more prisoners.

THE ADVANCE TO PETTYQUAMSCOT.

The English and allied tribes having now all arrived, their first great care was to obtain supplies, and to protect themselves against the cold storms of a New-England winter, as well as against the ambushed tribes of Philip, who lurked in every swamp that surrounded them.

Then on the next day the whole Massachusetts and Plymouth forces, with an intention to engage the enemy, advanced to Pettyquamscot.

The Connecticut forces, their house of *rendezvous* having been consumed, and for want of shelter from the extreme cold, now on that cold, stormy evening marched on through the snow at night, having and finding no protection better than the sharp air of the skies, and the fleecy, frosty snow that all night long fell upon their shoulders,

It was Dec. 19, 1675, at one o'clock, P.M., when they arrived at *Pettyquamscot*, after a march of fourteen miles through that country of the old *Snuke Squaw* of Narragansett. Still advancing, they reached a swamp, as they were told by their guide they would find Indians.

Capts. Mosely and Davenport were then on the lead; and Major Appleton and Oliver were following with the Massachusetts forces, Gen. Winslow with the Plymouth men in the centre; and the Connecticut troops were following on in the rear.

BATTLE OF NARRAGANSETT.

The front files, upon discovering Indians in the woods, fired at them; and their fire was returned from the swamp, the Indians flying farther in. Still they were followed by the invaders until they reached a fort, into which the tribes betook themselves. This battle-ground was an island of four acres in the wilderness, surrounded by a dense swamp. It is now an upland meadow a few feet higher than its adjacent lands, situated in *South Kingston*, Rhode Island. In the fort upon it, there was but one entrance: yet the Indians had many ways of coming out of it. It had been raised upon an island of four or five acres of rising land in the midst of a swamp. The sides of it were made of palisadoes set upright, compassed about by a dense, impenetrable hedge of almost a rod in thickness. Its usual Indian place of entrance was over a long tree extending over a pool of water, and *portended death*, such was its exposure, to any and to all who might venture to enter the fort in that direction. At one corner also there was a cap made up of a long log laying four or five feet from the ground over which files of men might also pass. Yet nearly opposite to it was a block-house.

The English filed in upon these, the only entrances; and from the block-houses, as well as the ambushes within, they were shot down nearly as fast as they arrived. Capts. Johnson and Davenport both fell. The soldiers were driven back: they threw themselves upon the ground to avoid the shots: many men were lost. At the last two fresh companies were brought up to another assault, who charged in upon them, raising the cry, "They run! they run!" This frightened the enemy, and encouraged their comrades, two fresh companies thus being brought in. They fought valiantly in the place of the four which had already been engaged. The enemy was driven from the fort, but not without great loss on the part of the assailants; but the enemy lay dead in great numbers in and about the fort and swamp.

No less than six brave leaders fell on the part of the English; to wit, Capts. Gallop, Siely, Marshall, and Lieut. Upham, as well as Davenport and Johnson already named.

The invaders then set fire to the wigwams of the fort, in which were remaining women and children, who many of them were destroyed in the general conflagration of five or six hundred dirty, smoky cells.

That night the English forces had to march back to their dreary headquarters, which then lay fifteen miles to the rear, bearing and carrying the bodies of their dead and wounded along with them through the snow.

And thus the war upon the Narragansetts who had threatened to join Philip had now in good earnest commenced.

CHAPTER XV.

BATTLE IN THE PETTYQUAMSCOT SWAMP.

Smoke of Wigwams on Fire. — Indian Dead and Dying. — English Force returning at Night, and bearing their Dead. — Prentice and Men are sent to Popham's Country. — Ninegret proposes Peace. — More Soldiers from Boston. — Canonicus asks a Suspension. — Tribes start Northward towards the Nipmucks. — Indians seize Two Hundred Sheep, Fifty Cattle, Fifteen Horses. — English follow; take Seventy, and kill some of them. — Philip's Force join the Nipmucks. — Massacres at *Lancaster*. — Mrs. Rowlandson's Captivity, and Narrative verbatim. — Her Conversations with King Philip. — Massacre at *Medfield*. — Mrs. Rowlandson describes the Indians' Return from this Battle. — A Rally for the Battle. — Tribes near *Patuxet*. — A Hundred and Forty of them killed. — At *Warwick*, Houses burned. — In *Plymouth*, Houses burned, and Eleven killed. — Indians near *Rehoboth* and *Swansey* burn Thirty Barns and Forty Houses. — Connecticut Colony sends *Dennison* with Forces to head them off. — Killed Forty-five without Loss. — *Canonchet* is shot. — Battle at *Sudbury*. — Capt. Wadsworth and Sixty Men slain. — Their Monument. — An Indian Dance. — Mary Rowlandson released from Captivity.

IT was night; and the smoke of the wigwams was still beclouding the heavens. The Indian dead, including their women and children slain by the sword or consumed in the conflagration of the fort, still haunted the frosty pathways of the wilderness.

all the way along, through that night, as the English bore their ninety dead and wounded back with them fifteen miles to their headquarters already consumed. Those gallant men, it will be remembered, had the preceding night marched through the perpetual snows to this battle-field, and again back all night long, burdened with the fatigue of the battle, and of their valiant dead through the woods. Was there ever a night more sad, more terrific, more hideous, than this? Is it to be wondered that many a gallant heart at this second great battle in Philip's war perished? Is it to be wondered that the English authorities thereafterwards sought safety in attempted fruitless treaties during what remained of the winter, making but few and feeble military movements against Philip and the Narragansetts until spring? Yet murders and skirmishes were common as usual.

The killed and wounded under the several commanders in this battle of December 19, 1675, were as follows:—

Mass. Companies.	Killed.	Wounded.	Connecticut Companies.	Slain and Wounded.
Major Appleton,	3	22	New Haven Co.,	20
Capt. Mosely,	9	10	Capt. Siely's Co.,	20
" Oliver,	5	10	" Watts's Co.,	17
" Gardner,	7	11	" Marshall's Co.,	14
" Johnson,	3	11	Plymouth Co., Commanders	
" Davenport,	4	15	Bradford and Gorham,	20
	31	79		91

THE TRIBES SEEK A SUSPENSION. 245

On the 27th of December, Capt. Prentice with a small force was sent into Popham's country; found no Indians, yet burned a hundred wigwams. He there learned, from one of Philip's squaws and others, that in the battle near Pettyquamscot the Narragansetts lost three hundred warriors.

On the 8th of January, Canonchet, a messenger from *Ninegret*, came into camp, who brought a letter from Stanton an interpreter, expressing from this old sachem friendship as ever, and who also said that corn was two shillings a pint among the tribes.

Jan. 10, a supply of soldiers were sent from Boston, in a severe snow-storm.

Jan. 12, a messenger came from Canonicus, asking a *suspension* of hostilities for *a month*, in which to negotiate a treaty; but the proposition was rejected.

By prisoners which were brought in, it soon appeared that the tribes had started, and were trailing away to the woodland swamps of the Nipmuck country; which country, as we have seen, lies between the Connecticut and Merrimack Rivers.

Capt. Prentice, Jan. 21, with his force, fell in with one of the tribes, took two prisoners and killed nine Indians. One of his men (Dodge of Salem), riding with his friend, met two Indians. — Dodge pursued one of them, his friend the other.— His pistol snapped; the Indian pulled him from his horse, and fell upon him with a knife in hand. Dodge, seeing it, caught hold of it, saved the life of his friend, and killed both Indians.

The English authorities are now beginning to discover the necessity of following the tribes in their hidden trails to the Nipmuck wilderness. But the Indians were already far ahead of their time of being ready to commence the pursuit; and, as the Indians advanced, they seized two hundred sheep, fifty head of cattle, and fifteen horses, belonging to one Carpenter; drove them along with them to be used as supplies among the Nipmucks.

The English forces followed them, troubling them in the rear, discovered the heads of fifty horses in one place, fell in with some of the tardy savages, killed and took about seventy of them, but could not obtain an open battle, as they would always, when assaulted, take to the swamps. After pursuing them far into the thickets between Marlboro' and Brookfield, towards Connecticut, our forces in the beginning of February returned to Boston.

Then the Narragansetts, thus left alone, joined the Nipmucks; and now on the 10th of February, 1675, we come to the

MASSACRE AT LANCASTER.

This was a village of about fifty families. The minister of that locality (Rev. Joseph Rowlandson)

was away; and the minister was generally the leader, if not the law-giver, almost everywhere in those days. That night, on his return from Boston, where he had been to consult the governor as to how Lancaster should be defended against the invaders, it was to meet the tragic news that Lancaster was in ashes, its inhabitants, including his wife and children, all *gone.*

His own mansion had previously been changed into a garrison; and within it were men to defend it. Yet the fortifications on the back side of it being closed up with firewood, the Indians forced their way to it, set it on fire; and its inhabitants within were then subjected to the alternative to yield to the merciless savages, or to be consumed in the crackling conflagration. It was thus the forty-two inmates of that minister's garrison fell: twenty-two of them were carried away captive, mostly women and children grown; the rest were murdered outright, or reserved for further misery. Several of them who were not killed in the fight were slain in their attempt to escape, as well as others who were not deemed valuable as captives.

MARY ROWLANDSON.

MARY was the *wife*, in whose care the household was left when her reverend husband left it to consult the governor at Boston. She with her children was among the captives of that day, was doomed to many months in captivity, saw and talked with King Philip; and in this matter I can give the reader no light more interesting than to allow Mary to speak here in her own words.

MARY ROWLANDSON'S "REMOVES."

Mary, in twenty chapters which she at the time denominated "REMOVES," wrote and published a full account of what she heard and saw of the tribes during her captivity in 1675. In this narrative, among other things, she says, —

"On the 10th of February came the Indians in great numbers" (Nashuas and Nipmucks, led by Sagamore Sam) "upon Lancaster. Their first coming was about sun-rising. Hearing the noise of some guns, we looked out: several houses were burning, and the smoke ascending to heaven.

"There were five persons taken in one house. The father and mother and an infant child they knocked in the head: the other two they took and carried away alive. There were two others, who, being out of their garrison upon occasion, were set upon. One was knocked on the head: the other escaped. Another there was, who, running along, was shot and wounded, and fell down. He begged of them his life, promising them money (as they told me); but they would not hearken to him, but knocked him on the head, stripped him naked, and mangled him.

"Another, seeing many of the Indians about his barn, ventured and went out, and was shot down.

"There were three others belonging to the same garrison who were killed. The Indians, getting up upon the roof of the barn, had advantage to shoot down upon them over their fortifications.

"Thus these murderous wretches went on, burning and destroying all before them.

"At length they came and beset our house; and quickly it was the dolefullest day that mine eyes ever saw.

"The house stood upon the edge of a hill. Some of the Indians got behind the hill, others into the barn, and others behind any thing that would shelter them; from all which places they shot against the house, so that the bullets seemed to fly like hail; and quickly they wounded one man among us, then another, and then a third.

"About two hours, according to my observation in that amazing time, they had been about the house before they prevailed to fire it, which they did with flax and hemp which they brought out of the barn. And there being no defence about the house, only two flankers at two opposite corners, and one of them not finished, they fired it once; and one ventured out, and quenched it. But they quickly fired it again; and that took.

"Now is the dreadful hour come that I have often heard of in the time of the war, as it was the case of others; but *now mine eyes see it.*

THE DREAD SCENE.

"Some in our house were fighting for their lives, others wallowing in blood, the house on fire over our heads, and the bloody heathen ready to knock us on the head if we stirred out.

"Now might we hear mothers and children crying out for themselves and one another, '*Lord, what shall we do?*'

"Then I took *my children*, and one of my sister's *girls*, to go forth and leave the house; but, as soon as we came to the door and appeared, the Indians shot so thick, that the bullets rattled against the house as if one had taken a handful of stones and threw them; so that we were forced to give back. We had six stout dogs belonging to our garrison; but none of them would stir, though at another time if an Indian had come to the door they were ready to fly upon him and tear him down. . . . But out we must go, the fire increasing and coming along behind us roaring, and the Indians gaping before us with their spears and hatchets to devour us.

"No sooner were we out of the house, but my brother-in-law (being before wounded in defending the house, in or near the throat), fell down dead; whereat the Indians scornfully shouted and hallooed, and were presently upon him stripping off his clothes.

A BULLET STRIKES HER.

"The bullets flying thick, one went through my side, and the same (as would seem) through the bowels and hand of my poor child in my arms.

"One of my elder sister's children, named William, had then his leg broken, which the Indians perceiving knocked him on the head.

"Thus were we butchered by those merciless heathens, standing amazed, with the blood running down our heels.

"My eldest sister, seeing her William and others *dead*, exclaimed, ' *Lord, let me die with them!* ' At the same moment a bullet struck her; and she fell down dead over the threshold.

"The Indians laid hold of us, pulling me one way and the children another, and said, ' Come, go along with us.' I told them they would kill me. They answered, '*If I were willing to go along with them they would not hurt me.*'

"There were twelve killed, some shot, some knocked down with their hatchets."

Mary says, "Those seven that were killed at Lancaster the summer before upon a sabbath day, and the one that was afterwards killed upon a week day, were slain and *mangled* in a barbarous manner by 'ONE-EYED JOHN,' and Marlborough's praying Indians which Capt. Mosely brought to Boston, as the Indians told her.

On the leaving of Lancaster she says, —

"One of the Indians carried my poor sick wounded babe" (a daughter six years old) "upon a horse. I went moaning along, '*I shall die, I shall die!*' I went on foot after it. *At length* I took it off the horse, and carried it in my arms till my strength failed, and I fell down with it. Then they set me upon a horse, with my wounded child in my lap."

There was a fall of snow; and Mary goes on to tell how she suffered with the wound in her side all the way through, with the child in her arms fast breathing out its life upon the broken boughs of the forest, and upon the cold snows of a February night.

This tribe dwelt a while at *Wenimesset*, now New Braintree, as they were on their way to Albany, which place had, for the time being, been adopted as the headquarters of King Philip.

For nine days she bore her sick and faint little

daughter along: at length, in the wigwam, as she says, "About two hours in the night, my sweet babe like a lamb departed this life, on Feb. 18, 1675, it being about six years and five months old."

Mary, as it seems, still hugged her dead daughter to her bosom for one or two nights; and at length, when the tribe next started upon the trail, she again clasped it in her arms to bear it along with her; but the tribe, with more show of humanity than usual, tore it away from her bosom, and buried it. Mary as yet had a daughter and son; but they were held by other tribes.

And here we may observe, there is an elevation of land in Warwick, near the place where the savages buried that little Grace Rowlandson, which has ever since borne her name. It is called Mount Grace.

MASSACRE AT MEDFIELD.

While Mary was still with them, Feb. 21, 1675, three hundred Indians advanced upon Medfield. It had a garrison supposed to be well guarded by soldiers and by its inhabitants; yet fire and slaughter followed.

The young growth in the surrounding woodlands afforded a thick-set shelter, and favored the schemes of the invaders. In these coverts, and in the barns, orchards, and under the fences, they hid themselves as usual; and then they leaped upon the villagers with the ferocity of tigers: thus they killed eighteen and wounded twenty of the inhabitants of Medfield. The houses in the centre, in the west, and in the south-west parts of the town were mostly burnt down: an old man was burnt in one of them. Lieut. Adams and wife among others were killed; and forty or fifty houses and barns were consumed. The loss to this town was upwards of two thousand pounds.

Of this battle *Mary*, being among their women and children, had been informed, and thus goes on to say, —

"The next day the Indians returned from *Medfield*, — all the company; for those that belonged to the other, smaller company came through the town that now we are at. But before they came to us, — oh the outrageous roaring and the whooping that there was! They began their din about a mile away. By their noise and whooping they signified how many they had destroyed. Those that were with us were gathered together as soon as they heard the whooping; and, every time they repeated the *number slain*, these at home gave a *shout* that the very earth rang again." And thus they continued till they arrived to the sagamore's wigwam. And then she goes on to tell "how hideous were their yells and triumphant exultation at and over the scalps of Englishmen which they had taken, and had brought along with them from Medfield."

These tribes, as we have said, were tending towards Albany. They advanced; and at her eighth remove Mary says, " We travelled on till night; and in the morning we must go over the river (Hudson) to see Philip's crew.

" While I was in the canoe, I could not but be amazed at the numerous crew of pagans that were on the bank on the other side. When I came ashore, they gathered all about me, I sitting alone in the midst. They asked one another questions, and laughed and rejoiced over their gains and victories.

MARY DINES WITH KING PHILIP.

" Then I went to see King Philip. He bid me come in, and sit down, and asked me *whether I would smoke it?* But this in no way suited me.

" Next " (she says) " the Indians gathered their forces to go against Northampton.

" Over night one went about yelling and whooping to give notice of the design; whereupon they went to boiling of ground-nuts, and parching corn (as many as had it) for their provision ; and in the morning away they went.

" During my abode in this place Philip spoke to me to make a shirt for his boy, which I did ; for which he gave me a shilling. I offered the money to my mistress; but she bid me keep it, and with it I bought a piece of horse-flesh. Afterwards he asked me to make a cap for his boy, for which *he invited me to dinner.* I went; and he gave me a pancake about as big as two fingers: it was made of parched wheat, beaten, and fried in bear's grease; but I thought I never tasted pleasanter meat in my life."

TRIBES AT PATUXET.

While Mary was still with Philip's Indians, within a month after their attack upon Medfield, constantly changing place, the tribes were seen to the number of six hundred near Patuxet and Providence. They did much mischief on the way.

On the 12th of March, eleven persons had been slain by them in Plymouth, and several houses burned. On the seventeenth they had beset *Warwick* near Narragansett, and had destroyed much property there; and on the 25th of March some of the tribes had fallen in upon *Weymouth,* and had destroyed dwelling-houses there.

Then on the 28th of March, 1676, they swept around towards the Narragansett country, and in the neighborhood of Rehoboth and Swansey burned nearly thirty barns and forty dwelling-houses.

In April, 1676, Canonchet, chief sachem, and

CANONCHET, A PRISONER. 257

Philip, being driven out from their own country the winter previously by the English, now from the westward, in order to obtain subsistence for the tribes in campaign of the spring and summer, had intended that all the plantations taken from the English should be planted to corn; and for that reason ventured with thirty men to bring his seed-corn from Seaconk (near Mount Hope), and started on his journey, leaving Philip's force of fifteen hundred men in and about Seaconk, to await his return.

But, as it happened, Capt. George Dennison of New London, who previously, on March 27, 1676, had started on an expedition made up of forty-seven English, eighty Indians, twenty of whom were Ninegret *Narragansetts*, led by *Catapazet*, the others were Pequots under *Cassasinamon*, and Mohegan under Oweneco, son of Uncas.

This force accidentally intercepted Canonchet. They slew one of his men; and from two squaws they learned that Canonchet was near. They started after him and his men, chased them around a hill, and finally captured Canonchet. In the race he cast off his lace coat, given him previously, in October, at a treaty in Boston. A young Englishman now speaking to him, the sachem replied in broken English, "*You much child, no understand matters of war.* Let your brother or your chief come: *him* I will answer."

He was as good as his word, and chose to die rather than to make concessions. He with two Pequots were imprisoned, and were shot at Stonington.

As soon as news of the enemy's returning was known, the Connecticut Colony, April 1, 1676, directed Capt. George Dennison, with his force made up of Mohegans, Pequots, and Nianticks belonging to Ninegret the Narragansett sachem, as we have stated; who followed the tribes, and killed there and on the way forty-five of them without much loss. Several of the sagamores were either slain or taken prisoners, among whom, as we have seen, was *Canonchet*, chief sachem of the Narragansetts, and son of Miantonimo, and the right heir of his nation's pride, as well as the avenger of the murder of his valiant father, who had been brutally murdered through the treachery of the English. The son, a prisoner, was now executed at Stonington.

It appears now that the war and the winter had wasted many from the ranks of that numerous nation. They numbered in the commencement, as was supposed, nearly two thousand warriors, with nine hundred stand of arms, yet now are very much reduced.

MASSACRE AT SUDBURY.

The next *raid* by Philip's returning forces, of much importance, was upon this ancient towr, April 18, 1676. And now, as the tribes had come in from Marlborough, they burned down several dwelling-houses and barns, and killed ten or twelve of the English soldiers who had been sent in from Concord, and who had been ordered to head off Philip, and protect the feeble, unfortified towns that lay open and exposed to his terrible encroachments on the way.

To the same end soldiers had been sent from Boston, under Capt. Samuel Wadsworth of Milton, who, on his destination to Marlborough, took the trail of Philip, and followed him through the woods to Sudbury. Within a mile of the town he discovered a body of a hundred Indians, who fled as if through fear, drawing the eager, incautious English into a place convenient to be surrounded by five hundred savages, who sprang forth and destroyed them. The most of this English force of about sixty men were slain; but a few of them were left alive to be tortured. Capt. Broclebank and Lieut. Sharp, who had joined Wadsworth on the way, also *fell* in this battle.

In 1852 a monument was erected here by the State of Massachusetts and the town of Sudbury, at the grave of the heroes of that bloody battle of long, long ago.

It will be remembered that Mary Rowlandson all this time had been a captive among Philip's forces. In her twentieth chapter and in her fourteenth month of captivity at this Sudbury onset, she says, —

"It was their usual manner to remove when they had done any mischief, lest they should be found out; and so they did at this time. We went about three or four miles; and there they built a great wigwam, big enough to hold an hundred Indians; which they did in preparation to a great day of dancing.

"They would now say among themselves, that the governor would be so angry for his *loss* at SUDBURY, that he would send no more about the captives, which made me grieve and tremble."

It was not long after this, however, before from the authorities a proposition came for her redemption; and then she says,—

"Philip called me to him, asked me what I would give him to tell me some good news and to speak a good word for me that I might go home to-morrow.

"I told him I could not tell what to give him, and asked him what he would have. He said, 'Two coats, and twenty shillings in money, half a bushel of seed-corn, and some tobacco.' I thanked him."

Soon this lady obtained a release, and returned home. Afterwards she travelled eastward to Newbury, Portsmouth, and other places; and with her the husband preached on the way; and finally they obtained the deliverance of their son and daughter from captivity.

Yet, sad to relate, this same husband, the Rev. Joseph Rowlandson, in 1697 was seized and murdered by the Indians.

CHAPTER XVI.

NEW LONDON, NORWICH, STONINGTON.

The Ten Expeditions. — Two Hundred and Twenty-nine Indians taken and slain. — Thirty killed on the Retreat from Narragansett. — Seventy-six slain by Dennison's Force. — Invasion of *Scituate, Bridgewater,* and *Taunton.* — Expedition to *Swansey.* — Assault upon *Bridgewater.* — Its Neighborhood. — Invasion of Groton. — Two Eruptions. — Expeditions there from Boston and Watertown. — Strategy in their Attack, and of the Black Sheep. — One-Eyed John. — His Threats. — His Capture and Execution. — Indian Spies. — Attack on Northampton. — Massachusetts Colonial Expedition. — Murder on the Highway. — Expedition from Sudbury. — Tribes begin to relent and vanish. — Depredations in many Places. — *Wamesit* Indians become Hostile. — Trespass on *Chelmsford* and *Woburn.* — Invasion of Concord, Mass. — Depredations at *Haverhill* and *Bradford.* — Expedition from Boston. — A Surprise on a Bear-Hunt. — Skulking Parties Numerous. — Indians at Wachusett Hills. — Expedition from *Hadley, Hatfield,* and *Northampton.* — Expedition by Twenty-five Men of Hadley. — Henchman at Brookfield. — Connecticut Expedition. — Another Assault on Hadley. — Tribes incline to surrender. — Proclamation to call them in. — Connecticut Expedition. — Battle at Warwick Neck.

IN the preceding chapter we have learned how Capt. Dennison's force had been made up, and of his success in his expedition; and now we come to a time when the inhabitants of New London, Norwich, and Stonington voluntarily enlisted under *Major Palmer,*

Capt. Geo. Dennison, and *Capt. Avery*, and during the year 1676 advanced, first and last, on ten expeditions against the tribes. On those several occasions they killed and took of the enemy in all two hundred and twenty-nine. In this they were assisted by small parties from the Pequots, Mohegans, and Narragansetts.

It may be noted, that a part of this force, on the 19th of December, 1675, during their long march after the fight in the Narragansett swamp, took thirty Indians; and sixteen others with fifty guns at other times not above reckoned.

After this it appears Dennison's force killed and took seventy-six Indians, among whom were two Narragansett sachems, and at the same time obtained a hundred and sixty bushels of corn.

Subsequent to this, but little damage was done by the Indians in Plymouth County, except in depredation, upon houses and barns.

SCITUATE AND SWANSEY.

On the 20th of April, fifty Indians burnt nineteen houses and barns at Scituate, and on the 8th of May seventeen houses in *Bridgewater;* and four of the inhabitants of *Taunton* were killed while at work in a field.

On June 20, 1676, an order from Gov. Winslow

directed the raising of twenty men well armed, and furnished with horses, to advance immediately to the relief of Swansey. Seventeen were sent away that night. On the 21st they were further directed by Capt. *Bradford* to advance to Bourne's garrison twelve miles away, to assist in the defence of the seventy inmates there. Six men from this garrison, while out on that day without a proper military protective force, were slain. On the following week fifteen of the force above named, while out in search of horses, discovering a party of Indians, fired at them; but they escaped, save one or two, afterwards found dead.

BRIDGEWATER.

On the 9th of May, Tisquagen, with three hundred warriors, made an assault upon *Bridgewater*, burnt an out-house and barn, rifled several houses, and committed other trespasses, particularly at the east end of the town. Another invasion was afterwards made; and thirteen dwelling-houses were destroyed in and about that neighborhood; and some barns and cattle were also lost.

Then, on the 18th and 19th of July, the English sent a military force to this same town, — to follow in pursuit of the tribes; and, advancing, they took sixteen of them. Some of the Bay Indians, under Capt. Brattle, also volunteered in the pursuit.

The conflicts at this date were not confined to Plymouth County. They extended almost everywhere. Trouble existed in the midst of the inland plantations, as well as all along the sea-coast; and the Colonies were at work by forces of considerable strength almost everywhere, in defence of the New-England settlements.

ATTACK UPON GROTON.

The town of Groton being invaded on the 2d of March, 1676, by the tribes of Philip, the news of it at once reached Boston; and on the following day *Major Willard* with seventy horsemen advanced from there, and forty foot-soldiers from *Watertown.* But the Indians, having burned all the houses in town save the four garrisons, the meeting-house among the rest being consumed, had all made a safe retreat to parts unknown.

CAPT. SILL AT GROTON.

Capt. Sill was also sent there to take away the inhabitants of Groton, their furniture, &c.; for which purpose some sixty carts were used, making a trail on the road, of some two miles in length.

While passing they were fired upon by the Indians in an ambush from the front, and two of the men were killed; the Indians being, as was supposed, a part of the same gang who the day before had burned some part of Chelmsford.

Chelmsford, being soon afterwards deserted, was destroyed by the enemy.

GROTON AGAIN.

This town was surprised as follows: —

The Indians came in on the night of the 2d of March, rifled seven or eight houses, and carried off some cattle.

On the 9th, about ten in the morning, a number of Indians, who had been secretly lurking about there, laid an ambush for two teams which had been driven from the garrison to bring in some hay; they were attended by four men, two of whom at sight of the Indians escaped. The other two being assailed, the one was killed, and left in a naked, mangled condition; and the other was carried away captive. He, however, finally escaped from them, and found shelter in the garrison at Lancaster.

Groton was again assailed by four hundred Indians on the 13th of March, 1676. The town had been previously startled by news of the attack upon Lancaster, and had concentrated its inhabitants into five garrisons, four of which were so near together as to afford assistance to one another; and between these the cattle were kept belonging to the various families. But the cattle at this time had been sent into the pastures, perhaps to obtain browse from the shrubbery.

In the night-time the Indians had secreted themselves in various places. Two of them at first made their appearance near one of the garrisons. The town did not anticipate such an advent. The day before they had searched the wilderness for many miles, finding none, and now were engaged in their usual business, — some feeding their cattle, some procuring fire-wood, and others doing other various things.

At sight of the two Indians an alarm was given; at which the men came forth from the *first* garrison, and some from the *second*, which were eight or nine rods apart, and started in pursuit of the two Indians, who remained stationary in the distance. But, when our men reached the brow of a hill, the Indians from an ambush fired upon, and routed them. One was slain, and three were wounded.

At the same time another squad had risen, and came in upon the back side of one of the garrisons so deserted of men, and pulled down the palisadoes. But the women and children had escaped from there to the stronger garrison, to which the soldiers also retreated; which left the first garrison to the mercy of the invaders, who consumed the most of the day in securing the spoils, which consisted mostly of corn and household materials. They fired upon the other garrison, and took a few cattle.

From the sound of the first volley, smoke ascended from nearly all parts of the town at once.

In the afternoon an old Indian came down the street, as if decrepit, with a black sheep upon his back. They made shots at him in the distance, and sallied forth to capture him, but, discovering an ambush, retreated; and the savage and his black sheep vanished from their sight. That night some of them remained in the deserted garrison, others in an adjacent valley, making the night hideous.

ONE-EYED JOHN.

Next morning they fired two or three volleys at the defended garrison, and then marched off, fearing perhaps that they might be overtaken by a strong force from abroad.

About forty dwelling-houses of the town were burned; and the head of the man slain was piked upon a pole, as well as the heads of others previously slain.

Before leaving the place, ONE-EYED JOHN, who led in this attack, announced his threats to Capt.

Parker then in the garrison, saying they had burned Lancaster and *Medfield*, and that next time they would burn *Chelmsford, Concord, Watertown, Cambridge, Charlestown, Roxbury*, and *Boston ;* adding in his own dialect, " *What me will, me will do.*"

THE RESULT.

Notwithstanding this braggadocio, the sagamore did not live to see his purpose entirely fulfilled.

Indeed, it was not long before these fellows, *One-Eyed John*, *Sagamore Sam*, and old Jethro, were all on the march to Boston, with halters about their necks, to be hanged.

Afterwards, April 17, Capt. Sill being appointed to keep the garrison at Groton, some Indians coming there and drawing near to the house, supposing it to have been deserted, the captain fired at them, killing three, — two at one shot.

INDIAN SPIES.

The Colonists, during this war of King Philip, found it very difficult to ascertain the precise localities of Philip's force. Hence, during the winter of 1675–6, they sent two Christian Indians, *James* and *Job*, through the woods into the Nipmuck and Narragansett countries as spies; who " having free liberty of discourse with them," and, in the end to obtain and bring information, performed at least favorable service to the English.

NORTHAMPTON.

On the 24th of March, 1676, the Indians made an assault upon Northampton, and broke through the fortification of palisadoes set up around it, but were repulsed after they had killed four men and two women, and destroyed four or five dwelling-houses.

A COLONIAL EXPEDITION.

In the beginning of March, Major Savage, commander of new forces, was sent out, to be joined by such as might be raised by the Connecticut Colony, with instructions to search for Indians at and about Wachusett Hill. But, on their arrival there, the Indians were somewhere else. The English, however, fell in with a few stragglers, slew some, took others, to the number of sixteen, and then turned back to the relief of Hadley and Northampton.

MURDER ON THE HIGHWAY.

About this time, March 26, sabbath, some families at Long Meadow, near Springfield, attending church under an escort of soldiers, on their return home, riding with women behind them, some, with children in their arms, fell in the rear of the rest of the company, and were fired upon from an ambush. Two of them were killed, and others wounded.

SUDBURY.

The inhabitants of this town, many of them on the 27th of March, 1676, started for the woods *in the night.* Towards morning they discovered the tribes, three hundred of them lying by their fires (within half a mile of a garrison-house), upon which forty of their townsmen fired upon them several times, wounded thirty, fourteen of which died then or soon afterwards.

THEY VANISH.

After this the tribes began to scatter; yet they were in fragment parties. We hear of their depredations at *Weymouth* and at *Billerica* (where *Timothy Farrer* was killed), at *Quaboag,* at *Braintree,* at Wrentham, and many other places all over the country; yet their main forces were lurking in the woods. Some of them were between the towns of Brookfield and Marlborough, and the Connecticut River.

They killed several persons, ten or twelve residents of Concord, Mass., who had marched to assist their Sudbury neighbors. On their journey back towards the garrison-house, they were all waylaid, killed, or taken.

Then again at Plymouth they burned eleven dwelling-houses and five barns. Our scouting parties, falling in upon a tribe of them, killed several; but within a few days seven houses and two barns were consumed in the same town.

By the ill-advised acts of some of the English, "*another sort of Indians*" from *Wamesit* (Lowell) had fired guns to the killing of some and wounding of others at *Chelmsford*, and also at *Woburn*. These, after winter was over, becoming enemies, set fire to Mr. Falkner's house in Andover, wounded one *Roger Marks*, and killed his horse; and at Shawshine, near it, on March 10, burned down houses; May 8, killed one, and carried away captive another, sons of George Abbott; killed some cattle on their way, cutting out their tongues, and passing away, being shot at from a garrison. Savages visited Thomas Fames of Sudbury, killed his wife, carried away his children, leaving his house in ashes. Two men were killed.

CONCORD, MASS.

In February, 1675, two boys, Isaac and Jacob Eames and a maid, were taken captives.

This maid, fifteen years of age, escaped from them; and in the May following, one of the captive boys, thirty miles through the woods alone, escaped, and returned home upon a horse which the Indians had stolen at Lancaster.

Also at Concord, on March 10, two men were killed; and on March 18, the hostile Indians, on the north side of the river

WAMESIT,

burned down three or four houses of Edward Colburn; and afterwards, April 15, about forty of them pursuing Colburn, Samuel Varnham and sons, shot at them, killing two of the sons, and at the same time burned fourteen dwelling-houses.

On May 3, after killing a man at Haverhill on the Merrimack, a party of them crossed over to Bradford, killed Thomas Kimball, and carried away his wife and five children into captivity, forty miles into the woods.

AN EXPEDITION.

To suppress these deadly eruptions, on April 27, 1676, the government at Boston started several fresh companies of soldiers, and sent them forth to range the woods under the command of Capts. Sill, Cutter, and Holbrook. The horse companies were commanded by Capts. Brattle, Prentice, and Henchman.

On the 6th of May, 1676, our Natick allied scout

discovered a party of the enemy, who were pursuing a bear, and, not perceiving the scout to be otherwise than friends, were easily pursued. Our horsemen fell in upon them, killing and taking sixteen.

It was charged, that the untimely sounding of a trumpet in the chase operated as a disadvantage to the English, and the tribes escaped.

After returning to their headquarters at Medford, although they could discover their fires at night in great numbers, yet the tribes had become too far scattered ever afterwards to be reached in any considerable numbers. English soldiers fell sick, and were temporarily dismissed on the 10th of May of that year.

But to return. The great body of Philip's men in the early spring, as we have seen, tended towards Plymouth; yet there were scattering skulking parties all about.

At Rehoboth a party went out, and killed ten or twelve. At *Springfield* Capt. Holyoke and his men entered the woods with ten or twelve resolute men, and near the great river killed three, and wounded another.

Previously, Oct. 5, 1675, about three hundred Indians made an attack on this town, killed three men and one woman, and reduced to ashes thirty dwelling-houses and twenty-five barns.

On the beginning of April, 1676, three of the Hadley men, at work under a guard of soldiers, Deacon Goodman being one of them, were slain. Two others, who had ventured to wander away from the guard, were also killed.

The largest company of Indians in this neighborhood were now in and about Wachusett Hills. They had been disappointed of their corn in the loss of Canonchet: yet they were now taking advantage of the fishing-season.

HADLEY, HATFIELD, NORTHAMPTON.

These towns now unite in revenge for the loss of life, of houses, and cattle, and, to rid the country of its common enemy, May 18, 1676, raised a hundred and fifty men, marched silently at dead of night, surprised the drowsy tribes at their wigwams in the woods.

Arriving there, they dismounted, fired into their wigwams, frightened them (killing some), drove others into the stream, by which many of them were borne down over the fall with the current, some perishing in the waters; others, hugging the shore, were killed there; and some, seeking the canoes, being shot or overset in the stream, sunk, and slept their last sleep. Capt. Holyoke killed five, young and old, with his own hand.

At the onset upon them, the Indians exclaimed, "*Mohawks!* THE MOHAWKS!" Their slain were nearly three hundred.

But the tribes, rallying after them on their retreat, fell upon their horse-guards, fired upon them in the rear; so that, on their return, thirty-eight men were missing. Holyoke's horse was killed. He was a valiant leader.

HADLEY'S TWENTY-FIVE YOUNG MEN.

These came forth May 30, 1676, crossed the river, and down upon a tribe which had been attacking their garrison, burning houses, and killing and driving away their cattle and sheep in large numbers; fired upon them, killing five or six on their flight far away.

This same force by the council at Boston was rallied again, with instructions to drive out the enemy from their fishing-places, from the woods, and from the plantations.

And then, on May 30, 1676, Henchman leading, advanced to *Brookfield*, intending to join others from the Hartford Colony, with *Tom Doublet* to trace out the Indian trails, overtook the enemy fishing in *Weshacom* Ponds, killed seven, and captured twenty-nine, mostly women and children. Previously, at Northfield, September, 1675, "Nine or ten persons were killed in the woods; and, on the day following this massacre, Capt. Richard Beers of Watertown, with thirty-six men, fell into an ambuscade, and several of them were slain. Retreating to Beers's Mountain, fought on the way; and only sixteen of Beers's company escaped. The conflict was severe. The heads of some of the English dead were elevated on poles: one of them was suspended by a chain from the limb of a tree. The fort there and the houses were destroyed."

BATTLE AT PAWTUCKET.

On Sunday, the 26th of March, 1676, a battle was sought by Capt. Pierce and his seventy men, twenty of whom were Indians. They fell in with the tribes at Pawtucket River, near Pawtucket Falls. The Indians led by Nanuntenoo decoyed them into an ambuscade, and surrounded them with a force of three hundred. Pierce and fifty-seven of his men were slain. The Indian loss was estimated at a hundred and forty.

NORTHFIELD (SQUAKEAG).

As it happened, Henchman did not meet the Hartford force until a week afterwards, who joined him at Hadley. The two forces then advanced towards *Squakeag*, arrived at Deerfield, encountered a severe storm, damaging their ammunition; yet seized and secured many stolen goods, and a quantity of fish from the enemy; found some places where depredations and murders had been committed; but from thence, supposing the tribes to have gone towards Plymouth, they returned home.

CAPT. HENCHMAN SAYS:

"Our scouts brought intelligence that the Indians were in continual motion, some towards Narragansett, some towards Wachusett, lying not above one night in a place. The twenty-seven scouts brought in two squaws, a boy, and a girl, giving an account of five slain. Yesterday they brought in an old fellow, brother of a sachem, six squaws, and children, having killed five men and wounded others. Eleven persons we had in all, two of whom by council we put to death."

DEDHAM AND SEACONK.

On their return, this force was ordered from Sudbury by the governor of Plymouth to Dedham, and so to Seakonk (Rehoboth), to join Bradford in pursuit of Philip, who, with his many hundreds, was besetting the plantations in that neighborhood, and whither, not long before, "Capt. Brattle with a troop of horse, and Capt. Mosely with a company of foot, were sent up from Boston to pursue them, now flocking in great numbers for the woods."

Here Hezekiah Willet of Swansey had been barbarously slain; and to these forces at their arrival a negro slave, escaping from their captivity, reported that Philip was preparing to attack *Taunton*, and that his army had slain twenty cattle over night, and that nothing was left of them in the morning.

Next, Major Talcot, advancing to meet our forces at Quaboag (Brookfield), as they came there from Norwich, surprised a gang of Indians, took fifty-one, nineteen being slain. Two other expeditions volunteered from New London, Stonington, and Norwich, having been left to guard that locality. The one under Talcot disposed of about thirty of the enemy, the most of whom were slain.

The other force killed and took forty-five, mostly women and children; yet (as the minister had it) they were "*serpents of the same brood.*"

HADLEY (POCUNTUCK).

The next day the Indians assaulted Hadley with seven hundred warriors, at six o'clock in the morning. But the Connecticut forces, made up of English, Pequots, Mohegans, and other friendly Indians, five hundred in all, being quartered near, were soon on hand. The Indians, leaving the town, had set it on fire. They fired, and killed three of the English, but made their escape.

The 29th of July, 1676, was observed as a day of thanksgiving. A body of Indians had been lurking about the Connecticut all the spring, suffering for food and of diseases; and, discouraged at losses, began to fall out with Philip, and resolved that the tribes might separate, and desired to return to their several homes; and that Philip and the Narragansetts might do the same. The Nipmucks and River Indians beat *westward;* others *northward,* towards Penacook on the Merrimack; and Philip's crew and the Narragansetts were left to drift in another direction, amid the swamps towards Mount Hope.

The tribes, in sight of events as of late they had drifted, began to despair at the impending fate of their race and of themselves.

The government at Boston, understanding this matter, published a

DECLARATION.

"*That whatsoever Indians should, within fourteen days next ensuing, come in to the English, might hope for mercy.*"

Thereupon *James* the printer came in, affirming, with others who came with him, that *more of his race had died* since the war by diseases than by the sword. And soon two hundred more came in.

SQUAW SACHEM OF SEACONET.

This squaw, allied to Philip as she had been, sent three messengers to the governor of Plymouth, suing for life and liberty, promising submission as above; but, before her messengers returned, the English troops came upon her. She submitted herself to Major Bradford, together with her ninety followers; and then, recklessly and without mercy, they were all murdered.

CONNECTICUT FORCES AT WARWICK NECK.

These, under Major Talcot and Capts. Dennison and Newbury, on the 2d of July, 1676, pursuing Philip, discovered a large force near Mount Hope in a swamp. They divided their forces in three divisions, and made a charge with Englishmen and Indians on all sides of the fort at once, by which all the tribes were either killed or put to flight. A hundred were killed at the outset, and the fugitives by both horse and foot, until the whole were either slain or taken prisoners. Two or three of the Mohegans and Pequots were wounded: none of the English were injured in the slaughter and capture of nearly three thousand savages, young and old.

Among these was the old squaw of Narragansett, commonly called the Old Queen.

CHAPTER XVII.

TRIBES IN TROUBLE.

War and Winter weakens them. — They murmur in Despair. — Treachery of their own Race. — They begin to distrust Philip. — Incline to abandon his Cause. — Two Hundred surrender. — Three Hundred led by Six Sachems come in. — Capts. Mosely, Battles, and Bradford Forces advance towards Mount Hope. — Philip escapes to Pocasset. — A Chief Sachem surrenders with Forty Attendants. — Also Sagamore John with a Hundred and Eighty. — Philip is slain. — Garrison-Houses. — An Epic. — An Expedition to Pasco Bay. — Depredations and Murders along the Piscataqua. — An Attack on the Upper Garrison at Salmon Falls. — Major Waldron sends a Team and Twenty Men to obtain the Dead. — The Men are attacked from an Ambush. — Capt. Plaisted killed. — Attacks at Kittery, Cocheco, and other Places. — Number slain.

THE winter of 1675–76 had fallen heavily upon them. From Mount Hope, Philip's main force had been routed, but with terrible loss to the English, in the beginning of the cold storms. Since then, the slaughter which his tribes had shared; their constant exposures to the inclemencies of winter, by the change of place from day to day, with their wives and little ones; and the devastating inroads which dire disease had made upon them, — overwhelmed their hearts with crushing despair and discontent.

281

And now, in early spring, their remnant tribes, as they perceived, were being beset with crushing forces not only by the English, but, most wicked of all, by the treachery from tribes of their own ancient race, to wit, the faithless Pequots, Mohegans, and others.

No wonder, then, that the hand of fate is now "seen writing upon the wall" this awful result, — that Philip's last great battle for the native freedom of an ancient race of red men had been fought, and is already lost; that Philip himself is to die speedily; that his tribes, *many more* of them, are yet to perish by the sword; that the others are to be driven beyond the deep seas, or farther and farther into the dark wilderness, there to be lost and forgotten.

In sight of all this, no wonder that Philip's warriors, for the sake of their women and children at least, should begin to throw down their weapons of war, and submit, however ingloriously, to the terms proposed by their faithless foes.

Next, then, two hundred of them, from within the Plymouth jurisdiction, through famine and fear came in, and submitted themselves to the government there; some of whom, to obtain favor, were, as induced, turned about, and were made to co-operate against Philip and his then trembling tribes.

And then five or six sachems from Cape Cod, with three hundred Indian attendants, came in and surrendered.

On the next day, July 7, 1676, the English with some Christian Indians, invading the woods not far from Dedham, killed *seven*, one of whom was a Narragansett sachem.

News then came that some of the Indians had fled to Albany, N.Y., and were obtaining ammunition there, on the pretext that Philip's war had come to an end.

On the 11th of July, Philip's whole remaining force made an attempt to destroy *Taunton;* but the plot, being seasonably discovered, was defeated. After the firing of two houses they were repulsed, and fled.

Up to the 22d of July, Capts. Mosely, Battles, and Bradford, operating from Concord, Mass., in and around the swamps of Mount Hope, had slain and taken of their enemies about a hundred and fifty.

It was feared Philip would now return to the Nipmuck country; and English horsemen were sent to guard the passage thither, as it led out from Mount Hope. They followed him into the swamps, oftentimes lodged near to him; always a little too late, yet sometimes found his camp-fires yet burning, his kettles still boiling over them, and his dead from sickness and war still unburied.

Philip, at length, with his followers much reduced, by means of a raft made his escape from the Metapoiset woods, over an arm of the sea on to another neck of land on the Pocasset side.

Capt. Church, commander of the Plymouth Colony, with eighteen Englishmen and twenty-two Indians, had long been on the chase of Philip, during which time he had slain seventy-six men from the faltering followers of Philip.

Philip's squaw was afterwards taken, one of his chief councillors also.

A chief sachem at Pocasset, and forty Indians, came in also, seeking life and liberty.

Other Indians heard of near Dedham, as being nearly in a state of starvation, were pursued by twenty-six of the English, and nine or ten Christian Indians, who took fifty prisoners without loss to the English, together with great quantities of wampum and powder; and they slew *Pomham*, one of the most valiant sachems of the ten commanders of the Narragansetts.

SAGAMORE JOHN.

This sachem, July 27, came in before the council at Boston, bringing with him a hundred and eighty warriors, their wives and children, all of whom surrendered.

On the 31st of July a party went forth from Bridgewater in search for Philip and his followers, and, coming near, killed some of them, among whom was Philip's uncle, who, standing by his side, was shot down; but Philip escaped, having previously shaved his hair off so as not to be known.

On the 6th of August, twenty volunteers, led by an Indian fresh from Philip, seized the whole party of twenty-six Indians except the squaw sachem, who escaped from them, but jumping into the river was drowned. It is a shameful truth, they cut off her head, and set it upon a pole in Taunton, at the sight of which the dusky prisoners, as they passed, were overwhelmed with grief, and passed on with wailings and heart-rending despair.

An Indian now came in, who, reporting Philip as having returned to Mount Hope, offered to pilot any force that would undertake to follow him. And then a company led by Capt. Church, part English and part Indians, advancing to the great swamp and surrounding it, Philip was discovered passing out from it. Church aimed to shoot him, but the gun missed fire: thereupon Alderman Seaconet, an Indian of his own nation, at the same moment, being with Church, fired; and Philip fell dead, shot through the heart. On the same day, Aug. 12, 1676, five of his strong men fell also. And here ended forever the last great struggle that foreshadowed the final fate of the red man on this continent.

Let us turn, that we may glance for moment at the landscape. New England even now is but little else than a wilderness. That wilderness is still inhabited by remnant, distracted tribes; some at present peaceful, some hostile, afflicted of painful scars, disease, and death; and some of these seeking refuge within the lines of neutral tribes; and some wandering afar off in quest of life and liberty in the far distance. Yet every wigwam in the woods, as well as every lonely cot, house, or hamlet in New England, is doomed to dread fear and consternation. At noonday, at midnight, consternation is now entailed upon all the generations of New England for the seventy tardy years now next to come. Philip is dead: but the embers in his ashes are still burning; and the war between the two races, under their surroundings, as a matter of course, could never die out but in the destruction or exit of the one or the other. Dread fear pervaded all. Garrison-houses were then standing in all the hamlets, and even in the more scattered neighborhoods. They must necessarily abound in New England, must remain; and they did remain.

Even now, after the lapse of two hundred years, some of those old structures, made mostly of logs, erected during the Indian wars, may be traced. They ought to be preserved forever. One of those

Deserted now within without,
  Alone aloof, upon a hill,
And rumor rife hath come about
That in those port-holes, looking out,
  The midnight spectre lingers still.

garrisons, with its terrible lessons, stood near the home of my boyhood. Not many years since, passing that way, I visited it at eve; met departed spirits, real or otherwise; and published as follows a conversation then had at

THE OLD GARRISON-HOUSE.

TALK WITH A GHOST,

At my native Barrington, N.H., Saturday Eve,
Oct. 20, 1866.

THEY'RE sacred now,— these walls of wood.
   Ah! what can bear comparison;'
From age to age they've nobly stood:
They've braved the conflict, storm, and flood,
   Of the olden time a garrison.

Deserted now within, without;
   Alone, aloof, upon a hill;
And rumor rife hath come about,
That, "in those port-holes looking out,
   The midnight spectre lingers still."

And now, ye ghosts, if ghost there be,
   Speak! speak, and tell us of the strife,
When you had life and limbs as we;
When panting Pilgrims had to flee
   The tomahawk and scalping-knife;

When, in that boundless forest wild,
   At sound of war-whoop from afar,
How anxious up and down ye filed,
And hewed the logs, and upward piled
   This fortress rude; how, in dread **war,** —

At humble huts far scattered wide,
   To toil ye gave the weary day,
Then, driven here at eventide,
The child and mother side by side,
   Fast winding through the thorny way.

Unheeded then the beasts of prey;
   The prowl of wolf no terrors brought,
Nor rancorous reptiles in the way:
The Pilgrim heart knew no dismay
   Save what the knife and fagot taught.

Within these doors, then bolted fast,
   Say, what of dreams? Pray speak, **and tell**
How oft, amid the tempest blast,
Ye heard the rattling arrows cast,
   The midnight gun, the savage yell.

What tearful thought, and what the **care,**
   That moved the matrons and the men
To hug sweet infants cradled there,
To guard the household, and to share
   The dangers dread impending then.

And what, when tedious years had passed,
    To mourn thy many kindred slain;
Here then, at peace, ye lived at last;
Yet did the sands of life fall fast,
    And dust to dust return again.

How then the spirit wafted high
    From lifeless nature 'neath the ground:
Then from the portals of the sky,
'Mid clouds of night, — oh! tell us why
    In this old fort ye still are found?

Whence are thy joys eternal bright? —
    As if ye had no faltering fear,
No sad bereavements, pain nor blight
Nor care, to cramp that calm delight
    Foretold of faith in such career.

Ye've seen the tribes that roamed of yore
    From Lovwell's Lake to the Falls of Berwick,
Or down Cocheco's woodland shore
Where *Wat-che-no-it* [1] dipped his oar,
    At Dover old, or Squanomegonic.

Since then, as now, to the market town,
    From the hills afar, yet blue and bland,
'Mid summer's heat or winter's frown,
How settlers teamed their treasures down,
    Proud in the products of the land.

Note 1. Wat-che-no-it was one of the chiefs who conveyed land-titles in New Hampshire.

Their footprints firm are on the plain
   'Mid blighting frost or blooming health,
Where varied life of joy and pain
Hath learned of Mother Earth how vain
   Is pride or fame or sordid wealth.

Then, tell me true, if well ye may, —
   Since tribe and pilgrim hither met, —
How generations lived their day,
How each in turn have passed away,
   But where — oh! where — untold as yet.

Of all that host some knowledge lend,
   That from the world the years have hurried:
Say, what of Waldron? — what his end?
Old " Mi-an-to-ni-mo "[2] his friend,
   And " Mossup,[3] slain yet kindly buried."

Say if, amid that spirit-sphere,
   Ye have full knowledge freely given,
Why thus withhold from mortals here
The glories grand, forever dear
   To thee and thine, of death and heaven?

NOTE 2. Mi-an-to-ni-mo was a chief, said to have been friendly, tall, and cunning.

NOTE 3. Mossup, a brother of Mi-an-to-ni-mo, was killed by the Mohawks, about twenty miles above the Piscataqua, and was buried by Major Waldron.

THE REPLY.

The spectre, listening, seemed to move,
    Half hidden still within the wall;
In garb of light and looks of love,
With cadence strange, as from above,
    Made answer thus, the one for all: —

"Why thus should men make search to know
    Their final fate forever hidden?
Beyond the world of weal and woe
Your vision finite ne'er can go.
    Enough for man it is forbidden.

"What truth in Abraham ye trace,
    And what of Israel's tribes are told,
What Bunyan wrote of the pilgrim race,
Ye well may know, and grow in grace,
    As the fathers faithful did of old.

"Enough! and why should we disclose
    The purpose grand ordained above,
Betray the trust that Heaven bestows,
And tempt the world from calm repose,
    Its tranquil life, and truthful love?

"Then banish care! Earth can but see,
    Far in the cloud, a guardian hand;
Nor heed the storm, alike as we,
True mariners upon the sea:
    Ye'll find the pilgrim's promised land."

The night-damp dark in curtains fell;
  Hushed were the hills and valleys green:
I bent my footstep down the dell;
A voice there whispered, "All is well;"
  And nothing more was said or seen.

JOHN.

In the winter which followed the downfall of Philip, under the Boston proclamation previously made, JOHN, a Nipmuck sachem, with many others, came in, and were protected of their lives; and Hubbard, who lived and wrote at that day, says, —

> "Yet did that treacherous villain make an escape this winter from Capt. Prentice's house, under whose charge he was put about Cambridge village, and with twenty more fled away into the woods to shift for himself, with the rest of his bloody companions. They were pursued, but had gone too fast and too far to be overtaken."

EFFICACY OF PRAYER.

Mr. Hubbard, who was a clergyman as well as historian, now at this date complaining of the pagan propensities of UNCAS, the Mohegan chief, says substantially that Parson "Fiske of Norwich," in the terrible drought of that summer, had prayed constantly and fervently for rain, but in vain; that the English were left to pray "*without any motion from the Indians;*" and that the drought long remained upon them; but that at length, by reason of dearth, Uncas and his tribes were induced to come in and join in the prayers, at which dense clouds at once covered the earth; a rain-storm followed; and that " the river rose more than two feet in height that night."

FIRST PLANTATIONS.

The first place taken and possessed in the East as a plantation was on the Sagadahock (Kennebeck); and in that neighborhood there was no serious trouble with the tribes until Philip's war; and even then the principal mischief was made by the Androscoggins. But westward of that locality, at Sturgeon Creek, at Salmon Falls, Cocheco (Dover), at Greenland, Lampre River, Exeter, and Swamscot, plantations were early commenced; and all of them suffered in 1675-6, and more or less during most of the Indian wars. In the East, some of the plantations were commenced as early as 1606, contemporaneously with the like commencements in Virginia.

At the inception of Philip's war, the Indians all through New England had been aroused; and in the East, although they had been peaceful from the beginning, they began to see force and justice in Philip's cause. And the tribes at Casco and Androscoggin, at Piscataqua, at Wamesit, being pinched with hunger and cold, had during the first winter risen against the

English, yet in the early spring and summer returned apparently to their good faith, and delivered up their English prisoners; yet in many instances, as in the case of *Simon* and *Andrew* in their violence at Bradford and *Haverhill*, returned their prisoners to Major Waldron at Dover, but soon afterwards joined the Kennebecks and Androscoggins in committing murders in that region.

By reason of these general uprisings, a meeting was held at the house of Capt. Pattishals near the Kennebeck; and an expedition was sent up that river to test the fidelity of the Indians. They succeeded in obtaining some arms and ammunition, and a promise of beaver-skins; the Indians, at the time, yielded to them for the sake of peace. Upon the condition if they cause no eruption, their arms, &c., were to be returned to them.

Robinhood then invited the tribes to a great dance, and sung songs attended with great applause, to evince a lively determination on their part to fulfil their agreement to keep the peace; yet many of them broke their covenants with the English, to their own injury as well as to that of their enemies. They at first assaulted the house of Mr. Purchase, took his liquor and ammunition, killed calves and sheep; but contented themselves, for the most part, with what they could eat and carry away.

Thereupon twenty-five Englishmen passed up Casco Bay in a sloop and two boats, to obtain Indian corn; and near Androscoggin River, they heard a knocking in and about the houses, and saw two Indians, who took towards the water. The English in pursuit killed one: the other escaped in a canoe.

CASCO.

And then at *Casco Bay* a tribe entered the house of Mr. Wakely, murdered him, his wife, his son, and daughter-in-law, and her three children.

Soon after, Sept. 18, 1676, the houses of Capt. Bonithon and Major Phelps were assaulted by about forty Indians, the one on the east and the other on the west side of the *Saco River*, and were set on fire; but the English rallied upon them, shot at them from from all quarters, wounded the leader of the gang, which caused them to " take leg-bail " for other more remote quarters. They killed several persons at Blue Point; surrounded a garrison having in it fifty persons, but none of the inmates were killed. Major Phelps was wounded; and his mills and other edifices were consumed. About the same time, five persons going up the Saco in a boat were all killed.

In September the tribes tended towards *Piscataqua*, and committed violence along that river, burnt the houses of the two Chesleys at Oyster River, killed two men on board a canoe there, carried away a young man and an old Irishman from Exeter, killed Goodman Robinson of Exeter, while on the road to Hampton. He and son were waylaid by *John Sampson* Cromwell, and *John Linde:* the son escaped, taking flight into the woods.

Then at Oyster River and Newechewanick great violence was done. At the latter place, on the 16th of October, 1676, a hundred Indians came in, and a half a mile above the upper garrison at Salmon Falls, amid other outrages, killed a man by the name of Tozer, and others, and took his son captive; from which a despatch was sent to Major Waldron as follows: —

SALMON FALLS, Oct 16, 1675.

MR. RICHARD WALDRON AND LIEUT. COFFIN,— These are to inform you that just now the Indians are engaging us with at least an hundred men, and have slain four of our men already,— Richard Tozer, James Barny, Isaac Bettes, and Tozer's son,— and burnt Benoni Hodsdan's house. Sirs, if ever you have any love for us and the country, now show yourselves with men to help us; or else we are all in great danger to be slain, unless our God wonderfully appears for our deliverance. They that cannot fight, let them pray. Nothing else; but I rest

Yours to serve you,

ROGER PLAISTED.
GEORGE BROUGHTON.

And thereupon Waldron sent twenty men with a yoke of oxen and cart to take away the dead bodies; and, obtaining a part of them, a hundred and fifty Indians in ambush fired upon them, frightened the cattle so that they ran back to the garrison carrying part of the dead, leaving the twenty men to fight it out on that line. Capt. Plaisted was killed: the others got back to the garrison, the Indians taking fright and running away. And the Indians advanced to Sturgeon Creek, to Kittery, to Cocheco, Exeter, Salmon Falls, Casco Bay, Wells: there and in other places were constantly depredations and murders; and in the conflicts in that direction between the Piscataqua and the Kennebeck, upwards of fifty of the English were slain, and nearly double that number on the part of the tribes. In this, from August to December, 1676, the Pugwakets of Saco, and Androscoggins of Pejepscot River, and some of the Pennacooks, took a part.

GARRISONS.

Besides the ordinary forts in these days, some of which have been named, there were garrisons or block-houses west, at George's, *Pemaquid, Richmond, Saco;* at *Fort Massachusetts, Pelham, Shirley, Colerain, Fall Town, Dinsdale, Northfield, Deerfield, Road Town, New Salem, Winchester, Lower Ashuelot,*

Upper Ashuelot, No. 4, *Pequiog,* Nashawog, Narragansett No. 2, Brown's, Leominister, Lunenburg, Townsend, Groton, New Ipswich, Salem, Canada, Souhegan West, New Hopkinton, Great Meadows, Contoocook, Rumford, Suncook.

In the eastern part, there were garrisons at Philip's Town, Berwick, Kittery, York, Wells, Arundel, Biddeford, Scarborough, Falmouth, Sacarappee, Narragansett No. 7 or Gorham's, New Marblehead, North Yarmouth, Topsham, Wiscasset or Unksechuset, Rice's of Charlemont, George Town or Arrowsick, Wiscasset, Sheepscot, Damariscotta, and East George's; being in all fifty-six, whereof fifteen are in another province, several in each of the many towns, and seven as we have seen in Penacook.

In the inland frontiers many of the out farm-houses had been reconstructed, having jets in their corners with loop-holes for small arms.

By means of garrisons erected almost everywhere, many lives were saved.

CHAPTER XVIII.

OTHER CONFLICTS EASTWARD.

Gen. Dennison in the East. — Tribes begin to disperse. — Canonicus is slain. — Warriors seek Concealment among the Neutral Tribes. — Four Hundred Indians surrounded and taken at Cocheco. — Some sold as Slaves, and Some hanged. — Tribes rebel at Casco and Falmouth. — Court at Boston appoint a Council of War. — Council obtain a Reconciliation. — War revives in the Summer. — Waldron pacifies the Piscataquas and Cascos. — Meets the Sachems on the Kennebeck. — Reasonings of the Squaw Sachem. — Massacres follow at *Hammond's*, at *Arrowsick*. — Settlers leave their Plantations. — Apply for Aid at Boston, but in Vain. — Indians again at Casco. — Again at Piscataqua. — At Cape Nedduck. — At Wells. — At Blackport. — The People Escape. — Tribes at Richmond Island. — Ransom from Boston stolen. — Mugg a Prisoner at Boston. — Remains as a Hostage. — More Forces sent. — Other Murders. — Forces reach Ossipee. — Indians have fled. — Mugg is shipped to obtain English Captives. — His Vessels return with Eleven Captives. — Forces sent under Major Waldron. — His Negotiation. — Returns to Boston. — War near Cocheco. — Alliance with Mohawks. — Mohawks at Dover. — Kill *Waldron's* Men. — Simon invades Portsmouth. — A Treaty of Peace. — Garrisons at Dover taken. — Major Waldron is slain. — Invasions.

DURING Philip's war, the governor and council of Massachusetts had enough upon their hands in the western towns; yet they had a care for the several counties eastward. That region of country was consigned more especially to the oversight of Major-Gen. D. Dennison, who raised soldiers; but, the winter setting in sharply in December, the snow, being deep, caused great delay. Yet the same winter's cold was bearing still more heavily upon the Indians, reducing them in some instances to starvation; and they began to sue for peace.

Their applications were made to Major Waldron of Dover, through whose mediation terms of peace were agreed upon, but which, as it seems, were not strictly fulfilled.

On the last of June, 1676, the Indians, by the terrible conflicts and exposures of the preceding year, were strangely dispersed and dispirited, every nation beginning to shift for itself. The faithful old Canonicus of the Narragansetts, distrusting the faith of the English, had been slain in the woods; but the life of his squaw was spared.

Some of the Lancaster warriors tried to obtain shelter beneath the wings of the peaceful Piscataquas. Some of them had mixed with the Penacooks, Pequawkets, and Ossipees, seeking thus to avoid danger. Thus at this time there was a strange admixture of the elements of peace and of hostility among nearly all the tribes.

Whereupon forces had been raised in Massachusetts, the commanders of which were Capts. Wm. Hawthorne and Joseph Still, to suppress insurrections. And these leaders joined Major Waldron and Capt. Frost of Kittery, and their men, in the scheme of seizing all the Indians that might be induced to assemble in Dover at their call.

Accordingly, on the 6th of September, 1676, Wonalancet with four hundred Indians had been induced to meet at Major Waldron's at Cocheco (Dover). They made a military parade, and, as was concerted, joined with the Indians in a sham-fight exercise. The Indians were put upon the dragropes of the artillery. The English, of course, were appointed to manage the guns; and a sham fight commenced. A gun exploded towards the Indians, at which the English infantry by a preconcerted manœuvre enclosed the Indians on all sides, secured and disarmed them all.

Hubbard says, "*They were handsomely surprised*, without the loss of any person's life," to the number of four hundred; by which device, after our forces had them all in their hands, they separated the peaceable from the perfidious. Wonalancet and the friendly Penacooks, Pequawkets, and Ossipees were dismissed to their homes, while two hundred or more, having taken part in the rebellion, were taken to Boston. Seven or eight of them were hanged for supposed murders; and the others were sent to other parts, and some of them at least sold into slavery.

Thus were they disposed of to prevent their union with the hostile eastern Indians.

By reason of certain friendly Indians at Cape Sable being taken under color of a legal warrant, but having fraudulently been sold into slavery, and the tribes having been deprived by the English of their ammunition, hunger and murmurings and animosity pervaded the eastern wigwams everywhere.

On the 11th of August, 1676, at *Casco*, a party of Indians commenced depredations, and carried away captive thirty persons, and burnt down their dwelling-houses, among whom was one Anthony Brackett of that place. Brackett's brother, offering to resist, was killed: the wife and five children were carried away prisoners. Thence they went to Corban's house, killed him, Humphrey Durham, and Benjamin Atwel, and thence onward to other places, killing others. So that from *Falmouth* and *Casco Bay*, thirty-four persons were carried into captivity.

The Indians up at Fort Totonic on the Kennebeck had done no wrong against the English: yet Capt. S. Davis and Capt. Lape of Boston thought fit to bring away all their powder and shot from their trading-house, and told them, if they would come down to their place they would supply them, and that if any of them refused to come down and deliver up their arms, the English would kill them.

MEETING OF THE SACHEMS.

These and other aggravating incidents caused so much trouble along the Kennebeck, that the General Court at Boston appointed a council of war there, and issued warrants to restrain all manner of persons from intermeddling with the Indians without further order, which within a few days should be had.

In the mean time the sachems met at Pemaquid; and, notwithstanding their many complaints made of the English on that river, they came to terms of peace, promised friendship as well as aid against the hostile Androscoggins.

A hard winter was over and gone; and then the English agent at Pemaquid attended a meeting of Indians in the East, praying that peace might be continued, at which the tribes were joyful, presents being passed in confirmation of a mutual good understanding. But when summer came the kidnapping of individual Indians by the English, which had previously transpired, of which we have spoken, came to light; and thereupon they again fell into a rage, making bitter complaints to Mr. Earthy the English agent, and others. They were told that their Indian friends thus kidnapped and transported should be returned to them. The Indians, thus outraged with mere promises which might never be fulfilled, were not easily appeased: for true it was in the summer and fall previously, they had been frightened away from their corn-plots; and, as it appeared also, the withholding of their powder and shot during the winter had tended to deprive them of their sustenance in that direction; and many of them in the winter's cold, almost starved, had died all along the Kennebeck.

Major Waldron of Dover had concluded a peace with the Piscataqua and Casco Indians; and now there was to be an attempt made to conclude a peace with the Androscoggins, including all the eastern tribes. Yet jealousies increased; and a meeting was sought as the agent had proposed.

Soon a notice came from Totonnock, desiring him to meet Squando and the "Amoscoggan" sachems there for a treaty.

Accordingly this agent, by advice from the council then sitting in Kennebeck, with others repaired thither. But at an English house on the way his suspicions were aroused by startling reports; yet our agent passed on, and met them in council.

Madokawando sat as chief; and Assimin, squaw, was their speaker.

Capt. Davis, speaking, told them in substance that the English were to *deal with them like men.* To which the squaw replied, —

HARD QUESTIONS PROPOUNDED. 305

"You did otherwise with us. When fourteen of our men came to treat with you, you set a guard over them, and took away their guns; and a second time you required our guns, and demanded us to come down unto you or you would kill us, which was the cause of our leaving our fort and corn to oui great loss."

MADOKAWANDO *appropriately asked what they were to do for the want of corn; what for the want of powder and shot; and whether the English would have them die, leave the country, or go entirely over to the French.*

The English messenger, on the other hand, among other things said, "You have admitted that the western tribes will not make peace. Now, if we sell you powder, and you give it to the western men, what do we do but to cut our own throats?"

Much was said, but no treaty was then had; and conflicts thereafterwards came to pass as formerly.

Hammond's house was invaded. On the 14th of August, 1676, on the island *Arrowsick*, early in the morning, the Indians hid themselves under the walls of its fort until the sentinel had gone from his place: then they followed him to the fort-gate, obtained a foot-hold at the port-holes, shot down all that were passing up and down within the walls of it, made themselves masters of it, and of all that was within it. Capt. Davis, within the fortification, was

26*

wounded there, but escaped. Two others, Capt. Lake and Major Clarke, also escaped ten or twelve miles away until they found some craft in which to get away; but, as it happened, that "good man" Lake was slaughtered before he reached a place of safety. He and Clarke were the owners, by purchase, of this island *Arrowsick* in the Kennebeck. Their fortifications there were extensive, with many convenient buildings for habitations and trade. The persons slain at Hammond's and Arrowsick were sixty-three.

From this all the white inhabitants along the Kennebeck and Sheepscot Rivers fled away. Help was sought at Boston. Some of the people tarried at Monhiggon, resolving there to stay to await some report from headquarters. Guarding themselves by a night watch of twenty-five men, they thus continued for a fortnight, within which time nearly all the houses in the country round about were consumed; yet Boston, having enough on its hands nearer home, had not been heard from. These people thereupon advanced farther out, some to Piscataqua, some to Salem, and some to Boston.

At the Arrowsick massacre, some of the people were away, some to bring corn; some were in boats obtaining fish. Among the latter was Richard Pots with two others. Mrs. Pots was washing by the water's edge, where she with her children were pursued in hot haste by the Indians. A little child cried, and called to its father from the shore in the distance for help; but the father in his prudence fled or paddled away, not deeming it wise even to shoot the Indian. From that place the Indians invaded Spurwinks and other places. At Casco on Sept. 23, 1676, some seven men went to Mountjoy's Island to obtain sheep. The Indians pursued them: they betook themselves to a stone house there, defended themselves, but in the end were all destroyed. One of them, George Felt, mortally wounded, survived but for a few days, and, being a valiant man, died much lamented.

From *this*, the Indians wandered nearer towards Piscataqua. A party advanced upon Cape Nedduck, killed or carried away nearly all the inhabitants of the scattered houses of that locality, leaving there unmistakable evidence of their heart-rending cruelties. The day before this a man was killed in Wells, and more soon afterwards.

On the 12th of October, 1676, one hundred Indians invaded Blackpoint. All the inhabitants had concentrated into one garrison. The Indians were led by the sagamore Mugg. He demanded of Joslyn, chief of the garrison, a surrender, offering them the privilege of taking away their goods. This was out a distance from it; and when Joslyn returned all his people had escaped, and had carried away their goods, so that none were left to stand by him but his servants who attended him; and he could do no better than to surrender. The invasion upon Richmond Island followed immediately upon that of Blackpoint. Many other wicked things happened hereabouts; and before the 1st of November, 1676, the said Mugg came to Piscataqua, bringing James Fryer, who, being disabled, soon died of his wounds.

Ray, in the mean time, had been sent east from Boston to ransom the eastern prisoners. But, as it seems, the ransom had been stolen by one of the tribes; and thereupon *Mugg*, their leader, was seized by the major-general of the Massachusetts Colony, or by his order, and was sent to the governor and council at Boston, that he might there, in the name of their chief, Madokawando, make arrangements for the giving-up of all the fifty or sixty prisoners which they then held; and with the understanding that said Mugg was to be held a hostage for the due performance of this understanding, Madokawando and Squando being the leading chiefs at war in the East.

Outrages in the mean time were daily heard of from the country farther north; and, to quell the eruptions there, a military force of one hundred and thirty Englishmen, and forty allied Indians, were sent there under the command of Capts. Hawthorne, Still, and Hunting, to be joined with others raised by Major Waldron and Capt. Frost. The force advanced in that direction, sweeping round *viâ* Casco, Wells, Winter Harbor, Blackpoint, in pursuit of Indians, but not finding many, yet killing now and then one or two, all others escaping. By these men, James George was shot from his horse while at Casco Bay going home from church; and Capt. Niddock on the 25th of September, 1676, was murdered, also George Farrow of Wells.

The enterprise proving fruitless thus far, this force swung around towards Ossipee.

Yet at Wells and vicinity some murders were still happening. Littlefield and Cross and Bigford were killed there about this time: thirteen head of cattle were also killed, their bodies left to their owners, ers, except that their tongues had been taken out.

In four days our forces had reached Ossipee, had taken quarters in an old fort built for the Indians by the English as a defence against the Mohawks, which was fourteen feet high, with flankers at the corners. Cold winter had now arrived: the soldiers made fuel of this fort, and advanced in scouting parties farther north into the woods among the lakes; yet finding no Indians, and coming to the conclusion after nine days' service in that direction, they marched back to Newitchewannock, having suffered more from frost than from Indian fire-arms.

In November *Mugg* had been despatched from Boston with two vessels, through whom the fifty or sixty prisoners were to be obtained in the East, pursuant to the articles of treaty entered into on the sixth day of that month, between the eastern tribes and the English; which treaty was signed by " *The X mark of Mugg, Indian,*" on the one side, and by " *John Earthy, Richard Oliver,* and *Isaac Addison,*" on the other.

Mugg with the vessels found *Madokawando* at Penobscot in the beginning of the next month, who delivered all the prisoners then there in his power, which were only eleven. Mugg then passed up into the wilderness to find other prisoners with other tribes; but, being gone too long, the vessels returned to Boston, where they arrived on the 25th of December, 1676 without him.

As to the other prisoners, they were still among their captors, and were not as yet obtained; the women being employed making garments for the natives from goods plundered from the English; the tribes not all seeking peace as their sachems had sought, and still desired.

In the first week of February, 1676, two hundred

and fifty soldiers, and sixty Natick Indians, were raised, and sent away by water to the East, under Major Waldron. On the 11th of February, Waldron sailed, touched in various places, established garrisons, searched for the captive prisoners, found *Mattahando*, who promised to deliver up those at Penobscot.

On the 20th of March, 1676, at Marlboro', the worshipping assembly was suddenly dispersed by a cry of "*Indians at the door!*" The confusion at the moment was instantly increased by a fire from the enemy. No one was injured, save Moses Newton, wounded in the arm. The people at once vanished to a place of safety. The meeting-house and all the defenceless dwelling-houses of the town were consumed. Much property was taken or destroyed.

The historian says, " The enemy retired soon after the first fire, declining to risk the enterprise and martial prowess of the young plantation. The people at once sought safer quarters by moving out of the place."

> " The hostile savage yells for prey
>   Along the pathless wild:
> The huntsman's track is watched by day;
>   By night his sleep's beguiled;
> His blazing cottage lights the gloom;
>   His infant shrieks the alarm;
> His wife sinks lifeless in a swoon,
>   Or bleeds within his arm."

BATTLE AT PEMAQUID.

At Gyobscot Point, Major Waldron espied two Indians in a canoe, who waved their caps, desiring to speak with him. Paine and Gendal were sent to them, from whom they learnt that there were many Indians at *Pemaquid* with the English captives; and the major bent his course in that direction, landed, saw an English captive with his master in a boat, and sought to speak with the captive, which was not allowed. But the Indians pretended peace, and promised to deliver up such captives as were at Penobscot the next morning. They desired to speak with some of the officers. Some of them went on shore; and three of the sagamores came on board the ship. After some talk the major went on shore with six men, carrying no arms with them. He found their words were uncommonly smooth; and, from the fact that all definite action in reference to the delivering-up of captives had been deferred to the next morning, his suspicions of their honesty began to be excited.

In the morning, Feb. 27, the major, with the same number as before, went on shore to treat with them; they with John Paine hailing them cheerfully. Their persons were searched on both sides, and all arms laid aside. They spent the forenoon in a treaty,

FAITHLESS TRIBES DEFEATED.

whereat they seemed much to rejoice, in expectation of a peace with the English. But when Major Waldron urged a present delivery of captives, with assistance of men and canoes to proceed against the Androscoggin Indians, enemies to both, it was denied; and they claimed pay for the keeping of the captives through the winter; as for their canoes, they had a present use for them, being bound to go to Penobscot: the price demanded was twelve skins. This proposition was yielded to; upon which they delivered up *William Chadbourn*, *John Winnick*, and *John Warwood*. The part of the pay which was to be *in liquor* was paid down: the rest was promised to be sent in the afternoon. Afterwards, and in the mean time, three of the sagamores came on board of the major's vessel; and, from their manner and talk, the major's suspicions of their evil intent were in no way abated.

BATTLE ON THE SHORE.

In the afternoon Major Waldron, with five attendants without arms, again went on shore to meet the Indians, to complete the treaty, and to pay the balance of the ransom; but upon arriving there, through a due circumspection, the major discovered, within a rod or two of the place of the hearing, some concealed weapons of death, in the shape of guns and lancets, obviously intended to be used by the warriors upon receipt of their full pay. He immediately seized up a lancet, and, springing towards them, charged falsehood and treachery upon them, at which guilt was seen in every countenance. One or two advanced towards him as if to get the weapon; but he, brandishing it, threatened death to any one that approached him, and passing his hand upward, raised his hat, which was a signal of distress to all his men in the ship, at which they rallied around him in full force. The Indians seized some of their weapons, but were put to flight. The soldiers fought valiantly: many of the tribe, before they could get away, as they took to their boats, were slain.

The remainder of the captives the major was left to seek elsewhere; and after establishing garrisons in the East, as we have noticed, and after visiting Sheepscot, from which they obtained plunder in which there were forty bushels of wheat, and at Arrowsick in the Kennebeck, after obtaining a hundred thousand feet of lumber, they returned home to Boston.

WAR IN WALDRON'S NEIGHBORHOOD.

This was in 1676. Previously, in 1675, while the war was going on westerly and in the remote East, *Squando* at Saco, and his tribes, were fruitful of conflicts in the country in which Dover and Major Waldron were the great centre. Men at Durham, at Exeter, at Hampton, at Newichewannock, at Concord, N.H., and many other places, had been slain, and many dwelling-houses consumed. Twenty young men, by leave of the major, had scattered themselves in the woods, discovered five Indians, and killed two of them. The people fled from their homes and from business to their garrisons. Fasting and prayer had become more common. At Salmon Falls, Lieut. Roger Plaisted sent out seven men from his garrison: they fell into an ambuscade, and three of them were killed. Two days after the taking of the four hundred Indians at Cocheco, of which we have spoken, Waldron's and Frost's men, with Blind Will, a sagamore of the Indians, as pilot, marched off to the eastward, and thence to the Ossipee Ponds, where the Indians had a strong fort of timber fourteen feet high with flanker; but, as we have seen, the tribes were somewhere else.

ENGLISH ALLIANCE WITH THE MOHAWKS.

Hitherto there had been conflicts between the eastern Indians and the Mohawks at New York; and at this crisis two messengers, Major Pynchon of Springfield and Richards of Hartford, repaired to that country, and made an alliance with the Mohawks. The Mohawks were valiant for a fight as against their enemies of old; and in March, 1677, they came down upon Amoskeag Falls. Wonalancet in the woods discovered fifteen Indians, who called to him in language not understood. He fled: they fired their guns at him; he escaped. Thence they appeared at Cocheco, against whom Waldron, not knowing them to be allies, sent out eight of his Indians led by Blind Will against them, or at least to obtain information; and the Mohawks fell upon them, and but two or three escaped. *Will* was dragged away by his hair, and perished in the woods at the confluence of the Isinglass and Cocheco Rivers. This place still bears the name of Blind Will's Neck. Hence it appeared that the Mohawks were intent upon the destruction of the *friends* of the English as well as their foes; and, in fact, they threatened the destruction of *all* the Indians in these parts without distinction. They thus proved fruitful of many calamities to the English. Then the garrisons at Wells and Blackpoint were beset: at the latter place the tribes lost Mugg, their leader and treacherous negotiator.

On a sabbath morning *Simon*, with twenty other Indians, surprised and took six of our Indians in the woods near *Portsmouth*. At night they crossed the river at Long Beach, killed some sheep at

TREATY AT CASCO. 317

Kittery, and turned off towards Wells; but in fear of the Mohawks they let their prisoners go. Four men were soon after killed at *North Hill.*

In 1678 *Shapleigh* of *Kittery*, Campernoon and Fryer of Portsmouth, as commissioners, entered into a treaty with *Squando* and other chiefs at *Casco*, and there obtained the remainder of the captives in the East; and here an end was put to this terrible war of three years.

We have said that Philip's war was ended; but this is to be taken at least with some allowance, as it is a very difficult matter to ascertain when an Indian war did end, their nationalities being numerous, and their impetuous notions various and uncertain.

At Cocheco (Dover), Major Waldron had a strong garrison-house; and near him were four others.

Rankamagus, a Pennacook chief, had, in league with others, on the 27th of June, 1679, contrived to surprise and destroy the town: accordingly squaws were sent, two to each garrison-house, to obtain lodgings for the night; and Massandowet, their chief sachem, that same evening took supper with the major, and, among other things, told him they were coming the next day to trade with him; but said, "Brother Waldron, what would you do if the strange Indians should come?" To which he forcibly replied, "*I could assemble an hundred men by lifting up my finger.*"

In the utmost quietude and security they retired to rest; but at midnight the gates were opened by the squaws, and death and consternation prevailed throughout the town. One garrison, having refused to admit the squaws, escaped: all the others fell.

They crowded Waldron's house, some guarding the doors, while others advanced upon their business of blood and death. Waldron, then eighty years of age, seizing his sword, defending himself, drove the savages from room to room, until, from behind him, he was knocked down with a hatchet, and then, being dragged away and placed upon a table, was stripped, and gashed, burned, and otherwise tortured, until death relieved him.

While gashing him, they would say thus, "*I cross out my account.*" While cutting off his fingers, they would say, "*Now will your fist weigh a pound?*"

While this was being done, other savages were compelling the women of the garrison to prepare supper for them.

In the garrison-houses and elsewhere, the inhabitants of Dover, to the number of twenty-three, were killed; and twenty-nine were carried away captive through the wilderness to Canada, where the most of them were sold to the French.

Previously, an Englishman at Chelmsford, Mass., had learned of some Indians of their proposed attack on Cocheco, and had sent a despatch to inform them; but, being delayed at Newbury Ferry, sad to relate, the despatch failed to reach its destination.

At ANDOVER, as we have seen, in Philip's war, several persons were killed by the Indians; others were captured; and some houses were burned, as was common: and now in 1698 Assacumbuit made an attack upon the town with forty Indians, "burned two dwelling-houses, and killed *Simon Wade, Nath. Brown, Penelope Johnson, Capt. Pasco Chubb*, his wife *Hannah*, and a daughter of *Edmund Faulkner*."

BILLERICA.

On this town, in 1695, an attack was made. As Nason describes it in his excellent Massachusetts Gazetteer, "Several were slain; and then again, on the 5th of August of that year, the Indians entered the house of John Rogers in that northerly part of the town, and discharged an arrow at him while asleep, which entered his neck, severing the main artery: awakened, he started up, seizing the arrow, withdrew it, but expired with the instrument of death in his own hand. A woman, being in a chamber at the time, threw herself out of the window, and, though severely injured, made her escape by concealing herself among some flags. A young woman was scalped and left for dead, but survived. A son and daughter of Mr. Rogers were made prisoners. The family of John Levestone suffered also severely: his mother and five young children were killed, and his oldest daughter captured. Capt. Thomas Rogers and his oldest son were killed. Mary, the wife of Dr. Roger Toothaker, and Margaret his youngest daughter, with four other persons, were slain."

The Indians were pursued by the villagers, but to no purpose. The tribes had covered their tracks, had even tied up the mouths of their dogs with wampum, to prevent all noise, and to avoid detection. That terrible shock to *Billerica* was long held by its inhabitants in painful remembrance.

In 1690, March 18, Sieur Hartel and Hopegood, with fifty-two French and Indians from Canada, invaded Salmon Falls, N.H. The attack was at daybreak, in three places. The people from their garrisons defended, but were overcome: thirty were killed, and fifty-four surrendered. Houses, mills, and barns were burned; and many cattle were killed. The inhabitants, gallantly following them into the woods, gave them battle, with the loss of some four or five on each side.

Hertel, on his way home, was joined by others, and fell in upon the fort at Casco. His mode of warfare was cruel.

CHAPTER XIX.

KING WILLIAM'S WAR.

New England is alarmed. — Wars as they advanced. — Three Detachments from Canada. — Attack on Salmon Falls. — Treaty with Penobscots and Others. — Attack on Oyster River. — Portsmouth invaded. — Skirmish at Breakfast Hill. — Dover and Kittery assailed. — Treaty at Casco. — Five Hundred French and Indians invade New England. — Invasion of 1704. — Col. Church's Expedition with Major Hilton. — Hilton's Expedition in 1705 on Snow-Shoes. — Patrol at Portsmouth. — Heroic Women. — Two Hundred and Seventy Warriors at Piscataqua and Dunstable. — Mohawks, painted Red, attack Oyster River. — Col. Hilton of Exeter slain. — Three Hundred and Forty-two French and Indians attack Deerfield. — A Flag-ship returns Prisoners. — *Raid* on Worcester. — On East Hampton. — On Sterling — Premium on Scalps. — Expedition to obtain Captives. — Church, Hilton, and Forces are sent East. — Col. W. Hilton slain. — Col. Walton's Expedition to the East. — Piloted by a Squaw. — Three Hundred Indians advance East with. Threats. — French and Indians by the Government declared Rebels. — Parson Rallé makes Trouble. — Arrowsick invaded. — Attack on Northfield. — Another Alliance. — Father Rallé, the French Jesuit, slain by Capt. Harmon.

IN the year 1689, New England was again startled with the news that King William had invaded England with the intention of dethroning the king. This, of course, at once led to combinations, and councils of safety. The French and Indians of Canada, as we might well suppose, came down upon the English here like an avalanche; and war here and war there continued until Jan. 7, 1699. Then upon the heel of this followed another foreign conflict, known as Queen Anne's War, commencing in Gov. Dudley's time, Aug. 10, 1703, and ending at the peace of Utrecht, March 31, 1713.

In consequence of encroachments by the English upon Indian lands, this peace proved to be of short duration; and war again gradually came on, became general in July 25, 1722, and continued to distress New England up to Dec. 15, 1725.

Thence with occasional troubles as the years advanced, until March 29, 1744, when Great Britain, under George II., declared war against France and Spain. This raged up to 1749. During all of these years, since the beginning of the war by Philip, (June 24, 1675), which we have detailed, and then again from 1689 up to the year 1763, there was, *all the way along*, more or less of Indian conflicts, afflicting the generations of men, and overwhelming the hearts of women and children with the pangs of sad bereavements.

In the winter of 1690 Count de Fontenac, governor of Canada, detached three parties of French and Indians on three different routes, upon the frontiers of New England. These parties, one of which went into New York, performed the offices for which they were organized, by killing the inhabitants, and burning and destroying their property.

On the 18th of March, 1690, Trois Rivières, with fifty-two French and Indians, made an attack on Salmon Falls, N.H., led by Hopegood, a noted warrior. They came in at daybreak in three parties. The people flew to arms, defended their garrisons valiantly; yet about thirty persons were slain, and the rest, fifty-four in number, surrendered to the tribes. The houses, mills, and barns were burned. They were pursued to the woods by a hundred and forty men, who overtook them at the bridge on Wooster's River. There, an engagement took place. The loss was small, — four or five on each side. The next day they destroyed the fort at Casco.

In 1693, Aug. 12, the Penobscots, Kennebecks, Androscoggins, and Sacos submitted to a treaty of peace at Pemaquid, in which they agreed to abandon the French interest, to deliver up all captives, and to sustain free trade. Yet July 13, 1694, they were induced by the French to other hostilities.

At Oyster River (which is a westerly branch of the Piscataqua) there were twelve garrisons, with dwelling-houses on both sides of the river. On the morning of the 17th of July, 1694, the Indians in two parties invaded the village on both sides, planted themselves in ambush in small parties near every house, and awaited the rising of the sun, as well as the firing of the first gun as a signal. John Dean, the earliest riser, was shot as he advanced from the threshold. This gave an alarm prematurely, as the Indians had not all obtained their several positions; and the inhabitants came forth, some to escape, and some to organize, and give battle to the tribes.

Of the twelve garrison-houses, *five* were destroyed; to wit, Adam's, Meader's, Drew's, Edgerley's, and Beard's.

Fourteen of the inhabitants were slain. A boy was made to run through their files. They threw their hatchets at him to carry out their sports, until he fainted and fell.

The defenceless houses were set on fire, and were nearly all consumed. Many persons were taken captive.

The other seven garrisons — viz., Burnham's, Bickford's, Smith's, Bunker's, Davis's, Jones's, and Woodman's — were resolutely and successfully defended.

Thence a part of these tribes proceeded westward, through Dover and Exeter, to Groton, Mass. They were led by Toxus, a Norridgewock chief.

In July, 1695, and 1696, men were killed by the Indians at Exeter; and in May (1696) John Church, who previously had been seven years a captive, was slain at Cocheco near his own house.

PORTSMOUTH, N.H.

On the 26th of June, 1696, an attack was made on Portsmouth, N.H., about two miles out from the village.

"The enemy came over from *York Nubble* to *Sandy Beach* in canoes which they had in the bushes near the shore. At early morn they pillaged five houses, took four prisoners, and killed fourteen persons. One man was scalped and left for dead, but recovered. The houses were consumed.

Thereupon, Capt. Shackford with a company of militia advanced in pursuit of the tribe, and, overtaking them at Breakfast Hill, rushed upon them from the top of it, retook the captives and the plunder; but the Indians, rolling themselves down the hill, and from thence into a swamp, reached their canoes, and escaped.

DOVER, N.H.

On the 6th of July of the same year the people of Dover were waylaid on their return from church. Three were killed, three wounded, and three were carried away to Penobscot.

In June, 1697, at Exeter, a body of Indians had in the morning placed themselves near the town for the purpose of an assault, but were frightened away; but in July they murdered Major Frost of Kittery in revenge, as they say, for the seizure of the four hundred Indians at Dover in which he had been concerned.

In 1699 the Indians were brought to a treaty at Casco, by the English commissioners, wherein the Indians once again promised better behavior.

During Philip's war, Douglas says about three thousand Indians had been slain or taken, and that the Narragansetts, one of the largest nations, had been reduced, not being able to rally more than a hundred men.

And again during King William's war much trouble within the Colonies of New England was constantly diminishing the population on both sides. Thus there were battles during this period at Haverhill and other places which we have named.

In 1689 there had been fights at North Yarmouth, at Sheepscot, and Cocheco; and forts and garrisons had been built at Sheepscot, Pegepscot, at Pemaquid, at Wells, York, Berwick, and Cocheco.

In 1690 Massachusetts sent a hundred and sixty men to Albany for protection, and to head off invasions from the Canadian French and Indians, and then to the East in 1692. William Phipps, having raised four hundred and fifty men, advanced against the enemy on the Kennebeck.

On the other hand, in 1696 the French landed

some soldiers at Pemaquid, as allies to the Indians. About this time the fort here, with ninety-five men and fourteen mounted cannon, was surrendered to the French by one Capt. Chub.

In 1697 a squadron from France was sent to operate against New England; but it was driven asunder in a storm. And then, Jan. 7, 1698, followed the French treaty of peace at Berwick; and the eastern Indians again submitted.

On June 20, 1703, Gov. Dudley, with delegates from his provinces, held a conference at Casco with the Norridgewocks, Penobscots, Pequawkets, Pennacooks, and Androscoggins. A treaty of peace was then and there entered into, with many mutual promises and much ceremony: yet, as it turned out, the Indians' guns were loaded. And on Aug. 10, 1703, M. Bobasier, with five hundred French and Indians in several divisions, invaded the New-England frontier from Casco to Wells, making barbarous havoc, sparing neither age nor sex, killing some, and taking others, — a hundred and thirty in all, burning and destroying all before them.

In the spring of 1704, the surrounding country was alarmed: the women and children fled to the garrisons. No laborers went to the fields without being fully armed, or surrounded by sentinels well posted.

On April 25 Nathaniel Meader was killed in his field at Oyster River. Edward Taylor was also slain by the tribes; and his wife and son were taken captive at Lamprey River.

In May of this year *Col. Church* was started on an expedition from Boston, with transports and whaleboats for going up the river. Major Hilton joined him at Piscataqua, and they were in the East all summer; destroyed Minas and Chiegnecto, and damaged the Indians at Penobscot and Passamaquoddy.

In the winter of 1705 Col. Hilton, with two hundred and seventy men, including Indians, advanced to Norridgewock on snow-shoes upon the snow, then four feet deep. They burned the wigwams, finding no Indians. This year the line of pickets which enclosed the town of Portsmouth was repaired; and a nightly patrol was established on the sea-shore from Rendezvous Point to the bounds of Hampton, the coast being infested with the enemy's privateers.

Thomas Dudley, governor at that time, kept a vigilant eye upon the enemy during the winter, and caused a circular scouting march to be taken once a month around the head of the towns from Kingston to Salmon Falls.

On the 24th of May, 1704, East Hampton, Mass.,

was destroyed by the Indians, and about twenty of its inhabitants were slain.

In 1706, at Reading, five Indians killed a woman and three children, and carried the remaining five into captivity.

In April, 1706, a small party of savages invaded the house of John Drew at Oyster River, killed eight, and wounded two. Not a man was in the garrison: *yet the* WOMEN *valiantly fired an alarm; putting on hats, and concealing their hair, they went into the fight, firing away fervently at the enemy. The Indians, frightened, fled before them, without plundering or even burning a house.*

In July, 1706, a rumor came that two hundred and seventy French and Indians were on the march to Piscataqua; and the people again took to their garrisons.

This enemy first fell in upon Dunstable, thence to Amesbury, and then to Kingston, at this time killing many cattle.

Again, a party of them lurked about Hilton's house in Exeter, where they saw ten men moving to the mowing-field. When the mowers had laid aside their arms, the Indians, creeping between them and their guns, rushed upon them, killed four, wounded one, and took three: two only escaped.

Sept. 15, 1707, a man was killed by them at Exeter; and, two days afterwards, Henry Elkins fell at Kingston.

Then again, at OYSTER RIVER, a company of men were at work in the woods, hewing timber; and a party of French Mohawks, painted red, came in upon them with a hideous yell, and at the first fire killed seven, and mortally wounded another. Capt. Chesley was among the slain.

During the winter of 1708, four hundred Massachusetts soldiers were posted within its province.

COL. WINTHROP HILTON.

This gallant officer, in 1710, July 22, was concerned in the masting business; being in the woods fourteen miles away from his house in Exeter, was ambushed by a party of Indians. Hilton, with two more, was killed at the first fire. His other men escaped. A hundred men followed the next day in pursuit; but no Indians were seen. They had left a lance in the colonel's heart. On the same day the savages ambushed the road in Kingston, and killed Samuel Winslow and Samuel Huntoon, and took and carried into Canada Huntoon and Gilman.

In the spring of 1711 the tribes renewed their ravages on the frontier; and *Thomas Downs, John Church*, and three others, were killed at *Cocheco;* and several were assaulted on their way from church. And from this, conflicts most cruel continued up to July 17, 1713.

THE OLD DOOR IN DEERFIELD.

On the night of Feb. 29, 1704, Major Hertel de Rouville, with three hundred and forty-two French and Indians, fell in upon Deerfield, entered its fort, embracing the church and several dwelling-houses then unguarded, and massacred many, and carried others away. At the onset Rev. Mr. Williams seized his pistol: it missed fire, and was knocked aside. Two of his children and servant were murdered. He and five of his remaining children were marched away into captivity. His wife, two days afterwards, was slain in Greenfield.

Two years after this a flag-ship, sent from Quebec to Boston, brought back Mr. Williams, his four children, and fifty-two other redeemed captives. As it happened, one of his children inclined to remain there, grew up among the Indians, accepted one of them as a husband, and in later years once or twice visited her early home in Massachusetts.

In this attack upon Deerfield (Mr. Nason says), the Indians, cutting a hole through the door of Mr. Sheldon's house, fired at and killed Mrs. Sheldon just as she was rising from her bed.

The old *door* of this house now hangs, enclosed in

a frame of chestnut, in the hall of the Pecomtuc House.

The peasant-bard of Gill thus speaks of it: —

"Bless thee, old relic! — old and brave and scarred;
And bless old Deerfield, — says the grandson bard.
Towns may traditions have, by error spun:
She has the door of history; that's the one."

At Worcester, in 1704, an invasion was made by the tribes. The inhabitants deserted the town; and the wife of Dickory Sargent became a captive, and was carried away. Years before this the place had been noted: the Indians here had been interviewed by the apostle *Eliot* and by *Gookin*; and then again, in Philip's time, Pakachoag had been visited by King Philip, while inducing the Indians to take up arms against the white men.

In 1704 Caleb Lyman at Cowwassuck on the Connecticut, with one Englishman and five Mohegan Indians, killed eight hostile warriors out of nine. The Assembly for this gave him thirty-one pounds.

In this same year, May 24, East Hampton (Passacomuck) was destroyed by the Indians, and about twenty persons killed.

In 1706 a party of Indians, visiting Reading, killed a woman and three of her children; and carried her other children, five in number, into captivity.

A PREMIUM FOR SCALPS.

On the 18th of August, 1707, a party of twenty-four Indians from the forest appeared to Mrs. Mary Fay and Mary Goodnow, while gathering herbs in a meadow. Mrs. Fay took to a garrison near by, and assisted in defending it until the men in the field came to their relief.

The next day, in Sterling, the same tribe invaded the town, and "got the worst of it:" nine of them were killed. In their packs was found the scalp of the unfortunate Miss Goodnow, whose lameness prevented an escape. Her lonely grave is still to be recognized near the place where she fell.

At this time the premiums for Indian scalps and captives had been advanced by the Assembly, per piece, to impressed men ten pounds, to volunteers twenty pounds, to volunteers serving without pay fifty pounds, with the benefit of captives and plunder. And Capt. Rowe was sent to Port Royal, N.S., with a flag of truce, to negotiate for prisoners.

Capt. Sheldon was also sent there twice for the same purpose.

Col. Hilton, with two hundred and twenty men, was also sent away to the eastern frontiers. He killed many Indians.

The colonel was himself killed by the Indians in 1711, in Exeter.

At this time Col. Church, March 13, 1707, sailed

east with two regiments to the same end. He obtained many prisoners.

And then Col. Hilton, with a hundred and seventy men, proceeded to Amarasconti and Pequawket.

In the spring of 1708, eight hundred French and Indians invaded New England; but, disagreeing among themselves, some of them returned back: the others fell in upon Haverhill and other places, as we have noticed.

In 1711, near Exeter, Col. Winthrop Hilton, with two others, was slain by the Indians in the woods: near Exeter two others were taken. The next day one hundred men followed in pursuit of the Indians; but they could not be traced. Soon they appeared again in the streets at Exeter, took captive four children and John Wedgwood, and murdered John Magoon; and again at Cocheco they killed Jacob Garland while on his return from worship.

In the winter Col. Walton, with 170 men, traversed the eastern shores, which were usually sought at that season by the Indians to obtain clams.

Some of the tribe, mistaking Walton's encampment at night, came near, and were taken prisoners. One of them was a sachem of Norridgewock, active, sullen, bold. He would make no discoveries, and was slain. Upon this his squaw and two others piloted the colonel to Saco River, where he overtook five Indians, and slew them all: also on the way he took two prisoners under her lead. Thomas Downs, John Church, and three others were killed at Cocheco; and on the sabbath, as the people were returning from church, Humphrey Foss was taken captive, and John Horn was wounded.

Walton, with two companies, advanced to the ponds in the fishing season; but the Indians had deserted their wigwams.

In Chelmsford Major Tyng was killed; and murders by the Indians were happening in other places.

SUSPENSION OF HOSTILITIES.

News now came of the suspension of arms between England and France; and the Indians applied for an accommodation.

In 1713, July 11, the New-England Colonies held at Portsmouth, N.H., a congress with the tribes.

The basis of this treaty was the same as that at Penobscot, Aug. 11, 1693; in which one of the articles provides, that, in case of a difficulty between the English and the tribe, the matter must be settled by an English court.

This conference included, as appears, the St. Johns, the Penobscots, Kennebecks, Ammoscoggins, Sacos, Merrimacks. Mauxis was their chief.

The tribes usually took the names of the rivers along which they hunted and obtained their fish.

HOSTILITIES AGAIN.

In 1717 the Indians began to murmur; and, after giving the settlers warning to leave their lands, advanced to the killing of cattle, and to other trespasses; and in 1719 the French again urged them to renew and set up their claims to the lands of New England.

But to a considerable extent thus far they are kept in awe of the English.

In 1719 (Shute and Dummer's time) the French again urged the Indians to set up claims to New-England territory, and proceeded to aid them in trespasses; but the English, with their allied tribes, soon discouraged them.

In 1720 the Indians are urged on again, and commence to kill cattle, committing depredations generally; but Col. Walton, with two hundred men, advancing against them, brought them to submission, and obtained hostages for their good behavior.

About this time the small-pox prevailed, which always operated as a terror to the tribes of New England. It tended to retard the general progress of hostilities.

In 1721 M. Croizer is sent here from Canada,

M. St. Casteen from Penobscot, and Rallé and De la Chasse (French missionaries), with about three hundred Indians, who made their appearance at Sagadahock (Kennebeck), with threats that if the English did not remove from the lands claimed by the tribes, within three weeks, they would kill the inhabitants, and burn their houses down.

On June 13, 1722, the French and Indians began in good earnest, and captivated *Love, Hamilton, Hansaid, Trescot,* and *Edgar.* Thereupon by the assembly in Boston in the following July they were declared rebels, and were proceeded against accordingly.

Parson Rallé, a missionary and Jesuit at Canada, about this time was telling the Indians that the lands of New England "*were given them of God,* to them and their children forever, according to the Christian sacred oracles."

BOUNTY.

In 1722, July 5, the government of Massachusetts Bay proclaimed the invaders to be rebels, and ordered a bounty of £100 per scalp to be paid to volunteers fitted out at their own charge; and afterwards it added and offered four shillings a day besides.

Soon after this Capt. Hanson on the Kennebeck slew several Indians; and many other captains advanced in search of the wigwams of the wilderness.

About this time (1722), at Arrowsick, a body of Indians killed several people, burned sixty dwelling-houses, and destroyed fifty cattle. They failed in their attempts upon the English forts at Richmond on the Kennebeck, and at St. George near the Penobscot. Yet they surprised sixteen fishing-vessels at Canso.

In 1723, Aug. 13, in Northfield (Squakeag), two men were killed by the Indians; and in October an attack was made on their block-house, and several others were slain; and, as late as 1748, Anson Bolding was slain there by the Indians. Here it was, as we have seen, Capt. Richard Beers with thirty-six men fell into an ambuscade in 1675, and only sixteen of them escaped after a desperate battle. On the previous day ten men by the same Indians had been slain there in the woods.

ANOTHER ALLIANCE.

On Aug. 21, 1723, sixty-three Indians from the six New-York nations visited Boston, proposing an alliance against the eastern Indians; their real object in this being to obtain presents. They, however, did not obtain many.

FATHER RALLÉ SLAIN.

In 1724, Aug. 12, a battle was had at Norridgewock on the Kennebeck River.

Capt. Harmon, with two hundred men in seventeen whale-boats, had moved up the Kennebeck River. He surprised the Indians there, took twenty-six scalps to be seen in Boston, among which was that of " Father Rallé," whose reckless advice had led to much of the bloodshed along the frontiers of New England.

The Indians killed and drowned in their attempt to cross the river, in that battle, were computed to be not less than eighty.

Belknap says, " In that battle they completely invested and surprised the village, killed the obnoxious Jesuit with about eighty of his Indians, recovered three captives, destroyed the chapel, and brought away the plate and furniture of the altar, with the devotional flag, as trophies of their victory."

Rallé was then in the sixty-eighth year of his age, and had resided in his mission at Norridgewock twenty-six years, having previously spent six years in travelling among the Indian nations in the interior of the American Continent.

Oft thus the powers with England disagree,
Which does portend what carnage hence shall be,
What man's estate must prove, — a varied life.
From quiet peace proceeds terrific strife;
From plenty, *dearth;* from faith and virtue, *sin;*

From health, *disease*, that wages war within. .
Thus strangely intermixed are good and ill,
True to the purpose of a sovereign Will:
Nature but thrives by fire that burns within:
From planets broken other worlds begin;
Yet bloody conflicts, such the world abhor
As mark the advent of avenging war —
Enough,— enough! yet others still there were
Of blood profuse. 'Tis man's estate to err:
Let pass Queen Anne's, the troubles of her day;
The craft of Jesuits, fruitful of dismay;
Nor need to note the French and Indian strife,
Nor trace the torch, the tomahawk, and knife
Farther. 'Tis now the olive-branch divine
We seek,— its beauteous benefits benign.

From my Merrimack, p. ⁑

CHAPTER XX.

BATTLE OF PEQUAWKET.

The Conflict of Fifty Years. — Its Inroads upon Civilization. — The Eventful Issues of 1725 still Pending. — Capt. Lovewell and his Forty-six Men. — His Fourteen Survivors pensioned. — Paugus of Pequawket slain. — The Battle poetized of Old. — An Ancient Battle, as from Tradition. — Depredations at Pennacook. — Garrison, and how Constructed. — Eruptions as started from Abroad. — Numerous Tribes allied to the French. — Inroads upon the New-England Frontiers. — Reckoning of Dates. — Expeditions against New England. — War of 1744. — Detachments sent out. — Bounties allowed. — Donahew's Expedition. — Conference at Albany. — Successive Invasions.

IN former chapters we have endeavored to give somewhat in detail, as they had transpired, the various leading eruptions, conflicts, and depredations, which, as between the English and the native Indians in New England, hitherto have happened. Up to this period, fifty years had elapsed since King Philip at Mount Hope had raised the battle-axe in behalf of his native soil and in behalf of his then dying race of red men. Philip died then: *still*, plain to be seen, the hatchet was not buried. And sad to relate, although the white race were destined in the end, as it were, by brute force to prevail, barbarism, for the time being, as against civilization, had been suffered to gain the mastery. Fifty years of bloody conflicts had made terrible havoc with the minds and morals of men, wherein a pure religion and a well-tutored civilization were of but little use, other than to sharpen the arrows which brought to an untimely grave thousands of innocent men, women, and children.

How could such a conflict, wherein law and religion for so long a period were substantially laid aside, do otherwise than to misguide and betray the public mind into the commission of devilish deeds? Hence the hanging of witches and of Quakers were but legitimate offshoots from the bloody barbarisms in New England, which, in spite of law and religion, had sprung forth, producing dreadful devastation on the right hand and on the left,— mutual barbarisms, which, taking a rabid form, worked inconceivable mischief in almost every direction. And yet when New England came out of its terrible trial, having learned much from the wars and bloodshed of tragic years, it thenceforth made haste to perfect itself in the organization of a noble, generous civilization, which at this time is every day exemplified through its thriving municipal corporations, as well as by individuals, in liberal laws and magnanimous deeds.

LOVEWELL.

We come now to other conflicts.

Capt. John Lovewell of Dunstable, previous to this time, had raised a company of thirty volunteers, and had advanced north of the Lake Winnipiseogee, and, finding an Indian and boy in a wigwam, killed the Indian, and, keeping the boy, brought him alive to Boston, and thereupon received the legal bounty as well as a gratuity from the government.

Upon another excursion he proceeded with seventy men to the same place in the forest above the Lake; but for the want of provisions thirty of his men thence returned. The remainder of them advanced into the deep forest, where they discovered a tribe encamped for the night. Concealing themselves, they remained; and at midnight, by the side of a frozen pond, they fell in with the Indians. Lovewell fired first, killing two. Five others fired instantly, and then the rest fired; and but one Indian remained alive. He, wounded, tried to escape, but, followed by the dog, was held fast until they killed him. This was at a place now known as Lovewell's Pond, in Wakefield, N.H., at the head of one of the branches of Salmon Falls River.

This "brave company on Feb. 24, 1725 [says Belknap], with the ten scalps stretched on hoops, and elevated on poles, entered Dover (Cocheco) in triumph, and proceeded thence to Boston: there they received the bounty of one hundred pounds for each, out of the public treasury."

On the 16th of April, Capt. Lovewell, raising another company, forty-six men, including a chaplain and surgeon, advanced again into the north-east. Two of the men becoming lame, and one falling sick, and the surgeon, were left behind in a stockade fort, on the west side of the great Ossapee Pond; and eight of the men were also left there as a guard. The remaining thirty-four men, led by Lovewell, advanced onward about twenty-two miles, and encamped on the shore of a pond. At their devotions in the morning, they heard the report of a gun, and discovered an Indian on a point of land extending into the pond nearly a mile away. Upon consultation they marched off in direction of the Indian, after disencumbering themselves of their knapsacks, leaving them at the north-east end of the pond without a guard. It happened that Lovewell's march had crossed a carrying-place wherein *Paugus* and Wahwa, with forty-one warriors from Saco River, were returning to the lower village of Pequawket, distant about a mile and a half from this pond.

They traced Lovewell's track back to their packs; and counting them, and ascertaining that the number was less than their own, they placed themselves in ambush to await their return.

The Indian who had stood on the point of land, while now returning to the village, received their fire, returned it with small shot, wounding Lovewell and one of his men.

Lieut. Wyman, firing again, killed him; and they took his scalp. And now returning to obtain their packs, the Indians arose, and fired upon them, raising a terrific yell. Capt. Lovewell and eight others were at once killed: Lieut. Farwell and two others were wounded. Several of the Indians fell; but, seeing their superiority of numbers, Lovewell's men took positions behind rocks and trees. On their right was the mouth of a brook; on their left was a rocky point; their front was covered partly by a deep bog, with the pond in their rear: there they kept up their fire for a long time. Jonathan Frye, Ensign Robbins, and one more were at length mortally wounded; and yet they continued the battle until the Indians near night left the ground, carrying off their killed and wounded, and leaving the dead bodies of Lovewell and his men unscalped.

Of the remnant of this brave company, three were unable to move from the spot, eleven were wounded but able to march, and nine had received no injury. It was sad to leave their wounded companions behind them, in the wilderness; but the fates had so ordered it. One of them, Ensign Robbins, desired them to lay his gun beside him, charged, so that, if the Indians should return before his death, he might be able to kill one more.

It was the 8th of May, at night. The moon had cast its light upon the fatal spot when they left it, and directed their march toward the fort where the surgeon and guard had been left. Lieut. Farwell and the chaplain, and one other wounded, perished in the woods. The others, after suffering the most severe hardships, came in one after another.

A generous provision was made for the widows and children of the slain; lands by the Commonwealth were given to the survivors of Lovewell's company, one tract of which now takes the name of Pembroke, N.H. Immediately afterward Col. Tyng of Dunstable visited that battle-ground, found and buried the bodies of twelve of the company, carved their names upon the trees, and then again left them alone in the dark, deep forest to a sweet repose.

Under the management of Gov. Dummer's administration, the Indians, on Dec. 15, 1725, begged and obtained a cessation of hostilities; and in the following May, at Casco, a treaty of peace was agreed upon, wherein the Indians were to have all their lands "not hitherto conveyed," with the privilege of hunting and fishing as formerly. This was signed by the government, and by the Norridgewock, Penobscot, St. Johns, and Cape Sable Indians, as represented by their several sagamores. And this treaty was ratified Aug. 5, 1726.

BETTER DAYS.

> Then Peace, that welcome harbinger of health,
> Of generous thrift, foreshadowing weal and wealth,
> Brings her glad tidings down, and cheers the land
> With prompt good will, and noble deeds at hand,
> To heal the broken heart, to make amends
> For wilful waste, which from the past descends.
> Thence this fair vale from mountain to the main
> In vernal grandeur buds to bloom again;
> And plenteous harvest with her golden ears,
> Crowning the prudence of progressive years,
> Adorns the field, and grace triumphant gives
> To honest toil. *My Merrimack*, p. 32.

Belknap says, "This account of Lovewell's battle is collected from the authorities (cited in the margin), and from the verbal information of aged and intelligent persons. The names of the dead on the trees, and the holes where the balls had entered and had been cut out, were plainly visible when I was on the spot in 1784. The trees had the appearance of being *very old;* and one of them was fallen."

Col. Tyng, while upon the battle-ground, dug up the bodies of the dead Indians, among which he identified that of Paugus, chief of the Pequawkets, who had fallen at the first shot in the engagement. Fourteen only, out of the forty-six who left Dunstable, lived to reach home.

The Indians centred no more at Pequawket during the Indian wars.

This battle, with its heroes, was poetized at that distant day; and we will try to interest the reader in a brief quotation:

> " Up then the tribes to battle rose,
>   Who'd hid themselves in ambush dread;
> Their knives they shook; their guns they **aimed**,—
>   The famous Paugus at their head.
>
> Thus Paugus led the Pequawket tribe;
>   As runs the fox would Paugus run;
> As howls the wild wolf would he howl:
>   A huge bear-skin had Paugus on.
>
> But Chamberlain of Dunstable,—
>   He whom a savage ne'er could **slay,**
> Met Paugus by the water-side,
>   And shot him dead upon that **day.**

> Then did the crimson streams that flowed
>   Seem like the waters of the brook,
> That brightly shine, that loudly dash
>   Far down the cliffs of Agio-chook.
>
> Ah! many a wife shall rend her hair,
>   And many a child cry, 'Woe be me!'
> When messengers the news shall *bear*
>   Of Lovewell's dear-bought victory."

DUNSTABLE, AND THE PENNACOOK BATTLE.

Lovewell's home, as we have seen, was at old Dunstable, within the dominions formerly of Passaconaway and of the peaceful Pennacooks.

Attendant upon this ancient town, are many memories. History as well as tradition follows it. Around it on either side, as well as within its lines, we now trace out, as it were, the ancient landmarks left us by Eliot the Apostle and by the peaceful Passaconaway. Before their time Indian wars had prevailed in this region, as we have seen. And at one time, as tradition has it, there was a great battle at Pennacook (now Concord, N.H.), between the Massachusetts, Pawtuckets, and Pennacook tribes, and the angry Mohawks from the eastern borders of New York. Of this conflict Dr. Bouton says, "The Mohawks, who had once been repulsed by the Pennacooks, came with a strong force, and encamped at what is now called *Fort Eddy*, opposite *Sugar Ball*, on the west of the river. Thence they watched their prey, determined either to starve the Pennacooks by a siege, or to decoy them out and destroy them.

"Having gathered their corn for the season, and stored it in baskets around the walls of their fort, the Pennacooks, with their women and children, entered within, and bade defiance to their foes." Skirmishes often ensued. Whenever a Pennacook left the fort he was ambushed. If a canoe pushed off from the bank, another from the opposite side started in pursuit. The Pennacooks would not venture an open fight in the field; nor did the Mohawks dare to assail the fort. At length one day a solitary Mohawk was seen carelessly crossing *Sugar Ball* Plain south of the fort. Caught by the decoy, the Pennacooks rushed out in pursuit: the Mohawk ran for the river. Band after band from the fort followed in the chase till all were drawn out of the fort, when the Mohawks, secretly crossing the river above, having approached in the rear, and secreted themselves, now suddenly sprang from their hiding-places, and took possession of the fort. At *this* a terrible war-whoop went up from the Pennacooks. They turned back; "and long and bloody was the battle." The fight by the Pennacooks was "*for their wives and children, for their old men, for their corn, and for life itself:*" by the Mohawks it was "*for revenge and for plunder.*"

How the victory turned does not appear: yet tradition has it that "the Mohawks left their dead and wounded on the ground," and that the Pennacook tribes were greatly reduced in numbers. A diversity in the skulls which used to be found there induces the belief that their dead were buried promiscuously.

This slaughter in the olden time, and that which followed it in 1617, attended by the plague, of which we have spoken in another chapter, were the only great battles among the tribes which happened prior to the landing of the Pilgrims, of which tradition gives any account: all others prior to 1617 being covered of oblivion.

All the way along from 1739 to 1754, there were great apprehensions of trouble from the Indians in the vicinity of Pennacook, caused in those years mostly by intrusions from Canada; and many garrisons were built.

In 1742 Jonathan Eastman's wife was carried away captive, but was afterwards redeemed.

In 1744, at the opening of the French War, the alarm to the Colonies was increased.

At that time, Capt. Ebenezer Eastman raised a

company of soldiers, and advanced against the fortress at Louisburg; and Pennacook (since Rumford, now Concord) was kept constantly on the alert for fear of invasions. The Massachusetts Government, in 1745, sent detachments there from Andover and from Billerica, to assist, if need be, in its defence.

Also, in 1746, *Capt. Daniel Ladd* and *Lieut. Jonathan Bradley*, with a company of soldiers from Exeter, were sent by the governor for the defence of Rumford and the neighboring towns.

MASSACRE AT RUMFORD.

On the 10th and 11th of August, 1746, Lieut. Bradley took seven men, and proceeded about two and a half miles to a town garrison: at about one and a half miles away, they were fired upon by thirty or forty Indians; and *Lieut. John Lufkin, John Bean*, and *Obadiah Peters* were killed. *Alexander Roberts* and *William Stickney* were taken prisoners.

The minute details of all these events are more fully given in Mr. Bouton's excellent "History of Concord."

GARRISONS.

Under the authority of Gov. Wentworth, additional garrison-houses were established in various places.

GARRISONS, HOW MADE. 353

In Pennacook there were seven in 1746.

They were usually made up of "hewed logs which lay flat upon each other: the ends, being fitted for the purpose, were inserted in grooves cut in large posts erected at each corner. They usually enclosed an area of several square rods;" were about the same height as a common dwelling-house. At two or more of the corners were projections (in box-form), wherein the sentinels kept watch by day and night.

In times of danger, all the houses not connected with the garrisons were usually deserted of the household, and were without furniture.

If the enemy approached, alarm-guns were fired; and the report was answered from *fort to fort*. In the house of worship, the men, with their powder-horns upon their shoulders, stacked their guns in the centre of it; "while the parson, having the best gun in the parish by his side, advanced to his preaching and prayer." — BOUTON.

CONFLICTS : 1743–1748.

The Indian eruptions, depredations, and invasions in New England, upon its English settlements, which transpired between the years 1743 and 1748, were too numerous to be detailed very minutely in these annals.

As we have already observed, the oft-repeated intrusions of the white man, and particularly the conflicts which occasionally came to pass in the Old World, were always to be regarded as the harbingers of depredations, violence, danger, and death in the New.

In Canada, at this bloody period, the French had five hundred Indians at their immediate control, independent of more distant allies, as follows:—

The Cacknawages, two hundred and thirty; Connestagoes, sixty; Attenkins, thirty; Neperinks, thirty; Missequecks, forty; Abenaquis at St. Frances, ninety; Obenacks at Becancourt, fifty; Hurons at Lorette, forty.

Ever jealous of the English, and entertaining a deep interest to appropriate these domains to themselves as a distinct race, and having an abiding alliance, in their marriages and in their traffic, with the tribes, those French leaders controlled the masses, and from time to time urged them forward to deeds of blood throughout the English frontiers.

Hence Massachusetts, as well as the Districts of Maine, New Hampshire, and Vermont, constantly suffered more or less in all their settlements; as well as Rhode Island and Connecticut, to whose Indian battles we have already adverted.

Aside from their Indian tribes, the French force

in Canada had nearly thirteen thousand of their own race, all ready and able to bear arms.

At that date, the then Territory of Massachusetts contained a thin population of only two hundred thousand, many of its inhabitants living in lonely cots, hemmed in by the old native forest: others lived in little villages, few and far between.

My friend Drake, the historian of "long ago," estimated the *New-England* population of that time at four hundred thousand.

In this place, it may be of use to the young reader to understand the mode in which our time is reckoned, as by the

OLD OR NEW STYLE.

It should be remembered that the English did not reckon dates by the Gregorian calendar until Jan. 22, 1752. Their year previously had commenced on the 25th of March.

Up to that date, their rule or mode of computation during a long series of years had, by degrees, carried the *winter* too far into the *spring*.

To remedy this irregularity, Parliament adopted this new rule, ordering eleven days to be dropped out from the calendar; so that, for instance, the 30th of March, 1697 (the date of the Contoocook slaughter) should in our time be reckoned as the eleventh day of April of that year.

The French adopted the same rule previously. Our dates, when taken from their records, will of course accord with our own reckonings at the present day.

The war which had broken out between Great Britain and Spain involved France in its flame; and in New England it took the name of the

FRENCH AND INDIAN WAR.

The contest opened in Nova Scotia, that province at first being the debatable ground. Such had been the invasions, depredations, and murders by the French and their allied Indians, that, on the 2d of June, 1744, our English Government at Boston proclaimed war against *France*, and, as a guard against the common enemy, called into the service five hundred men, fifty from each of the militia regiments of Pepperell, Gerish, Berry, Plaisted, Saltonstall, and Phipps, and two hundred men for the western frontier; to wit, fifty from each of the regiments of *Chandler*, *Ward*, *Willard*, and *Stoddard*.

Also twenty-five men were raised from each of the regiments of *Wendall* and *Gouge* at Boston, for reenforcing the various garrisons; to wit, to be sent to George's Fort forty men, to Pemaquid twenty, to

Richmond twenty-five, to Brunswick twelve, and to Saco twenty.

No detachment was made from the militia of the Plymouth Colony. Gunpowder (ninety-six barrels) was conveyed to the several townships, to be sold to the inhabitants at prime cost.

Other provisions were made; and, of course, many other things were done in that and other directions.

In the summer of the same year the Cape Sable and St. John's Indians, having made an attempt on Annapolis, were by the government in Boston proclaimed rebels. And in November, 1744, in and over all the territory east of the River Passamaquoddy, they offered a bounty of £400, old tenor, to be granted for every scalp or captivated Indian obtained; and when it was learned that the Penobscots and Norridgewocks had joined them, then, Aug. 23, 1725, a declaration of war was also extended to them. Previously those Indians had burned the fort, St. George, at Annapolis Royal, also English dwelling-houses, had murdered the master of a sloop, and killed many cattle.

REWARDS.

On the 26th of October, 1744, the General Court enacted laws offering other premiums as follows:—

"To any company, party, or person singly, of His Majesty's subjects, to or residing within this province, who shall voluntarily, and at their own proper cost and charge, go out and kill a male Indian of the age of twelve years or upwards, of the Indians above named, after the twenty-sixth day of October last past, and before the last day of June, 1745 (if the war lasts so long), anywhere to the east of the Penobscot beyond a fixed line, the sum of £100 in bills of credit, new tenor; and £105 for a male Indian captive of the like age; and the sum of £50 for women; and the like sum for children under the age of twelve years killed in fight; and £55 for such of them as shall be taken prisoners.

On Nov. 2, 1744, the "precise line" above named, to the east of which they were to operate by the killing, scalping, and taking captives, was fixed and published. It was to begin on the sea-shore, three leagues from the most easterly part of Passamaquoddy River, and from thence to run north.

DONAHEW'S EXPEDITION.

In 1645, May 15, Capt. David Donahew embarked in the sloop "Resolution," with two other armed vessels, with nine hundred men, to advance against the French and Indians at Louisburg.

In this undertaking Massachusetts had enrolled and sent out 3,250 men, including Donahew's force; New Hampshire, 304; Connecticut, 516. The train of artillery consisted of eight twenty-two-pounders, twelve nine-pounders, two twelve-inch mortars, one eleven and one nine inch mortar.

Ten eighteen-pounders were borrowed of Gov. Clinton of New York.

"Brig-Gen. Samuel Waldo was the leader. Col. Samuel Moore commanded the forces from New Hampshire, Lieut.-Col. Simon Lothrop those of Connecticut, and Lieut.-Col. Gridley the artillery.

"Lieut.-Gen. Wm. Pepperrell supervised the expedition."

DONAHEW'S FATE.

After this expedition and its results were known, a considerable time elapsed before the fate of the gallant Col. Donahew was known, who, as it proved, had fallen into the hands of the Indians. "*Picket*" relates that he with eleven others went on shore in the Gut of Canso, and was at once nearly surrounded by two hundred and fifty-three French and Indians.

"That, being cut off from retreating to their vessel, defended themselves for a quarter of an hour, in which time the captain, his brother, and three others were killed."

That the rest, six in all, being wounded, were taken prisoners: two of the enemy were killed, and several wounded. That the Indians cut the flesh and sucked the blood of the captain's brother, and brutally mangled his dead body, and repeated the same upon others who had been slain.

This captain previously had commanded a privateer, which went out from Newbury, Nov. 7, 1744.

VARIOUS DEPREDATIONS.

In these years depredations by the tribes were being committed continually. We give place to a few of them.

"In 1745, July 10, an Indian party who previously had assaulted the Great *Meadow* Fort in Putney, Vt., came to the Upper Ashuelot, now the town of Keene, N.H., waylaid the road; and an early proprietor of the town, Deacon Fisher, while on his way to a pasture with his cows, was shot and scalped. On the 19th an express came to Falmouth, from Capt. Bradley at Fort George, that a garrison had been burnt by the Indians, having seventy inmates, and that one man and forty cattle had been killed. On the 30th, news arrived at Boston that two men had been beaten down by the Indians with clubs, and scalped, the one being dead, the other yet alive. And then on the 23d of August, 1745, Lieut.-Gov. Phipps, in the absence of Gov. Shirley, declared war *against 'the Eastern and Canada Indians*,' because, as he averred, the Norridgewocks, Penobscots, and others had 'broken out in open rebellion.'"

On Sept. 5, Lieut. Proctor and nineteen men gave battle to some Indians near Fort George, and two noted chiefs were killed who had been known as *Col. Morris* and *Capt. Samuel;* another of them, "*Col. Job*," was taken prisoner, and afterwards died in prison at Boston.

News came that a son of Col. Cushing was killed by unseen Indians at Sheepscot, and that two boys, James and Samuel Anderson, were taken and carried captive to Canada. Their father was killed. And thus the fight progressed.

On the 5th of October, 1745, by request of Gov. Clinton, a conference was held at Albany, N.Y., between the English and the *Six Nations*.

"Pursuant to notice, MASSACHUSETTS sent delegates, *John Stoddard, Jacob Wendall, Samuel Wells,* and *Thomas Hutchinson;* Connecticut, *Roger Walcot, Nath. Stanley;* Pennsylvania, *Thomas Lawrence, John Kinsey,* and *Isaac Norris.* Arent Stevens and Coenrat Weiser were the Interpreters. The nations represented there were the *Mohawks,* the *Oneydas,* the *Onondagas,* the *Tuscaroras,* the *Caeuges,* and the *Senekes.*"

The result of this conference was on the 20th of October announced in Boston, that, —

"The Six Nations readily renewed their covenant with the several governments; that they had taken the hatchet against the French and Indian enemy, and only wait till the Governor of New York shall order them to make use of it."

Still depredations were advancing almost everywhere, and particularly on the borders of New York. About this time a large body of three hundred French and two hundred Indians came down upon the Dutch settlements at Saratoga, and murdered

31

many of the inhabitants, ravished the country, burned houses, saw-mills, and lumber.

"For the years 1745-6-7 the premium in New York for Indian scalps and captives was £1,000, old tenor, per head, to volunteers, and £400 to impressed men, their wages and subsistence money to be deducted."

In this year, 1745, *James McQuade* and *Robert Burns* of Bedford, N.H., while returning home from Pennacook, were fired upon by Indians. McQuade was killed: Burns escaped.

A man by the name of Bunten, while on his way from Pelham to Pennacook, near Head's Tavern in Hooksett, N.H., was shot. And thus it was that the English as well as the tribes suffered dreadfully in murders and in battles, daily and nightly.

> "Such was the bloody fight and such the foe:
> Our gallant force returned them blow for blow,
> By turns successfully their force defied;
> And conquest wavering seemed from side to side."

CHAPTER XXI.

CONFLICTS 1746-1780.

Various Invasions. — Rewards are offered to Volunteers. — War declared against the Eastern Tribes. — Aid from the Penobscots sought, but in Vain. — Invasion against Royalton, Vt. — War wanes away. — Chocorua's Boy poisoned. — The suspected Family murdered. — Chocorua slain. — His Curse upon the White Man. — The Truth of his Squaw. — An Epic.

WE have seen how the wars commenced in Philip's time, — how in May, fifty years previously to this (1746), the Indians had made an attack upon the town of Scituate, burnt a saw-mill, killed *William Blackmore*, and mortally wounded *John James*, and burned down nineteen dwelling-houses, but at the close of the day were repulsed, and driven out of town.—

How at about the same period, six hundred Indians entered *Hatfield*, set fire to twelve buildings within the fortifications, and then made an attack upon the men in the meadow, and upon the fortified houses. The people, twenty-five from Hadley, rallied, killed twenty-five Indians, one apiece to each of the gallant volunteers. How in October they again beset the town, as we have shown. How again in September, 1677, fifty Indians came down the Connecticut upon Hatfield, shot three men outside of the fortifications, took captives, and made sad havoc among the women and children. And how in *Wrentham* the Indians burnt every house in town save two; and from these they were only prevented by the small-pox, which prevailed within.

Conflicts like these were going on throughout the New-England settlements *then;* and, although fifty dreary years had elapsed, there was as yet no delivance from daily and nightly anxieties, from the fagot, torch, nor from the sight of blood.

Forts and garrisons were as common as the cot.

It was thus, from town to town, for fifty years, the war went on, nearly all the way continually; and now, Aug. 26, 1746, nine hundred French and Indians invade the town of *Adams*, Mass. It had a fort which had been constructed in 1744, and is now gallantly and successfully defended under the lead of Col. Hawks, who kills forty-five of the assailants.

Three hundred French and Indians again invaded it, Aug. 2, 1748; and Col. E. Williams, with a gallant force, defended it.

In 1746, at Athol, Mass., *Ezekiel Wallingford,*

while on his way to a garrison, was slain by the Indians; and, in the following year, *Jason Babcock* was carried into captivity.

In August, 1747, *Elisha Clark* of South Hampton was killed by the Indians at his barn; and Capt. *Ephraim Williams*, *Eliakim Wright*, and *Ebenezer Kingsley* were killed near Lake George at about the same time.

In 1754 Stockbridge, Mass., was attacked by heartless savages. A Mr. Owen and his children were slain; and again in the next year, several persons fell by the blade of the tomahawk in the same neighborhood.

Many invasions and many murders had thus transpired, and were still happening up to 1763.

CONFLICTS AGAIN AMONG THEMSELVES.

During 1757 the Mohegans were again obliged to defend themselves against the Narragansetts and Nehantics, who were assisted, at times, by two Massachusetts tribes, the Pocomtocks and Norwootucks. On one occasion some Pequots allured a Mohegan canoe to shore, and thus enabled a party of Pocomtocks, who were lying in ambush, to surprise and massacre the crew. Pessicus, with a large force, invaded the Mohegan country, and once more held Uncas besieged in his fortress. A small body of

English was sent by the Colony of Connecticut to relieve him. Its very appearance caused the Narragansetts to retreat; and the Mohegans, rushing out upon them, changed their retreat into a rout. The invaders fled tumultuously towards their own country, and were furiously pursued by the Mohegans, who overtook and killed many of them while struggling through the thickets, or floundering across the streams.

In the early part of 1661, Uncas attacked the Indians of Quabaug in the eastern part of Massachusetts, killed some, made others prisoners, and carried off property, as the sufferers alleged, to the value of thirty-three pounds sterling.

WAR FARTHER NORTH, 1746-1780.

The Indians usually extended their wigwams along the banks of rivers, and sought the sea-shores rather than the deeper woods in the north. Hence Vermont suffered less from their invasions than the other New-England States: yet (1746) in the town of Vernon, Bridgman's Fort was taken and destroyed by them, and several of the inhabitants of the town were slain. On the 27th of July, 1755, *Caleb Howe*, *Hilkiah Grout*, and *Benja. Gaffield* were waylaid and fired upon while on their return from their labor in the field. At the Fort the tribes made prisoners of the families of those above named, including their wives and eleven children, and sold them into captivity in Canada.

Other depredations were committed. In 1756 Capt. Melvin with twenty men, on his way from Charlestown, N.H., to Hoosic Fort, was fired upon by Indians. A conflict followed, and several were killed. During the wars the frontier towns were frequently alarmed by Indian scouts, but were not often molested. On Aug. 9, 1780, they took three men captive in BARNARD; and in October of that year they invaded ROYALTON on White River, then a town of three hundred inhabitants. The invaders were made up mostly of Indians, and were led by one Horton, a British lieutenant. Their first design was to attack Newbury; but, upon hearing of its being fortified, they fell in upon Royalton. It was on Monday morning, Oct. 16; *first* they searched the house of *John Hutchinson*, near the line of Tunbridge, and took him and his brother prisoners; thence advanced to *Robert Haven's;* killed *Thomas Pember* and *Elias Button;* thence to *Joseph Kneeland's*, and took him, his father, *Simeon Belknap, Giles Gibs*, and *Jonathan* captives; thence to the house of *Elias Curtis*, and made him, *John Kent*, and *Peter Mason* prisoners. Thence they divided into parties, and proceeded to plunder the dwelling-houses, and bring in other prisoners.

By this time the inhabitants had taken the alarm, and were flying; and the Indians were still at work, filling the air with yells. One party proceeded towards SHARON, taking prisoners, and burning houses and barns there: another went up the river, made prisoner of *David Waller*, set fire to *Gen. Stevens's* house, plundered it, and thus on three miles, killing cattle, plundering, and setting fires all the way.

Thence they returned to their starting-point; and then they advanced across the hill to Randolph, and camped down for the night, on the second branch of the White River. During the day they had killed two persons, burned twenty houses and as many barns; had killed one hundred and fifty head of cattle, and all the sheep and hogs that fell into their paths on the way. By night the people had gathered from Connecticut River and elsewhere, organized with Capt. John House commander, and followed on in pursuit of the enemy. At length they were fired upon from an ambuscade, one man being wounded: they returned the fire, killing one, and wounding two others.

The captain then halted, and remained till daylight. The savages then sent an aged prisoner to inform the Americans that if they made an attack upon them they would put all their English prisoners to death; that *two* had already been killed, — the one to retaliate for the death of the Indian who had been slain; and the other was slain for refusing to march, in the expectation that the Americans would relieve him. These were tomahawked as they lay upon the ground.

Having placed their warriors in the rear, they silently proceeded to Randolph, took one prisoner there, thence through Brookfield by the way of Winooski River and Lake Champlain to Montreal. House and his men followed them to Brookfield, and thence returned, but without further conflict.

PEACE.

Soon after the close of this French war the Indians, withdrawing from their rivers and ponds, and from their hunting and trapping grounds in New England, gradually vanished away. Thus by degrees the way was opened to English settlers, who ventured farther into the forests thus vacated, and, sequestering and taking possession of the lands, built houses, and otherwise made progress, sometimes aggressively excluding the red man, until at length he became unheard of, except now and then from the far-off wilderness.

In his departure he left behind him not the ruins of desolated cities, nor of lofty castles, nor of world-renowned monasteries: he left nothing, absolutely nothing, but mere samples of the bow and arrow, the chisel, and the mortar.

About this time there was a last lingering remnant of a tribe in New Hampshire, led and cared for by

CHOCORUA.

Oh, what clusters of historical incidents seem to rally around that name! Chocorua (pronounced *Cheh-corruah*) was the last chief of the Pequawkets then wandering in the woods north of the great lakes, in territory of which the town of Burton became the centre, and where the world-renowned mountain is still lifting its bloody cliffs to the skies, beclouded as they are as if to weep over it. Chocorua had a family. His squaw died, and was buried by the brook-side, where he had first found her. His little Indian boy still continued to follow at his heels, in this then wilderness.

One day, at the house of one Campbell (a white settler), the boy got poisoned, and came home to the wigwam, and died. Chocorua thought he was poisoned purposely.

Soon afterwards *Campbell* left home; and when at night he returned, his family were all dead in the house.

A few days elapsed; and the white settlers followed CHOCORUA into that mountain which now bears his name, about fifteen miles north of the lake, in Burton, now Albany, N.H. Campbell discovered him on the pinnacle of the mountain cliff, and commanded him to jump off. "Ah!" said the Indian, "the Great Spirit gave *Chocorua* his life; and he will not throw it away at the bidding of the white man." They shot him; and while dying he pronounced awful curses upon the English.

In describing that scene, Mrs. L. Maria Child, in a vigorous legend, gives the words of Chocorua's *curse* thus: —

"A curse on ye, white men! May the Great Spirit curse ye when he speaks in the clouds, and his words are fire! Chocorua had a son; and ye killed him when the sky looked bright. Lightnings blast your crops; winds and fire destroy your dwellings! The Evil Spirit breathe death on your cattle! Your graves lie in the pathway of the Indian; panthers howl and wolves fatten over your bones!"

Ever since that day the want of vegetation in and about that mountain, all its dearths, and all the diseases upon the cattle and upon the inhabitants of that region, have been attributed to that *curse* of Chocorua.

The faithfulness of Chocorua's squaw has been celebrated in epic verse, wherein the story is briefly told: it was published in one of my books. And I here give place to the

BRIDE OF BURTON.

[AT MY TENT IN THE MOUNTAIN.]

"Chocorua goes to the Great Spirit: his curse stays with the white man. The prophet sank upon the ground, still uttering inaudible curses. And there they left his bones to whiten in the sun."

1.

The tired hounds at length are sleeping;
And over our tent wild night is weeping.
  Dark dews in the Burton Wood;
While from her distant radiant fountain
The queenly moon lights up the mountain,
  Where brave Chocorua stood.

2.

To this the ills of earth had brought him;
'Twas here the white man sought and fought him,
  In daring, dashing numbers.
From whence despair had deigned to dwell,
Chocorua, wounded, faltering, fell;
  And here in death he slumbers.

3.

Entranced beneath thy cragged peak, —
Creation vast! — thy summit bleak,
  Thy varied vales, I ponder.
I reverence Him who shaped the hills,
These silvery lakes, those glittering rills,
  Wild, in a world of wonder.

4.

Up 'neath the stars, yon glimmering slope,
Piled range on range, they fill the scope
   Of man's enchanted vision.
Bold there above a heaving sea,
For aye to vie in majesty,
   Earth's grandest proud position.

5.

Life and its joys Chocorua sought:
His tribe he trained as Nature taught,
   Mild in these magic mountains;
With bow and arrow known of yore,
Vast woodlands wild he hunted o'er;
   Dame fed him at her fountains.

6.

Of what wild waters yield in view,
Chocorua launched his light canoe
   On many a rapid river.
Fierce falcons faltered in the air,
And the wild deer bounded from his lair,
   At the rattle of his quiver.

7.

From boyhood brave a priest he roved;
Faithful at heart, he fervent loved
   Keoka, ne'er to sever.
No happier pair could earth produce:
Keoka true, and a proud pappoose
   Inspired that wigwam ever.

8.

With truth and trust and patient pride,
At morn, at noon, or eventide,
  She calmed the cloudy hour;
Her heart was full of love and song;
She cheered Chocorua's life along;
  She brought him many a flower.

9.

Such was the life Chocorua sought;
Such were the charms Keoka brought:
  Unselfish, unpretending.
Kings of the earth I'd envy not:
Give me to know Chocorua's lot,
  Such faith, such favor, blending.

10.

Soon then, alas! sad, fatal years,
That moved heroic hearts to tears,
  Fell heavy on Pequawket.
Dread death, that brought Keoka blind,
Had mazed Chocorua in his mind:
  The tribes began to talk it.

11.

Of rushes rude they made her shroud,
In crooked form a casket proud;
  And laid her in the wildwood,
Beside a rippling river shore,
Where many a song and dance of yore
  Had cheered her happy childhood.

Ten times a day Chocorua wept,
Ten times a day his shadow swept
In plumy form around her.

12.

Six logs laid high on either side, —
Embraced they hold that sainted bride,
　With a rail-made roof around her,
Deep, calm, at rest, devoid of fears,
Of loves, of hopes, or tender tears,
　Where first Chocorua found her.

13.

A white flag fluttered in the air;
Sweet stars from heaven glittered there;
　And the zephyrs came to love her.
Deep woodlands whispered sighs unknown;
The plaintive pines their loss bemoan;
　And the wild-rose creeps above her.

14.

Ten times a day Chocorua wept;
Ten times a day his shadow swept
　In plumy form around her;
The partridge fluttered from his trail;
And the she-wolf nightly heard his wail:
　To a troubled trance it bound her.

15.

Where'er he turned, where'er he roamed,
Or when around the grave he mourned,
　There, prompt and true to mind him,
His little lad, with lifted eye,
As if to hail that mother nigh,
　Tripped on, and stood behind him.

16.

'Twas thus Chocorua's heart was pressed:
Long months moved on, but gave no rest;
  Sad thus, dread Fate had made it.
Still there is grief as yet unknown:
" One trouble never comes alone,"
  Our dear old mothers said it.

17.

Next then indeed, how true it proved!
Another fate, as Fortune moved,
  Came, cruel quite as t'other.
By hidden drugs in malice made,
Alas! that beauteous boy is dead,
  To moulder with his mother.

18.

Then wailed Chocorua wilder still,
Without a heart, without a will,
  A ghostlike, lurking wonder;
Yet in his flesh there's native fire,
Though earth and hell in crime conspire
  To drive the soul asunder.

19.

As now the story oft is told,
Chocorua cursed the English old,
  For deeds unholy certain.
And ever since, from then to this,
Not a breath of hope, or breeze of bliss,
  Hath moved the woods of Burton.

20.

Dark shadows came to chase the sun;
The Indian hunter's day was done;
   And the woodlands wild were sighing.
'Twas then a shaft his heart had broken;
Vengeance the eternal Fates betoken:
   Chocorua is dying.

21.

On that dread night, and hitherto,
The heavens let fall malarious dew,
   Far down these murky mountains.
Not a flower in all the waste is known;
The maple-leaf is dry half-grown,
   And death is in the fountains.

22.

The moping owl hath ceased to hoot,
The scrub-oak falters at the root,
   And the snail is lank and weary.
The fated fawn hath found his bed;
Huge hawks, high-flying, drop down dead,
   Above that apex dreary.

23.

Faded, the vales no fruits adorn;
The hills are pale with poisoned corn;
   The flocks are lean, repining;
No growth the panting pastures yield;
And the staggering cattle roam the field
   Forlorn, in death declining.

24.

'Tis thus we're made the slaves of earth,
Mope in miasmas, deep in dearth,
  Sad, from some bad beginning, —
From cruelty to friend or foes.
Our morbid pains and mental woes
  Prove but the pangs of sinning.

25.

High now a voice is in the air,
As if Chocorua still were there,
  With wood-nymphs wild attending;
'Tis heard far up the mountain-side, —
That plaint of earth's down-trodden tribe,
  Bleak, with the zephyrs blending.

26.

O God, forgive our Saxon race!
Blot from thy book, no more to trace,
  Fraternal wrath infernal,
That taints the atmosphere we breathe,
The sky above, and earth beneath,
  With dearth and death eternal.

27.

Come, boys! we'll take our tents away
To better vales. 'Tis break of day;
  And the hounds are awake for duty.
Blow, blow the horn! A gracious sun
Hath brought a *brotherhood* begun
  In life, in love, and beauty.

CHAPTER XXII.

DUSTON MONUMENT.

Preliminary proceedings to its erection on the
ISLAND CONTOOCOOK.
Its Inscriptions, and Programme at its Unveiling,
June 17, 1874;
together with an
Historical Oration
and Poem, by
ROBERT B. CAVERLY,
then and there addressed to the
Sons and Daughters
of
New England.

THUS, in the foregoing pages, have we endeavored to recount the successive events which startled New England for nearly a hundred years,—events in which the most terrible conflicts, as well as the heroism of Hannah Duston, with others, are prominently delineated.

And now, at the distance of nearly two centuries, as appears, the faith, valor, and endurance of our ancient mothers, still remaining in the human heart, have been faithfully recognized in the building of a monument to their memories. This enterprise affords the materials which are to fill our last chapter; and here it may be well to learn and remember, that noble deeds are never to be lost; that the fair fame of the mothers is not to be forgotten.

The granite rock, deep in the mountain, which had held concealed the image of Hannah Duston for thousands of years, has of late been dug out. A New-England sculptor, and two artists, the one from Scotland, and the other from the far-off Italy, have carved her out, and have made her image to stand forth to the world heroic in all of her native strength, faith, and beauty.

STATUE.

This tribute to the ancient mothers, which for these many years had been contemplated and promised, took its start to be erected in January, 1872.

To that end, Messrs. John C. and Calvin Gage, then the owners of the Island Contoocook, conveyed to Messrs. Bouton, Nutter, and Caverly, gratuitously, all that part of it east of the Northern Railroad track between the rivers, for the purpose of the monument.

Thereupon a paper was issued, as follows:—

SUBSCRIPTION-PAPER, AND PLAN OF THE WORK.

To the benevolent sons of New Hampshire, and to whom it may concern:—

The undersigned propose to erect a monument to the memory of HANNAH DUSTON as a representative of New-England mothers; to be of granite, and of form and dimensions as in the diagram, at the cost of about six thousand dollars; to be completed within two years from this date, and to be erected on the island at the mouth of the Contoocook River, near to, and in sight of the Northern Railroad, and on the precise spot where the wigwam stood, and where Mrs. Duston and her assistants liberated themselves from their cruel captors.

It seems to belong to us, as a generous people, after a lapse of so many years, to erect such a monument, and it will be the duty as well as the pleasure of all coming generations to protect and perpetuate it.

This statue, when completed (the title to the land being in us), is to be assigned to the State, or to some corporation, municipal or otherwise, who shall forever protect and preserve it.

We respectfully call your attention to this undertaking, trusting it will meet your approval: if it does, you will please append your name to this, carrying out against it such sum as you will be good for to us for the purpose of accomplishing the design herein set forth.

        N. BOUTON,
        E. S. NUTTER,
        ROBERT B. CAVERLY.

CONCORD, Jan 23, 1873.

DONORS.

Names of those who volunteered, and generously accomplished the work: —

FRANKLIN, N.H.

Jonas B. Aikin, Esq.
Hon. Geo. W. Nesmith.
Rev. Wm. T. Savage.
Walter Aikin, Esq.
Hon. Austin F. Pike.
H. F. Aikin.
Burleigh & Bro.
Charles H. Clark, Esq.
C. B. Nichols, M.D.
Wesley Sawyer.
Alexis Proctor, Esq.
H. N. Stevens.
Daniel C. Burleigh, Esq.
W. F. Daniel, Esq.
J. H. Rowell.
Daniel Barnard, Esq.
D. Gilchrist.
Lowell Scribner.
A. W. Sulloway, Esq.
Isaac N. Blodgett, Esq.
Stephen Kenrick, Esq.
Daniel A. Brown.
M. B. Goodwin, Esq.
J. W. Swett.

FISHERVILLE.

Almon Harris, Esq.
John A. Holmes.
Samuel F. Brown.
John S. Rollins.
W. H. Allen.
Chas. H. Amsden.
H. M. Fisher.
Henry F. Brown.
D. Arthur Brown.
N. Butler, Esq.
John S. Brown, Esq.
A. G. Howe.
Ebenr. F. Elliott.
A. M. Gage, Esq.
John C. Gage, Esq.

Dr. S. M. Emery.
J. P. Hubbard.
Isaac K. Gage, Esq.
John A. Coburn.
H. M. Fisher.
Daniel A. Brown.
T. S. Jacobs.
D. Warren Fox.
C. C. Zopbliff.
Geo. P. Meserve.
W. Walter Eastman.
John McNeal.
J. P. Sanders.
Calvin Gage.
John Chandler Gage.
Isaac Kimball Gage.
Moses H. Bean.
Hiram M. Fisher.
Charles V. Fisher.
John P. Rowe.
Northern R. R. Co.
C. J. C. Gage.
Gage, Porter, & Co.
Calvin Gage.

LOWELL, MASS.

Dr. James C. Ayer.
Gen. B. F. Butler.
Artemas L. Brooks, Esq.
Mrs. C. L. George.
Hon. Sewell G. Mack.
Hapgood Wright, Esq.
Hon. Josiah B. French.
J. F. Kimball, Esq.
Hon. John A. Butrick.
George Wright, Esq.
C. J. W. Maynard.
F. F. Battles, Esq.
A. F. Jewett, Esq.
Hon. John A. Knowles.
Stone, Huse, & Co.
Marden & Rowell.
John L. Hunt.

Knapp & Morey.
George M. Elliott, Esq.
Emily Rogers and Elizabeth Rogers, descendants of Zadock Rogers, Esq.
Mrs. Jefferson Bancroft, descendant of Mrs. Duston.
John L. Corliss.
John F. McEvoy, Esq.
Erastus Stearns.
Chester W. Rugg.
A. G. Norcross.
John R. Wentworth.
Charles Kimball.
Frederick Ayer, Esq.
Edward Caverly.
Wm. L. Clark.
Alanson Folsom.
Thomas H. Elliot, Esq.
Wm. W. Duncan, Esq.
Jona. Hope.
Dr. Joseph R. Hayes.

LAWRENCE.

Hon. J. C. Hoadley.
Wm. A. Russell, Esq.
Morris Knowles, Esq.
S. Dockham.
J. S. Bennett.
M. B. Ames.
Rufus Reed.
H. A. Prescott.
Abiel Chandler.
E. Jaslyed.
A. Morrison, Esq.
Geo. S. Merrill, Esq.
Horace A. Wadsworth, Esq.
R. Bower & Son.

BOSCAWEN, N.H.

Hale Atkinson, Esq.
E. E. Graves.
Amos Webber.
James F. French.
C. E. Chadwick.
C. W. Webster, Esq.
N. S. Webster.
L. M. Chadwick.
John Seavey.
E. G. Wood.

J. E. Hosmer.
B. R. Dow.
John Lang.
C. J. Chadwick.
N. S. Webster.
L. T. Boyce.
S. A. Ambrose.
S. B. Chadwick.
Roswell Swetland.
Geo. W. Prichard.
F. S. Swetland.
Richard Pervere.
Dearborn Glines.
Peter Coffin.
E. Raymond.
John E. Rives.
John K. Chandler.

CONCORD, N.H.

Ch. Jus. Henry A. Bellows.
"   " Ira Perley.
Hon. Edward L. Knowlton.
Hon. Geo. G. Fogg.
Hon. E. C. Bailey.
C. H. Kelley, Esq.
Hon. Asa Fowler.
L. Downing, Jun.
F. L. Blood.
James L. Mason.
Geo. P. Harvey.
Alonzo Downing.
Joseph H. Abbott.
George F. Whittridge.
George A. Pillsbury, Esq.
J. V. Barron, Esq.
Franklin Moseley.
Albert Foster.
J. E. Clifford.
Solon A. Carter.
Hon. B. F. Prescott.
A. B. Thompson.
Hon. N. White.
Franklin H. Rice.
M. T. Willard.
Oliver Pillsbury.
Peter Sanborn, Esq.
B. F. Caldwell.
Dunkler & Allen.
Chas. P. Moore.
Rufus M. Morgan.
J. C. Harvey.

M. W. Tappan.
Joseph D. Taylor.
J. P. Bancroft.
J. H. Rowell.
Walter Bates.
Jacob B. Rand.
John Abbott.
S. C. Whitcher.
Geo. L. Stratton.
Joseph Stickney.
Geo. A. Blanchard, Esq.
Geo. W. Brown.
Wm. H. Brown.
Joseph Eastman.
Daniel Marden.
David Blanchard, Esq.
Republican Press Association.
John L. Tallant.
Daniel Holden, Esq.
P. E. Blanchard.
W. B. Durgin.
J. H. Albin.
Calvin Howe.
W. W. Cochran.
T. W. Pillsbury.
Isaac Clement.
Wm. M. Chase.
Samuel B. Page.
Ira Rowell.
Henry Martin.
R. R. Abbott.
Daniel Farnam.
Atkinson Webster.
Henry McFarland.
Chas. Woodman.
Chas. Nutting.
William Pecker.
Cyrus R. Robinson.
J. T. Clough.
Joseph Smith.
Herman Sanborn.
Mrs. E. A. Pecker.
Ira Abbott.
B. W. Sanborn.
A. C. Holt.
W. Odlin.
J. N. Lander.
Samuel E. Clifford.
Mrs. E. L. Staniels.
Harrison Bean.
Benja. L. Larkin.
Mrs. Mary A. Larkin.

Simeon Abbott.
Reuben N. Myers.
Geo. A. Cummings.
S. C. Morrill.
Geo. H. Done.
M. B. Abbott.
Mrs. Mary D. Eastman.
Daniel Sanborn.
James Frye.
Andrew Bunker.
S. Seavey.
John Ballard.
Horatio G. Belknap.
Ichabod C. Weeks.
D. A. McCurdy.
W. M. Abbott,
Albert Stevens.
Thomas W. Perkins.
M. Critchel & Son.
Woodbury Flanders.
J. Palmer.
David Fowler.
Abel Hutchins.
Samuel Butterfield.
Chas. H. Farnum.
Moses M. Davis.
Lowell Brown.
John B. Sanborn.
Horace Call.
Daniel S. Webster.
Hon. Onslow Stearns.
C. W. Blake.
J. S. Lund.
Dutton Woods.
Stephens & Dunkler.
F. S. Abbott.
Geo. P. Harvey.
C. H. Norton.
G. W. Wadleigh.
A. J. Prescott.
George D. B. Prescott.
John Jackman.
G. A. Young.
S. G. Lane.
B. F. Holden, Esq.
Gust. Walker.
John H. Pearson.
William E. Chandler.
Enos Blake.
S. S. Kimball.
John Kimball.
John Hackman.

ITS BUILDERS.

Stephen Carleton.
E. S. Barrett.
B. A. Kimball.
C. H. Martin & Co.
M. H. Farnum.
S. Farnum.
George W. Crockett.
John McNeal.
George P. Cleaves.
W. G. Shaw.
N. S. Bachelder.
J. N. Patterson.
D. J. Abbott.
Frank H. Pierce.
G. H. H. Silsby.
J. Frank Hoit.
Robert Hall, M.D.
Noah Ranlet.
C. C. Flanders.
T. W. & J. H. Stewart.
O. V. Pitman.
Moses H. Bradley.
A. H. Crosby.
John M. Haines.
D. M. Morrill.
H. W. Ranlet.
A. Langmaid.
J. P. Tenney.
J. T. Bachelder.
H. B. Tebbetts,
J. C. Pillsbury.
J. C. A. Hill.
Stanley & Ayer.
John H. George, Esq.
George E. Lawrence.
Charles R. Corning.
C. W. Moore.
Bradley Gill.
Richmond Smith.
E. B. Hutchinson.
Naham Robinson.
H. L. Rand.
Daniel Wyman.
George W. Brown.
Hamilton E. Perkins.
John C. Kilburn.
Amos Hadley.
Luther McCutchins.
O. E. Sheldon.
Andrew S. Smith.
Marsh Richardson.
A. A. Blanchard.

J. H. Morey.
A. S. Marshall.
Charles Butters.
G. H. Adams.
George H. Davis.
Joseph P. Stickney.
W. C. Sargent.
L. Johnson.
George J. Sargent.
George A. Boswell.
Elbridge Dimond.
Timothy Carter.
F. B. Carter.
R. B. Hoit.
Mrs. Harriet N. Runnels.
John Sawyer.
Sherman D. Colby.
Daniel C. Tenney.
Lyman Sawyer.
Anson S. Marshall.
J. Frank Webster.
Jonathan Clough.
Aaron Tay.
D. A. Morrill.
John W. Carter.
John G. Tallant.
Mrs. Caroline Clark.
Mrs. Mary E. Pecker.
Hon. N. S. Berry.

MANCHESTER, N.H.

Gov. E. A. Straw.
Hon. B. F. Martin.
Hon. Isaac W. Smith.
Hon. Daniel Clark.
C. W. Stanley, Esq.
William Shepherd.
Phineas Adams.
Dr. Josiah Crosby.
Hon. Daniel Cross.
Hon. Moody Courier.
D. B. Varney.
Att'y Gen. L. W. Clark.
Hon. J. P. Newall.
J. W. Fellows.

NASHUA, N.H.

Josiah G. Graves, M.D.
T. H. Woods, Esq.
H. W. Gilman.
Dr. C. G. A. Eayers.

Edward Spaulding, M.D.
B. B. & T. P. Whittemore.
Moore & Langley.
Myron Taylor, Esq.

OTHER TOWNS.

SMITHVILLE, N.J.
H. R. Smith, Esq.

BUFFALO, N.Y.
Hiram Lewis.

PEMBROKE, N.H.
George P. Little, Esq.
James Dodge.
Mrs. B. Whitehouse.
Aaron Whittemore.
William Parker.
Truworthy L. Fowler.

ALLENSTOWN.
Rev. H. H. Hartwell.
D. L. Jewett.

PORTSMOUTH.
Ex-Gov. Ichabod Goodwin.
Hon. W. H. Y. Hackett.

CANTERBURY.
D. M. Clough, Esq.
David Morrill.
Joseph Ayers.

BOSTON, MASS.
Ira Bradley, Esq.
John F. Banchor, Esq.
Dana B. Gove, Esq.
John E. Lyon.

HOOKSETT, N.H.
Hon. Natt Head.
W. F. Head, Esq.

WILMOT.
John Bachelder, Esq.

DANBURY.
Alonzo Wilkins.

BOW.
Parker Brown.
John Brown, 2d.
W. W. Storrs.
Betsey Stark.
Robert Hall, M.D.
Andrew Gault.

ANDOVER.
John Proctor, Esq.

GUILFORD.
John J. Morrill.

SUNCOOK, N.H.
Mary Bean.
Clark E. Humphrey, Esq.

BROOKLYN, N.Y.
Edward Caverly.

TYNGSBORO, MASS.
Hon. Nath. Brinley.

SUNCOOK.
Philip Sargent, Esq.
David Hayes, Esq.

WEARE.
M. A. Hodgdon.

BRADFORD.
M. M. Tappan.

WARNER.
C. G. McAlpine.
W. R. Bartlett.

SUTTON.
Enoch Page.

DUNBARTON.
C. M. Stark.

BRISTOL.
Geo. T. Crawford.

HILL.
S. T. Johnston.

CHICHESTER.
Edward Langmaid.

LOUISVILLE, KY.
Samuel L. Avery, Esq.

HOPKINTON, N. H.
Horace Chase.

ENFIELD.
William Potter.

KEENE, N.H.
Sentinel Printing Co.
Julius N. Morse.
C. S. Faulkner, Esq.
Adam Poor.
F. A. Faulkner, Esq.
Gen. S. G. Griffin.
Hon. Wm. Dinsmoor.
A. T. Colony, Esq.
Hon. Horatio Colony.

DEXTER, ME.
Nath. Duston.

WARNER, N.H.
C. G. McAlpin.

NOTE.— In the completion of this extraordinary work of art, much has depended on the generous, untiring exertions of our friend and associate E. S. NUTTER, Esq., of Concord, N.H., who was the chief marshal in its erection as well as in the ceremonies through which it is to be unveiled. Long, *long* may he live! R. B. C.

SCULPTOR.

WILLIAM ANDREWS , ... Lowell, Mass.

ARTISTS.

ANDREW ORSOLINI . . . . . . Carari, Italy.
JAMES MURRAY . . . . . . Aberdeen, Scotland.
CHARLES H. ANDREWS . . . . . Lowell, Mass.
PORTER E. BLANCHARD, Builder . . . Concord, N. H.

INSCRIPTIONS.

On its westerly side, in deep letters, is the following :—

HEROUM GESTA.
Fides —— Justitia.
Hannah Duston
Mary Neff
Samuel Leonardson
March 30, 1697
Mid-night

On its easterly side is the following : —

March
15   1697   30

The War-whoop — Tomahawk — **Fagot**
and
Infanticides
were at Haverhill.

The Ashes of the Camp-fires
at Night
And ten of the Tribe
are here.

On the northerly side is the following: —

DONORS.

John S. Brown	(F)	Morris Knowles	(La)
John Proctor	(A)	Walter Aikin	(Fr)
Jonas B. Aikin	(Fr)	Edward Spaulding	(N)
Almon Harris	(F)	Henry F. and D. A. Brown	(F)
Edward K. Knowlton	(C)	Joseph Stickney	(C)
Artemas L. Brooks	(L)	John C. Gage	(F)
George W. Nesmith	(Fr)	George A. Pillsbury	(C)
Josiah G. Graves	(N)	James C. Ayer	(L)
Onslow Stearns	(C)	Calvin Gage	(F)
Benj. F. Butler	(L)	Mrs. Jefferson Bancroft	(L)

Emily and Eliz. Rogers (L)
and
many, *many* others.

On the southerly side is the following : —

STATUA
1874.

Know ye that we with many plant it;
In trust to the State we give and grant it,
That the tide of Time may never cant it,
Nor mar, nor sever;
That Pilgrims here may heed the mothers,
That Truth and Faith and all the Others,
With banners high in glorious colors,
May stand forever.

Witnesses.   NATH. BOUTON [S]
B. F. PRESCOTT,   ELIPH. S. NUTTER [S]
ISAAC K. GAGE.   ROB'T B. CAVERLY [S]

HISTORICAL ADDRESS

TO THE

SONS AND DAUGHTERS OF NEW ENGLAND,

ISLAND CONTOOCOOK, JUNE 17, 1874,

By ROBERT B. CAVERLY.

THE same genial sun in the heavens is moving. — The moon and the stars have once again given place to it.—

The same round earth is advancing, revolving as of yore; and the generations are *upward* and *onward* as in the days of Hannah Duston.

Yet of all the inhabitants of the wilderness that then were here; of the birds of the air, that filled the heavens with the melody of their music; of all the finny tribes in these waters, as they sported up and down then, in the vivacity of sweet life, — *none*, not one, of all that innumerable throng, now lives.

Since then, sad to relate, the entire race of red men in New-England, as they ingloriously fled from civilization, faltering, fell, and have vanished away.

This, indeed, came to pass, partly through the aggressive intrusions of English settlers, oft repeated; partly through the cruel interference of the Canadian French, who tainted the tribes; yet mostly, perhaps, through the inordinate, unbridled infirmities of the tribes themselves.

To-day, in spite of the Indian wars of a hundred years, during all which time New England was but little else than one common battle-field of blood, we stand here upon this island, — an island fraught with tearful tragedy and touching memories. Hither to *this*, the tribes came up; and here at midnight, nearly two hundred years ago, the camp-fires in front of the wigwams sent forth for the last time their flickering lights.

We stand here to-day as if upon the ruins of a fallen race, to revive reminiscences of the past, and, as well as we may, to transmit them down to the far-off coming generations. The soil beneath, the rivers around, and the skies above, are all sacred. Here it was that the poisoned arrow, which had pierced the harmless hearts of women and children, fell to the earth. Here, too, the keen edge of the Indian battle-axe was broken: it began to crumble; and in the then distant years it wasted away.

This, of all others, was the primeval standpoint from which the wild forest of New England began to discard its barbarisms.

This, indeed, was the turning-point at which the combined forces of French and Indians were first made to know and feel, that, in such a warfare, there were blows to take, as well as blows to give.

In fact, from this standpoint the tribes were made to take the hint, that, in dealing with *Hannah Duston*, "they had been waking up the wrong passenger."

Nay, it was from this spot, and from kindred points, that the cruel, devastating inroads made by barbarous Indians in this then wilderness, began to yield to the progress of Pilgrim settlers, and to the transcendent march of civilization in a new world.

Hannah Duston was a native of Haverhill, Mass. On the 15th of March, 1697, the tribes divided themselves into separate squads, and surrounded the town.

And then at her own threshold she heard the terrific war-whoop cry of savages seeking blood. There and then she had witnessed the twelve captives, other than herself, driven away from Haverhill, to be murdered or to be sold as slaves. There and then she had heard the wail of helpless women and children at the slaughter of twenty-seven of her own dear neighbors; had seen the blood-stained tomahawk; had seen the apple-tree, crimsoned over as it had been with the life-blood of an infant, her own little Martha. Nay, she had witnessed in the distance the devouring flames, crackling and bursting from eight dwelling-houses as well as from her own, as she calmly gazed back from the cold snow-banks of a dark wilderness.

In truth, that mother then was too sedate to mourn, too sad to weep; too sagacious, too *valiant*, to evince the least emotion.

These traits of character in the calm demeanor of this heroine, as they appeared throughout that terrible trial-day, must ever be regarded as a transcendent climax in true heroism.

Next, they arrived upon this island.

Fifteen long, weary days they had been meandering, now in the deep wilderness, now along the shores of the Merrimack, and then in boats of birch, up here to the Contoocook.

Just before arriving at this fort, the one-half of the tribe (with whom Hannah Bradley was a captive), turned away to another locality, and encamped in other wigwams not far away.

The other Indians, twelve in number, came over here, and started their camp-fires on this ground.

As usual, they feasted on the slaughtered game of that day. Night came on; and the clouds of heaven cast their dark shadows upon the drowsy earth. The tired tribe camped down, fell asleep here, and probably slept soundly.

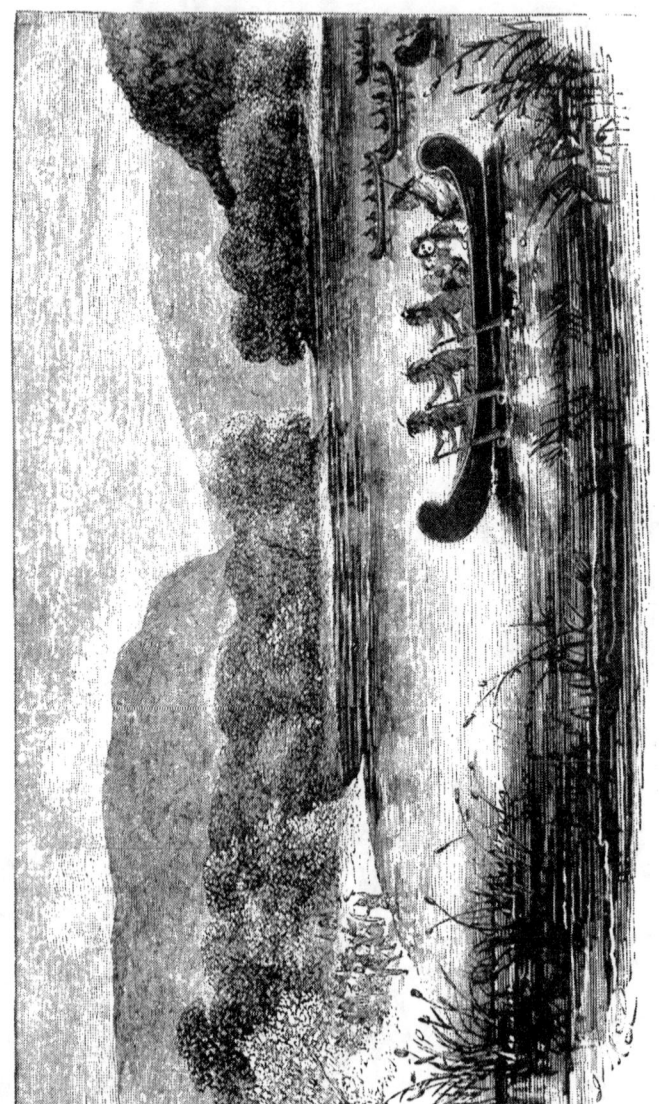

CROSSING TO THE CONTOOCOOK.

Then at midnight, pursuant to a previous appointment which Mrs. Duston had made with Mary Neff her maid, and Leonardson the boy, they rose up while their oppressors were still asleep.

They silently, stealthily creeping about, obtained from the belts of their enemies three of those blood-stained weapons of death which had been used at Haverhill.

Now they are taking their positions.

Alas! how much depends on the eventful happenings of a moment! Every step of the foot, every breath that moves the air, is taken cautiously; the snap of a brittle twig, the rustle of a leaf, or the least mishap or mistake in their concert of action, must have been the startling signal of death to themselves. Ah! a strange divinity attends them. Their wigwam camp-fires, hitherto brilliant, had begun to fade.

That noisy old forest which had been waving above the slumbering tribes, ominously, as if by magic, ceased to move. The whispering west winds, previously boisterous in the lofty tree-tops, are hushed to silence.

The stars of night, and the ghosts of a thousand slaughtered pilgrims, are looking down.

Three tomahawks uplifted are seen to glimmer in the light of the camp-fires, and ten savages, in garments crimsoned with the blood of men, women, and children, slept their last sleep.

Their scalps, taken as evidence of what had transpired, a hatchet, and an Indian gun,—these also they took along with them to Haverhill and to Boston.

In the dread darkness which followed, Mrs. Duston, Mary, and the boy, as they in a canoe from this island floated down the Merrimack, not much could be seen. Nor was there much to be *heard*, save the suggestive ripplings of waters, and the howlings of the hungry wolf in the boundless wilderness beyond them.

Still quietly, cautiously, downward they wended their way towards Haverhill,—

> Sedate, impressed, while now and then
> A siren voice invades the glen;
> A peaceful prayer, a trite, *Amen*,
> Goes up to the gracious Giver.
> And though the owl was moping still,
> And Death is seen, go where they will,
> God's candle-lights the heavens fill:.
> They burn upon the river.

Since that day two hundred years have run their circuit nearly through. Time has swept away the red man and the Pilgrim, as we have seen. It is now fast overwhelming the revered, yet half-forgotten fame of our own immediate mothers and fathers. Yet some things are eternal.

THE ISLAND — ITS INSPIRATIONS.

This island, preserved as it is of nature's God, still remains; and its incidental sublimities are among the wonders of the world.

Its inspirations move us. We stand here to-day *collectively, individually, duteously.* We look about us to the east, to the west, to the north, and to the south; and *June* — lovely June! — has spread the landscape with its most beautiful colorings. The bleating flocks are *playful;* and the cattle upon a thousand hills are abundant, awaiting the pleasure and the profit of an industrious, God-serving yeomanry. The wicked wars are over; and peace, "the sweet peace of Jerusalem," is here.

Alas! how unlike it were the cloud-covered, crimson days of our ancient mothers!

The God of nature is here as of yore. As if to honor this occasion, and to animate us, the balmy breezes of heaven are full of inspiration-giving discourses. The nightly zephyrs have come, and even at noonday are whispering forth their sweet pæans. The young and beautiful forest of this tragic island puts on airs to-day, as if in an effort to wave obeisance to this occasion, and as if in the glow of its ancient beauty it tries to speak of the heroic deeds of old Mother Duston. Again the once angry yet now tranquil waters of the old Contoocook and Merrimack are moving beautifully.

On their endless round from ocean to mountain, and from the mountains to the sea, they have come down to us to-day, in the knowledge of tragic years; yet, turning hither as if in familiar converse, they tender to us the inspiring harmonies of peace and of holiness. And then again, as of yore, they move onward, everywhere on the way imparting and promulgating impressive lessons of constancy, of endurance, of divinity, and of duty. Onward as from the creation let them live, and let them rejoice.

Forever shall they bear and keep unchanged the beautiful euphonic names, which in the beginning of the world they had taken from the old Pennacooks. Nobler, brighter than ever, they discourse sweet music, as if to vie with the daughters of New England in generous deeds, and in the glorious inspirations of faith and of truth and of loveliness.

To-day this vast assemblage, as representatives of a generation, constitute a connecting link between the past and the great future. We, at this hour, are here to bring back from oblivion, as best we may, impressive yet fast-fading reminiscences; to take note of the advancing generations; and to add at least a brief chapter to our common history.

To record and perpetuate the annals of an ancestry, is among the noblest achievements of life.

To adorn and enliven such a history, there are no

better examples in all the events of the world, than are to be found in the lives and characters of the old New-England mothers. Try them; measure their faith, if you please, as in the days of dearth and disappointment. Measure them in the midst of conflagrations, war, and blood, or in the tranquil years of peace and plenty; or try them in the appalling perils of an Indian raid upon their houses, their little ones, and their lives. Stern in integrity, strong for endurance, firm in truth, and fervent in valor forever, they never faltered.

God give us heroism like theirs, force like theirs, and faith like theirs, through all the events of advancing time!

[*An Interlude of Music.*]

1.

Ye daughters fair, from many a town
Of the noblest stock in the world's renown,
We've come to lay our trophies down
    Here at thy feet.
Your hopeful halves, your little ones,
The force and valor of your sons,
Your love at heart, warm as it runs, —
    We grateful greet.

2.

We've come inspired of the fond old mothers:
Their sainted care still o'er us hovers;
Daring in deeds transcending others
    Mid life's relations.

Their kindly natures, firm defial,
Their souls triumphant through all trial,
To truth and faith and self-denial
    We bring oblations.

3.

To this we've come from the mountain side,
Far out from where wild waters glide,
Up where old ocean turns her tide
    To memories dear;
From where Monadnoc pours her rills,
From Franklin's favored wild-wood hills,
From floods afar that roll their mills,
    We volunteer.

4.

We've roamed where the red man roamed of yore,
On many a highland hunted o'er,
On the shores where oft he dipt his oar,
    Trailing along.
We've stood where the heaven-taught Pilgrim stood;
Out from the fields once stained of blood,
We bring glad tidings of our God;
    We swell the throng.

5.

Down from the lakes uncounted numbers,
From mountains mighty, full of wonders;
From where Niagara's torrent thunders,
    Vast for renown;
Far up from Massachusetts Bay,
From the Heights of Abram, the other way,
We hail old Contoocook to-day,
    Still rolling down.

6.

Onward as ever, balmy, beauteous,
'Neath sun or cloud, serene, salubrious,
To God and man forever duteous,
    Ye move amain;
Thy banks, thy waves, the wild deer loved
Thy power the tribes of yore approved:
Of thee the pilgrim heart was moved:
    Hail, once again!

7.

Hither we've come in pathways winding,
Mid light and shade, and sorrows blinding;
Yet do we heed fond mothers minding;
    From above they look;
Our fathers, too, brave spirits they,
Stand high on many a cloud to-day,
To greet creation on the way
    To the Contoocook.

8.

Sons of New-England, daughters too,
There's many a heart in faith for you,
True thanks to bring, and honors due
    In measures double.
For generous natures, ways of winning,
For faithful house-wives, frugal spinning,
For orators, your dead and living,
    And patriots noble.

9.

For husbandry to gladden the soil,
For hearts that beat for truth and toil;

Whose rectitude could ne'er recoil
    In thought or deed;
For men of learning, men of light,
Valiant for justice, God, and right;
Translated many, they're still in sight,
    We give them heed.

10.

Your Hiltons, Thompsons, Pilgrims pure,
Their fame, their faith, shall ever endure;
Your Putnams, Stark, and Molly, sure, —
    All, all are here.
Your natives and primeval comers,
Your Waldrons, Wentworths, and your Plummers,
Uncounted souls of bygone summers,
    Bring memories dear.

11.

Your Sullivans, your Masons meet us;
Your Websters, Greeleys, Woodburys weet us;
Most graciously they've come to greet us:
    We hail them nigh.
Brave, welcome spirits, sainted, fair;
They linger in the purpled air
With whisperings vague, yet vocal there:
    They're from on high.

12.

They mind us of primeval years,
Of Indian war-whoop, death, and tears;
When faith in Pilgrim pioneers
    Came forth revealed.

How, when the British lion roared,
And tax and tea went overboard,
And shot and shell and powder poured
   On the crimson field.

13.

How then the fathers fought the battle,
While out upon old England's cattle,
They made the bones of nations rattle,
   And thrones to fear 'em.
Then how the fire-lock rusty, old,
True Yankee valor did unfold;
Of this the one half ne'er was told:
   We live to revere 'em.

14.

And how, when seven years had flown,
Victorious veterans to the town,
Homeward in squads came limping down
   In broken ranks;
The uniform, the cornered hat,
The gaiters, breeches, and all that;
And hearts of maidens "pit-a-pat"
   Made mazy pranks.

15.

Grave men and mothers gathered nigh;
Strange acclamations fill the sky:
Magnanimous manhood stands on high,
   In garnished glory.
They'd waded through tempestuous war,
Their flesh all furrowed, seam, and scar,
Ten thousand tongues proclaimed afar
   A tragic story.

16.

Peace came, and plenteousness combine,
Good manners crowned that olden time;
And the God of love gave days divine
    To the Pilgrim sons.
Their daughters too, taught well of the mothers,
Loved labor then as did their brothers,
And held it high to all the t'others,
    Their little ones.

17.

Health moved that meek advancing train:
From war and blood it bloomed again;
And the night-cloud dark at length became
    Fair, glorious morn;
The forest fed her buds anew;
The flowery fields beamed bright with dew;
And the harvests, prompt, were generous too,
    In golden corn.

18.

Thus had the generations flown,
Prolific, true in faith their own,
When a war-trump bleak again is blown
    These vales along.
It doomed the port to a sad seclusion,
Inflated fear to a fierce confusion,
A waste of wealth and destitution
    To the Yankee throng.

19.

It roused the realm to resolution,
At Little Harbor, constitution,

Vociferous crowds for revolution,
    Flagrant they swell;
They'd come to beard the British lion,
In Devil-daring to defy 'em,
With bombshells huge to tease and try 'em,
    And give 'em h—ll.

20.

Hail, hail, that hero here to-day,
Who stood high up in battle array
With a soul on fire, came forth to obey
    His country's call!
They're like the leaf last on the tree,—
Mild mariners of a stormy sea:
They're a glorious pattern for you and me:
    Thanks, thanks for all!

21.

Then fifty years of plenteous peace
Fed well the folds with a rich increase,
And gave to the land a full release
    From waste and care;
Meanwhile old Dame inspired her throngs,
And the beauteous birds sung well their songs,
To the heavens afar triumphant tongues,
    Made music there.

22.

Earth pregnant filled her ranks humane,
Full many a state, a vast domain;
And the gods on high were proud again
    Of a nation noble.

High, then, alas! revolving time
Upturned the world to a dread decline:
Rebellion born of hell and crime
    Draped earth in trouble.

23.

Thence came forebodings of the **morrow,**
A people pale, oppressed of sorrow,
Portentous war of blood and horror,
    A world of woe.
But victory turned that cloud away;
And brighter glimmered, o'er the way,
All round the world a better day,
    Above, below.

24.

Thus do the waves of strife betide
The path of mortals in their pride;
And Fate and Fortune side by side
    Trudge in the train;
High now, afar from foe or fears,
We've *never* a danger, dearth, nor tears:
Entranced we greet the happy years:
    (Hail!) all hail again!

25.

Brief thus hath history told the tale,
That saw the sunshine, storm, and gale
Since Mother Duston followed the trail
    Of the Pennacook;

DUSTIN STATUE.—FIRST DRAFT.

Down thence, they say, there's been no lack
Of sainted souls on the Merrimack,
Far in the cloud oft coming back
   To the Contoocook.

26.

Thanks, *thanks!* — we give for a world begun,
For duties daily, promptly done,
For glorious victories *nobly* won,
   For life and love;
For holiness and hearts upright,
For peace and plenty, gospel light,
For sun and moon and the stars at night,
   And a heaven above;

27.

For a God *who* moves the minds of men
To generous deeds, *illustrious when*
They lift the heart, the hand, the *pen*,
   To a lofty custom;
To a gift from the sculptor's graphic hand, —
An emblem glorious and grand,
Unveiled to the world for aye to stand, —
   Old Mother Duston!

[*Unveiled.*]

DUSTON MONUMENT.

Its Unveiling.

JUNE 17, 1874.

THE assembly, large and attentive, was briefly addressed by Samuel B. Page, Esq., of Concord, N.H., President of the day, followed by music from the "Cornet" Bands of Fisherville and Franklin, N.H.

Exercises then proceeded.

1. *Prayer.* — By Rev. Dr. N. Bouton.
2. *Solo and Chorus.* — "Come Back to New England." Sung by Mrs. G. C. Brock, and by Prof. J. Jackman, of Concord, with a hundred vocalists sustained by the bands.
3. *The Oration and Poem* by Robert B. Caverly, Esq., interluded with a duet by his daughters, was well received. When the speaker, as he advanced to the conclusion of his epic, announced the words, —

"*An emblem glorious and grand,*"

the American Flag, which thus far had concealed the monument, instantly fell from it; and the giant *image* of HANNAH DUSTON, on a pedestal of Concord granite, *stood forth* in all of its heroic beauty, saluted by the multitude, by the bands, and by the booming of cannon from the hill-tops.

4. *An hour's recess.*

Previously, as appeared, ladies from the neighboring towns had bounteously supplied the tables of the various tents in the wild and beautiful grove; and, as of old, the multitude was generously fed beneath its cool, inspiring shades.

AFTERNOON.

The spacious stand which had been erected a few rods north of the statue again being filled with the choirs, the donors, and speakers, the audience, at the inspiring music of the bands under direction of the marshal, J. Whittaker, Esq., returned; and orators, as in the programme, answered to sentiments as follows: —

5. "*The soldiers of New England, since the days of Hannah Duston.*"

The announcement of this by the presiding officer elicited a patriotic, appropriate response by Maj.-Gen. S. G. Griffin of Keene, N.H.

6. "*Orators of New England, from the days of yore.*"

By *this*, many reminiscences relating to the eminent men of the olden time were recalled in a glowing historic address by David O. Allen, Esq., of Lowell, Mass.

Hon. Benj. F. Prescott of Concord, N.H., then interposing, offered a resolution as follows, which was adopted :

"*Resolved,*—That the thanks of the people of New Hampshire be hereby tendered to R. B. Caverly, Esq., of Lowell, Mass., a native of our State, for his energy and perseverance in causing to be erected one of the finest monuments in New England in commemoration of a most daring act of heroism."

Mr. Caverly briefly responded, paying tribute to *others* who had contributed largely in its erection.

7. "*The Law and the Lawyers.*"

To this sentiment, Col. John H. George of Concord, being called, responded eloquently in commendation of the faith and strength of the lawyers of New England, particularly the bar of New Hampshire, now as well as in the olden time.

8. *A Duet.* — By the Misses Caverly.

9. Rev. Elias Nason, next being called, in the midst of enthusiasm responded to the sentiment,— "*Ye ancient Psalmody.*" Holding up to the gaze of the multitude the first old singing-book published in New England, he humorously quoted old poems, with anecdotes of the early settlers. His eloquent address elicited much merriment and applause.

10. *A Hymn.* Tune : Complaint. — By the choirs and the bands, in these and other words : —

> "*Spare us, O Lord, aloud we cry ;*
> *Nor let our sun go down at noon.*
> *Thy years are one eternal day ;*
> *And must thy children die so soon?*"

Many eloquent speakers were still present, ready with

contributions to the occasion, as named in the Programme of the day, among whom were the *Hon. Natt Head* of Hooksett, *Rev. W. T. Savage, Judge Geo. W. Nesmith* of Franklin, the *Hon. Onslow Stearns* of Concord, N.H., and others; but as they sought to be excused by reason of an intervening shower of rain, and lateness of the hour, the exercises were accordingly abbreviated.

11. DEED OF THE STATUE.

This was now delivered to his Excellency the Governor (his state counsellors standing near him) by Mr. Caverly and associates Messrs. Nutter and Bouton.

To their address the Governor briefly, eloquently replied, and in behalf of the State of New Hampshire accepted the

DEED. (A COPY.)

To His Excellency JAMES A. WESTON, *and to all the Governors of New Hampshire:* —

Know ye that we the underwriters,
For reasons rightful, valid, divers,
By deed of quit-claim do deprive us
    Of title traced

To all our lands in the Contoocook,
However bounded, knoll or nook,
On which that block we undertook
    Is built and based.

A generous people, grateful, plant it;
To the State in which it stands we grant it,
That the tide of time may never cant it,
    Nor mar nor sever;

That Pilgrims here may heed the Mothers;
That Truth and Faith and all the Others,
With banners high in glorious colors,
    May stand forever.

To witness what this deed reveals,
We've given our hand, and set our seals:

    NATHANIEL BOUTON. [Seal]
    ELIPHALET S. NUTTER. [Seal]
    ROBERT B. CAVERLY. [Seal]

Witness: B. F. PRESCOTT,
         ISAAC K. GAGE.

Then were the grantors all agreed
And true; 'tis made their act and deed.

MERRIMACK, ss. — June 17, 1874. Before me,
    ISAAC K. GAGE, *Justice of the Peace.*

www.ingramcontent.com/pod-product-compliance
Lightning Source LLC
Chambersburg PA
CBHW050426240426
43661CB00055B/2286